FRENCH
at a Glance
Phrase Book & Dictionary for Travelers

Fifth Edition

P9-APE-626

BY GAIL STEIN, M.A.
Former Teacher of French
Department of Foreign Languages
Martin Van Buren High School, New York

HEYWOOD WALD, Ph.D., Coordinating Editor
Former Chairman, Department of Foreign Languages
Martin Van Buren High School, New York

BARRON'S

All inquiries should be addressed to:
Barron's Educational Series, Inc.
250 Wireless Boulevard
Hauppauge, New York 11788
www.barronseduc.com

International Standard Book No. 978-0-7641-4777-7

Library of Congress Control No. 2011934873

PRINTED IN CHINA
9 8 7 6 5 4 3 2 1

CONTENTS

PREFACE

So you're taking a trip to one of the many fascinating countries of the world. That's exciting! This phrase book, part of Barron's popular *At a Glance* series, will prove an invaluable companion.

In these books we present the phrases and words that a traveler most often needs for a brief visit to a foreign country, where the customs and language are often different. Each phrase book highlights the terms particular to that country, in situations that the tourist is most likely to encounter. Travel tips found throughout the book have been updated. With a specially developed key to pronunciation, this book will enable you to communicate quickly and confidently in colloquial terms. It is intended not only for beginners with no knowledge of the language, but also for those who have already studied it and have some familiarity with it.

Some of the unique features and highlights of the Barron's series are:

- Easy-to-follow *pronunciation keys* and complete phonetic transcriptions for all words and phrases in the book.
- Compact *dictionary* of commonly used words and phrases—built right into this phrase book so there's no need to carry a separate dictionary.
- Useful phrases for the *tourist*, grouped together by subject matter in a logical way so that the appropriate phrase is easy to locate when you need it.
- Special phrases for the *business traveler*, including banking terms, a computer mini-dictionary, computer terms, and a list of helpful websites.
- Thorough section on food and drink, with comprehensive food terms you will find on menus.
- *Emergency phrases* and terms you hope you won't need: legal complications, medical problems, theft or loss of valuables, replacement or repair of watches, camera, etc.
- *Sightseeing itineraries*, with shopping tips, practical travel tips, and regional food specialties to help you get off the beaten path and into the countryside, to the small towns and cities, and to the neighboring areas.
- A *reference section* providing important signs, conversion tables, holidays, abbreviations, telling time, days of week, and months of year.
- A brief *grammar section*, with the basic elements of the language quickly explained.

Enjoy your vacation and travel with confidence. You have a friend by your side.

Travel Tips There are many theories on how to survive jet lag—the adjustment to a long trip into a different time zone. Some multinational corporations take jet lag so seriously they do not allow employees to make business decisions on the first day abroad. Most experts agree on several techniques: Eat lightly for several days before departing, avoid dehydration while flying by drinking plenty of nonalcoholic liquids; take frequent strolls around the plane to keep your blood circulating; if possible, get some rest on the flight; use ear plugs, an eye mask, and an inflatable neck collar to make sleep easier. If you arrive early in the morning, take an after-lunch nap, get up for some exercise and dinner, then go to bed at the regular new time. If you arrive at your destination in the afternoon or later, skip the nap and try to sleep late the next morning. In countries where massage or saunas are standard hotel service, indulge yourself on the evening of arrival to help you sleep soundly that night.

ACKNOWLEDGMENTS

We would like to thank the following individuals and organizations for their assistance on this project:

Nora Brossard, Assistant Director Public Relations, French National Tourist Office, New York, New York; Professor Pierre François, SUC New Paltz, New York; Marie-Charlotte Iszkowski, Foreign Service Institute, Washington, D.C.; Michel Lalou, Phonelab, New York, New York; George Lang, George Lang, Inc., New York, New York; Dr. Gladys Lipton, Coordinator of Foreign Languages and ESOL; Marek Pukteris, Quebec Tourist Information Center; Anne Arundel County Public Schools, Annapolis, Maryland; François Mead, Alliance Française, New York, New York; Professor Henry Urbanski, Chairman, Department of Foreign Languages, SUC New Paltz, New York; Herta Erville; and Andrée Katz.

Also, Air France, Association of American Travel Writers, French National Tourist Office, *New York Times*, *Signature Magazine*, *Travel-Holiday Magazine*, *Travel and Leisure Magazine*, U.S. Tour Operators, and U.S. Travel Data Center.

QUICK PRONUNCIATION GUIDE

Although all the phrases in this book are presented with an easy-to-use key to pronunciation, you will find speaking French quite a bit easier if you learn a few simple rules. Below are some tables that give the sounds represented by each French letter along with the symbols used to indicate them in this book. Although a French sound is quite different from ours, with a little practice and repetition you will be able to make yourself understood by native French speakers.

After studying the phonetic pronunciation system below, begin to practice the vocabulary words and then progress to the longer phrases. Bonne chance! *Bohn shah<u>n</u>ss*

STRESS

As an aid to pronunciation, words in this book have been divided into syllables. Since all French syllables have approximately the same amount of stress, pronounce each syllable with equal emphasis and put a slightly stronger emphasis on the last syllable of a word group.

CONSONANTS

In French, final consonants are usually silent, except for final C, R, F, and L (as in CaReFuL), which are usually pronounced.

FRENCH LETTER	ENGLISH SOUND	SYMBOL	EXAMPLE
b, d, f, k, l, m, n	same as English		
p, t, v, z	same as English		
c (before e, i, y)	SS (S at beginning of word)	S	cigare *see-gahr*
ç (before a, o, u)	SS (S at beginning of word)	S	garçon *gahr-ssohn*
c (before a, o, u)	K	K	comme *kohm*

FRENCH LETTER	ENGLISH SOUND	SYMBOL	EXAMPLE
g (before e, i, y)	S as in plea*s*ure	ZH	rouge *roozh*
ge (before a, o)	S as in plea*s*ure	ZH	mangeons *mahn-zhohn*
g (before a, o, u)	G	G	gant *gahn*
gn	nyuh as in o*n*ion	NY	oignon *oh-nyohn*
h	always silent		hôtel *oh-tehl*
j	S as in plea*s*ure	ZH	je *zhuh*
qu, final q	K	K	cinq *sank*
r	Say the R at the top back of the mouth as if you were gargling or spitting.	R	rue *rew*
ss	S	SS	poisson *pwah-ssohn*
s	beginning of word	S	six *sees*
s	next to consonant	SS	disque *deessk*
s	between vowels	Z	poison *pwah-zohn*
th	T	T	thé *tay*
x	S in these words only	SS	six *seess*, dix *deess*, soixante *swah-ssahnt*
x	X	KSS	excellent *ehkss-eh-lahn*
x	X	GS	exemple *ehg-sahn-pluh*

NOTE: When combined with a word beginning with a vowel or *h*, *x* has a *z* sound. Beford a word beginning with a consonant, it is silent.

VOWELS

FRENCH LETTER	ENGLISH SOUND	SYMBOL	EXAMPLE
a, à, â	A as in yacht or A in after	AH	la *lah*
é, final er, final ez, et	A as in day	AY	musée *mew-zay*
e + 2 consonants e + final pronounced consonant e, ê, è	E as in ever	EH	sept *seht*
e	sometimes like E of early with no R sound	UH	le *luh*
i (î), y	EE as in meet	EE	île *eel*
i + vowel or ll	Y as in yes	EE	famille *fah-mee*
o + final pronounced consonant	O as in love	OH	homme *ohm*
o, o before se, o last sound in word, au, eau	O as in open	OH	au *oh*
ou	OO as in tooth	OO	où *oo*
oy, oi	WA as in watch	WAH	trois *trwah*
U	There is none. Round lips and say E and U at same time.	EW	du *dew*
U + vowel	WEE as in wee	WEE	huit *weet*

NASAL SOUNDS

Nasal sounds are produced through the mouth and the nose at the same time. Nasal sounds occur when N or M follows a vowel in the same syllable. There is NO nasal sound for VOWEL + NN, VOWEL + MM, VOWEL + N + VOWEL, VOWEL + M + VOWEL. NOTE: n means there is a nasalized pronunciation of the "N" sound. The tip of the tongue does not touch the roof of the mouth.

FRENCH LETTER	ENGLISH SOUND	SYMBOL	EXAMPLE
AN, AM, EN, EM	similar to on	AHN	France *Frahnss*
IN, IM, AIN, AIM	similar to an	AN	pain *pan*
IEN	similar to yan of Yankee	YAN	bien *byan*
ON, OM	similar to on of long.	OHN	bon *bohn*
UN, UM	similar to un of under.	UHN	un *uhn*

LIAISON and ELISION

Liaison and elision are two linguistic devices that add to the beauty and fluidity of the French language.

Liaison means linking. In French, the final consonant of a word is usually not pronounced. Sometimes, however, when the final consonant of one word is followed by a beginning vowel or H of the next word, liaison occurs.

EXAMPLE:

Nous arrivons.   *noo zah-ree-vohn*

With the following words in French, the final vowel is dropped if the next word starts with a vowel or H. The dropped vowel is replaced by an apostrophe. This is called elision.

EXAMPLE:

la auto = l'auto   *(loh-toh)*

le homme = l'homme   *(lohm)*

THE BASICS FOR GETTING BY

MOST FREQUENTLY USED EXPRESSIONS

The expressions in this section are the ones you'll use again and again—the fundamental building blocks of conversation, the way to express your wants or needs, and some simple question forms that you can use to construct all sorts of questions. It's a good idea to practice these phrases until you know them by heart.

Sir	**Monsieur**	*muh-ssyuh*
Madame	**Madame**	*mah-dahm*
Miss (Ms.)	**Mademoiselle**	*mahd-mwah-zehl*
I'm American.	**Je suis américain/ américaine (f.)**	*zhuh swee zah-may-ree-kan/ ah-may-ree-kehn*
Do you speak English?	**Parlez-vous anglais?**	*pahr-lay voo ahn-gleh*
I speak a little French.	**Je parle un peu le français.**	*zhuh pahrl uhn puh luh frahn-seh*
Do you understand me?	**Vous me comprenez?**	*voo muh kohn-pruh-nay*
I understand.	**Je comprends.**	*zhuh kohn-prahn*
I don't understand.	**Je ne comprends pas.**	*zhuh nuh kohn-prahn-pah*
What did you say?	**Qu'est-ce que vous avez dit?**	*kehs-kuh voo zah-vay dee*

Please repeat.	**Répétez, s'il vous plaît.**	*ray-pay-tay seel voo pleh*
How do you say ____ in French?	**Comment dit-on ____ en français?**	*kohn-mahn dee-tohn ____ ahn frahn-seh*
What does this/that mean?	**Qu'est-ce que ça veut dire?**	*kehs-kuh sah vuh deer*
My name is ____.	**Je m'appelle ____.**	*zhuh mah-pehl*
What is your name?	**Comment vous appelez-vous?**	*kohn-mahn voo zah-play voo*
What is your name, address, phone number?	**Quelles sont vos coordonnées?**	*kehl sohn voh koh-ohr-doh-nay*
How are you?	**Comment allez-vous?**	*kohn-mahn tah-lay voo*
Very well, thanks.	**Très bien, merci.**	*treh byan mehr-see*
And you?	**Et vous?**	*ay voo*
How's everything?	**Ça va?**	*sah vah*
Everything's fine.	**Ça va.**	*sah vah*
I'm lost.	**Je me suis égaré(e).**	*zhuh muh swee zay-gah-ray*
I'm looking for ____	**Je cherche ____**	*zhuh shehrsh*
Where is ____?	**Où est ____?**	*oo eh*
▒ the exit	**la sortie**	*lah sohr-tee*
▒ the taxi stand	**l'arrêt de taxis**	*lah-reh duh tahk-ssee*

▨ the bus stop	**l'arrêt de bus**	*lah-reh duh bewss*
▨ the metro station	**l'arrêt de métro**	*lah-reh duh may-troh*
▨ the train station	**la gare**	*lah gahr*
Where are _____?	**Où sont _____?**	*oo soh<u>n</u>*
▨ the bathrooms	**les toilettes**	*lay twah-leht*
▨ the telephones	**les téléphones**	*lay tay-lay-foh<u>n</u>*
▨ the taxis	**les taxis**	*lay tahk-ssee*
It's _____.	**C'est _____.**	*seh*
▨ to the left	**à gauche**	*ah gohsh*
▨ to the right	**à droite**	*ah drwaht*
▨ straight ahead	**tout droit**	*too drwah*
What's that?	**Qu'est-ce que c'est?**	*kehs-kuh seh*
I (don't) know.	**Je (ne) sais (pas).**	*zhuh (nuh) seh (pah)*

Do you have ___?	**Avez-vous ___?**	*ah-vay-voo*
I'd like ___.	**Je voudrais ___.**	*zhuh voo-dreh*
I need ___.	**J'ai besoin de ___.**	*zhay buh-zwan duh*
Please bring me ___.	**Apportez-moi, s'il vous plaît ___.**	*ah-pohr-tay mwah seel voo pleh*
Please give me ___.	**Donnez-moi, s'il vous plaît ___.**	*doh-nay mwah seel voo pleh*
Please show me ___.	**Montrez-moi, s'il vous plaît ___.**	*mohn-tray mwah seel voo pleh*
How much is it?	**C'est combien?**	*seh kohn-byan*
I'm hungry.	**J'ai faim.**	*zhay fan*
I'm thirsty.	**J'ai soif.**	*zhay swahf*
I'm tired.	**Je suis fatigué(e).**	*zhuh swee fah-tee-gay*
Good-bye.	**Au revoir.**	*oh ruh-vwahr*
See you later.	**À tout à l'heure.**	*ah toot ah luhr*
See you tomorrow.	**À demain.**	*ah duh-man*

QUESTIONS

| Where is (are) ___? | **Où est (sont) ___?** | *oo eh (sohn)* |
| When? | **Quand?** | *kahn* |

At what time?	**À quelle heure?**	*ah kehl uhr*
How much/many?	**Combien?**	*kohn-byan*
Who?	**Qui?**	*kee*
What?	**Que?/Quoi?**	*kuh/kwah*
Why?	**Pourquoi?**	*poor-kwah*
How?	**Comment?**	*kohn-mahn*
Which?	**Quel/Quelle/Quels/Quelles?**	*kehl*
Which one(s)?	**Lequel/Laquelle/Lesquel/Lesquelles?**	*luh/lah/lay-kehl*

EXCLAMATIONS, SLANG, COLLOQUIALISMS

Wow!	**Oh là là!**	*oh lah lah*
Darn!	**Zut!**	*zewt*
Well!	**Eh bien!**	*eh byan*
Great!	**Chouette!**	*shoo-eht*
Wonderful!	**Formidable!**	*fohr-mee-dahbl*
Fantastic!	**Génial!**	*zhay-nyahl*
My goodness!	**Mon Dieu!**	*mohn dyuh*
That's it!	**C'est ça!**	*seh sah*
That's awful!	**C'est affreux!**	*seh tah-fruh*

It's marvelous!	**C'est magnifique!**	*seh mah-nyee-feek*
Cheers!	**Santé!**	*sah<u>n</u>-tay*
Quiet!	**Silence!**	*see-lah<u>n</u>ss*
That's enough!	**Ça suffit!** **C'est assez!**	*sah sew-fee* *seh tah-say*
Too bad!	**Tant pis!**	*tah<u>n</u> pee*
So much the better!	**Tant mieux!**	*tah<u>n</u> myuh*
Never mind!	**N'importe!**	*na<u>n</u>-pohrt*
Of course!	**Bien sûr!**	*bya<u>n</u> sewr*
OK.	**D'accord.**	*dah-kohr*
With pleasure.	**Avec plaisir.**	*ah-vehk pleh-zeer*
Let's go!	**Allons-y!**	*ah-loh<u>n</u>-zee*
What a shame!	**Quel dommage!**	*kehl doh-mahzh*
How annoying!	**Que c'est ennuyeux!**	*kuh seh tah<u>n</u>-nwee-yuh*
Nonsense!	**C'est ridicule!**	*seh ree-dee-kewl*
What a drag!	**Quelle barbe!**	*kehl bahrb*
You're kidding!	**Vous rigolez!**	*voo ree-goh-lay*
Good luck!	**Bonne chance!**	*bohn shah<u>n</u>ss*

PROBLEMS, PROBLEMS, PROBLEMS (EMERGENCIES)

Hurry up!	**Dépêchez-vous!**	*day-peh-shay-voo*
Look!	**Regardez!**	*ruh-gahr-day*
Watch out!	**Attention!**	*ah-tahn-syohn*
Be careful!	**Soyez prudent(e)!**	*swah-yay prew-dahn(t)*
Calm down!	**Calmez-vous!**	*kahl-may voo*
Take it easy!	**Allez-y doucement!**	*ah-lay zee dooss-mahn*
Listen!	**Écoutez!**	*ay-koo-tay*
Wait!	**Attendez!**	*ah-tahn-day*

I have lost ____.	**J'ai perdu ____.**	*zhay pehr-dew*
What's the matter?	**Qu'est-ce qu'il y a?**	*kehs-keel yah*
What's the matter with you?	**Qu'est-ce que vous avez?**	*kehs-kuh voo zah-vay*
What do you want?	**Que voulez-vous?**	*kuh voo-lay voo*
Stop bothering me.	**Laissez-moi tranquille!**	*leh-say mwah trahn-keel*
It's none of your business!	**Ce n'est pas votre affaire!**	*suh neh pah vohtr ah-fehr*
Go away!	**Allez-vous-en!**	*ah-lay voo zahn*
Get out!	**Sortez!**	*sohr-tay*
I'm going to call the police!	**Je vais appeler la police!**	*zhuh veh zah-play lah poh-leess*
Help, police!	**Au secours, police.**	*oh skoor, poh-leess*
Someone has stolen ____.	**Quelqu'un a volé ____.**	*kehl-kuhn ah voh-lay*
my car	**ma voiture**	*mah vwah-tewr*
my passport	**mon passeport**	*mohn pahss-pohr*
my purse	**mon sac**	*mohn sahk*
my suitcase	**ma valise**	*mah vah-leez*
my wallet	**mon portefeuille**	*mohn pohr-tuh fuhy*
my watch	**ma montre**	*mah mohntr*
This person is bothering me.	**Cette personne m'embête.**	*seht pehr-sohn mahn-beht*
That person is following me.	**Cette personne me suit.**	*seht pehr-sohn muh swee*

Stop that person!	**Arrêtez cette personne!**	*ah-ruh-tay seht pehr-sohn*
I haven't done anything.	**Je n'ai rien fait.**	*zhuh nay ryan feh*
It's a lie!	**C'est un mensonge!**	*seh tuhn mahn-sohnzh*
It's not true!	**Ce n'est pas vrai!**	*seh neh pah vreh*
I'm innocent.	**Je suis innocent(e).**	*zhuh swee zee-noh-sahn(t)*
I want a lawyer.	**Je voudrais parler à un(e) avocat(e).**	*zhuh voo-dreh pahr-lay ah uhn ah-voh-kah(t)*
I want to go ____.	**Je voudrais aller ____.**	*zhuh voo-dreh zah-lay*
▓ to the American Consulate	**au consulat américain**	*oh kohn-sew-lah ah-may-ree-kan*
▓ to the American Embassy	**à l'ambassade américaine**	*ah lahn-bah-sahd ah-may-ree-kehn*
▓ to the police station	**au commissariat de police**	*oh koh-mee-sah-ryah duh poh-leess*
I need help, quick!	**Vite. Aidez-moi!**	*veet eh-day mwah*
Could you help me, please?	**Pourriez-vous m'aider s'il vous plaît?**	*poo-ree-yay voo meh-day seel voo pleh*
Does anyone here speak English?	**Il y a quelqu'un ici qui parle anglais?**	*eel yah kehl-kuhn ee-see kee pahrl ahn-gleh*
I need an interpreter.	**Il me faut un interprète.**	*eel muh foh tuhn an-tehr-preht*

NUMBERS

You will use numbers the moment you land in France, whether it be to exchange money at the airport, purchase a bus ticket for a ride into town, or describe the length of your stay to a customs official. We list here first the cardinal numbers, then the ordinal numbers, fractions, and other useful numbers.

CARDINAL NUMBERS

0	**zéro**	*zay-roh*
1	**un**	*uh<u>n</u>*
2	**deux**	*duh*
3	**trois**	*trwah*
4	**quatre**	*kah-truh*
5	**cinq**	*sa<u>n</u>k*
6	**six**	*seess*
7	**sept**	*seht*
8	**huit**	*weet*
9	**neuf**	*nuhf*
10	**dix**	*deess*
11	**onze**	*oh<u>n</u>z*
12	**douze**	*dooz*
13	**treize**	*trehz*
14	**quatorze**	*kah-tohrz*
15	**quinze**	*ka<u>n</u>z*
16	**seize**	*sehz*
17	**dix-sept**	*dee-seht*

18	**dix-huit**	*dee-zweet*
19	**dix-neuf**	*deez-nuhf*
20	**vingt**	*va<u>n</u>*
21	**vingt et un**	*va<u>n</u>-tay-uh<u>n</u>*
22	**vingt-deux**	*va<u>n</u>-duh*
23	**vingt-trois**	*va<u>n</u>-trwah*
24	**vingt-quatre**	*va<u>n</u>-kah-truh*
25	**vingt-cinq**	*va<u>n</u>-sa<u>n</u>k*
26	**vingt-six**	*va<u>n</u>-seess*
27	**vingt-sept**	*va<u>n</u>-seht*
28	**vingt-huit**	*va<u>n</u>-tweet*
29	**vingt-neuf**	*va<u>n</u>-nuhf*
30	**trente**	*trah<u>n</u>t*
31	**trente et un**	*trah<u>n</u>-tay-uh<u>n</u>*
32	**trente-deux**	*trah<u>n</u>t-duh*
40	**quarante**	*kah-rah<u>n</u>t*
41	**quarante et un**	*kah-rah<u>n</u>-tay-uh<u>n</u>*
42	**quarante-deux**	*kah-rah<u>n</u>t-duh*
50	**cinquante**	*sa<u>n</u>-kah<u>n</u>t*
51	**cinquante et un**	*sa<u>n</u>-kah<u>n</u>-tay-uh<u>n</u>*
52	**cinquante-deux**	*sa<u>n</u>-kah<u>n</u>t-duh*
60	**soixante**	*swah-ssah<u>n</u>t*
61	**soixante et un**	*swah-ssah<u>n</u>-tay-uh<u>n</u>*
62	**soixante-deux**	*swah-ssah<u>n</u>t-duh*
70	**soixante-dix**	*swah-ssah<u>n</u>t-deess*
71	**soixante et onze**	*swah-ssah<u>n</u>-tay-oh<u>n</u>z*

72	**soixante-douze**	*swah-ssahnt-dooz*
73	**soixante-treize**	*swah-ssahnt-trehz*
74	**soixante-quatorze**	*swah-ssahnt-kah-tohrz*
75	**soixante-quinze**	*swah-ssahnt-kanz*
76	**soixante-seize**	*swah-ssahnt-sehz*
77	**soixante-dix-sept**	*swah-ssahnt-dee-seht*
78	**soixante-dix-huit**	*swah-ssahnt-dee-zweet*
79	**soixante-dix-neuf**	*swah-ssahnt-deez-nuhf*
80	**quatre-vingts**	*kah-truh-van*
81	**quatre-vingt-un**	*kah-truh-van-uhn*
82	**quatre-vingt-deux**	*kah-truh-van-duh*
90	**quatre-vingt-dix**	*kah-truh-van-deess*
91	**quatre-vingt-onze**	*kah-truh-van-ohnz*
92	**quatre-vingt-douze**	*kah-truh-van-dooz*
100	**cent**	*sahn*
101	**cent un**	*sahn-uhn*
102	**cent deux**	*sahn-duh*
110	**cent dix**	*sahn-deess*
120	**cent vingt**	*sahn-van*
200	**deux cents**	*duh-sahn*
201	**deux cent un**	*duh-sahn-uhn*
330	**trois cent trente**	*trwah-sahn-trahnt*

1000	**mille**	*meel*
1001	**mille un**	*meel-uhn*
1100	**mille cent**	*meel-sahn*
	onze cents	*ohnz-sahn*
1200	**mille deux cents**	*meel-duh-sahn*
	douze cents	*dooz-sahn*
1350	**mille trois cent cinquante/treize cent cinquante**	*meel-trwah-sahn-san-kahnt/trehz-sahn-san-kahnt*
2000	**deux mille**	*duh-meel*
5000	**cinq mille**	*sank-meel*
10,000	**dix mille**	*dee-meel*
100,000	**cent mille**	*sahn-meel*
1,000,000	**un million**	*uhn-mee-lyohn*
200_	**deux mille___**	*duh meel*

ORDINAL NUMBERS

first	**premier/première (1er)**	*pruh-myay/pruh-myehr*
second	**deuxième (2e)**	*duh-zyehm*
third	**troisième**	*trwah-zyehm*
fourth	**quatrième**	*kah-tree-yehm*
fifth	**cinquième**	*san-kyehm*
sixth	**sixième**	*see-zyehm*
seventh	**septième**	*seh-tyehm*
eighth	**huitième**	*wee-tyehm*
ninth	**neuvième**	*nuh-vyehm*
tenth	**dixième**	*dee-zyehm*

QUANTITIES

a half	**une moitié**	*ewn mwah-tyay*
half a	**un/une demi/e**	*uhn/ewn duh-mee*
half of	**la moitié de**	*lah mwah-tyay duh*
a quarter	**un quart**	*uhn kahr*
three-quarters	**trois quarts**	*trwah kahr*
a third	**un tiers**	*uhn tyehr*
two-thirds	**deux tiers**	*duh tyehr*
a bag of	**un sac de**	*uhn sahk duh*
a bottle of	**une bouteille de**	*ewn boo-tehy duh*
a box (can) of	**une boîte de**	*ewn bwaht duh*
a cup of	**une tasse de**	*ewn tahss duh*
a dozen of	**une douzaine de**	*ewn doo-zehn duh*
a kilo of	**un kilo de**	*uhn kee-loh duh*

a liter of	**un litre de**	*uhn leetr duh*
a package of	**un paquet de**	*uhn pah-keh duh*
a pair of	**une paire de**	*ewn pehr duh*
a pound of	**une livre de** **cinq cents grammes de**	*ewn lee-vruh duh sank sahn grahm duh*
a slice of	**une tranche de**	*ewn trahnsh duh*

a little bit of	**un peu de**	*uhn puh duh*
a lot of	**beaucoup de**	*boh-koo duh*
enough of	**assez de**	*ah-ssay duh*
too much of	**trop de**	*troh duh*

Travel Tips There was a time when buying an airline ticket was simple. Since the airline industry was deregulated, however, travelers must shop and compare prices, buy charter or discount tickets far in advance, join frequent flier clubs to become eligible for free tickets, and do research on the Internet. Read the fine print in ads and ask questions when making reservations. Often, discount fare tickets cannot be exchanged for cash or another ticket if travel plans must be changed. If you must change plans en route, talk to an airline ticket agent. Sometimes they have soft hearts!

WHEN YOU ARRIVE

PASSPORT AND CUSTOMS

In France at last! Your vacation can't begin until you've shown your passport to the proper authorities and passed through customs.

The following chart shows what duty-free items visitors over 17 years of age from the United States or those coming from the European Union (EU) countries may bring into France.

DUTY-FREE ITEMS	FROM U.S.* & NON-EC COUNTRIES	FROM EC COUNTRIES
cigarettes	200 *or*	"Reasonable amounts" of tobacco, alcohol, and perfumes destined for personal use
cigars	50 *or*	
tobacco	250 grams	
table wine	2 liters *and*	
spirits	1 liter	
coffee	500 g	
tea	100 g	
perfume	50 ml	
toilet water	250 ml	
other goods	175 euros	
	90 euros	
	under age 15	

*Goods purchased in a duty-free shop within the U.S.

And when you return to the United States: •

DUTY-FREE ITEMS FROM EUROPE
$800 worth of foreign goods if you have been out of the U.S. for at least 48 hours and have not used the $800 allowance or any part of it in the past 30 days
1 liter of alcohol if you are 21 or older 200 cigarettes *and* 100 non-Cuban cigars gifts or articles up to a value of $100

Generally all items for personal use enter duty-free in France and most tourists have little trouble passing through customs. Baggage in hand, you must follow the sign that applies to you: Articles à déclarer or Rien à déclarer (Nothing to declare). Good luck! You're on your way!

ARTICLES À DÉCLARER	RIEN À DÉCLARER

My name is _____.	**Je m'appelle** _____. *zhuh mah-pehl*
I'm American, Canadian, British, Australian.	**Je suis américain(e), canadien(ne), anglais(e), australien(ne).** *zhuh swee zah-may-ree-kahn (kehn), kah-nah-dyan (dyehn), ahn-gleh (glehz), ohs-trah-lyan (yehn)*
My address is _____.	**Mon adresse est** _____. *mohn nah-drehss eh*
I'm staying at _____.	**Je reste à** _____. *zhuh rehst ah*
Here is (are) _____.	**Voici** _____. *vwah-ssee*
■ my documents	**mes papiers** *may pah-pyay*
■ my passport	**mon passeport** *mohn pahss-pohr*
■ my driver's license	**mon permis de conduire** *mohn pehr-mee duh kohn-dweer*
I'm _____.	**Je suis** _____. *zhuh swee*
■ on a business trip	**en voyage d'affaires** *zahn vwah-yahzh dah-fehr*
■ on vacation	**en vacances** *zahn vah-kahnss*

I'll be staying here _____.	**Je resterai ici _____.**	*zhuh rehss-tray ee-ssee*
▦ a few days	**quelques jours**	*kehl-kuh zhoor*
▦ a few weeks	**quelques semaines**	*kehl-kuh suh-mehn*
▦ a week	**une semaine**	*ewn suh-mehn*
▦ two weeks	**quinze jours**	*kanz zhoor*
▦ a month	**un mois**	*uhn mwah*
I'm traveling _____.	**Je voyage _____.**	*zhuh vwah-yahzh*
▦ alone	**seul**	*suhl*
▦ with my husband	**avec mon mari**	*ah-vehk mohn mah-ree*
▦ with my wife	**avec ma femme**	*ah-vehk mah fahm*
▦ with my family	**avec ma famille**	*ah-vehk mah fah-mee*
▦ with my friends	**avec mes ami(e)s**	*ah-vehk may zah-mee*
Here are my bags.	**Voici mes bagages.**	*vwah-ssee may bah-gahzh*
I have nothing to declare.	**Je n'ai rien à déclarer.**	*zhuh nay ryan ah day-klah-ray*
I have only _____.	**J'ai seulement _____.**	*zhay suhl-mahn*
▦ a carton of cigarettes	**une cartouche de cigarettes**	*ewn kahr-toosh duh see-gah-reht*
▦ a bottle of whisky	**une bouteille de whisky**	*ewn boo-tehy duh wheess-kee*
They're gifts.	**Ce sont des cadeaux.**	*suh sohn day kah-doh*
It's for my personal use.	**C'est pour usage personnel.**	*seh poor ew-zahzh pehr-soh-nehl*

Travel Tips Students traveling abroad should inquire about the International Student Identity Card issued by the Council on International Educational Exchange and the Youth International Educational Exchange Card issued by the Federation of International Youth Travel Organizations. These agencies offer many enticing discounts to students at a very reasonable price.

Do I have to pay duty?	**Dois-je payer des droits de douane?** *dwahzh peh-yay day drwah duh dwahn*
May I close my bag now?	**Puis-je fermer ma valise maintenant?** *pweezh fehr-may mah vah-leez mant-nahn*

IDENTITY CARD

Upon entering the country you will be required to fill out an identity card, usually with the following information.

Nom de famille _____ Last name _____

Prénom _____ First name _____

Nationalité _____ Nationality _____

Date de naissance _____ Birthdate _____

Profession _____ Profession _____

Adresse _____ Address _____

Passeport (de) _____ Passport (from) _____

BAGGAGE AND PORTERS

If you can find a porter to help you with your luggage, it is customary to give him/her a tip. It will probably be simpler and less expensive, however, to avail yourself of a handcart or to purchase luggage with wheels.

Where can I find a baggage cart?	**Où puis-je trouver un chariot à bagages?** *oo pweezh troo-vay uhn shah-ryoh ah bah-gahzh*
I'm looking for a porter.	**Je cherche un porteur.** *zhuh shehrsh uhn pohr-tuhr*
Please take our (my) bags.	**Prenez nos (mes) valises, s'il vous plaît.** *pruh-nay noh (may) vah-leez seel voo pleh*
Be careful with that one!	**Faites attention avec celle-là!** *feht zah-tahn-syohn ah-vehk sehl lah*
I'll carry this one myself.	**Je porterai celle-ci.** *zhuh pohr-tray sehl see*

I'm missing a suitcase.	**Il me manque une valise.** *eel muh mahnk ewn vah-leez*
Thank you (very much).	**Merci (beaucoup).** *mehr-ssee (boh-koo)*
This is for you.	**C'est pour vous.** *seh poor voo*

AIRPORT TRANSPORTATION

Where can I get a taxi?	**Où puis-je trouver un taxi?** *oo pweezh troo-vay uhn tahk-ssee*
What buses go into the city?	**Quels bus vont en ville?** *kehl bews vohn tahn veel*
Where is the bus stop?	**Où est l'arrêt de bus?** *oo eh lah-reh duh bews*
How much is the fare?	**Quel est le tarif?** *kehl eh luh tah-reef*
Where can I rent a car?	**Où puis-je louer une voiture?** *oo pweezh loo-ay ewn vwah-tewr*

Travel Tips Luggage is sometimes lost or arrives long after you do. To avoid problems, some people travel light and carry everything with them. At the very least, take one complete change of clothing, basic grooming items, and any regular medication aboard with you. Because airlines will not replace valuable jewelry when paying for lost luggage, it should be carried on your person. Safer yet, select one set of basic, simple jewelry that can be worn everywhere—even in the shower—and wear it during your whole trip. Remember, carry-on bags must be small enough to fit in overhead compartments or to slide under your seat.

BANKING AND MONEY MATTERS

BANKS

Many of the world's major banks have branches in large French cities. The two main types of banks in France are commercial banks and cooperatives, which have independent local branches.

Banks generally open between 8:30 and 9:00 and close between 4:00 and 5:30. Some larger banks may have extended hours one day per week. Some local banks in smaller towns may close for a lunch break. Most banks provide a large range of Internet banking services and telephone banking, with multilingual support staff. Banks will change foreign currency at the most favorable rate of exchange. *Bureaux de change* at airports or railway stations give a less favorable exchange rate. Some *bureaux de change* on the streets of Paris give very favorable exchange rates. Many hotels will exchange money and travelers' checks, but the rate will be the least favorable.

The current exchange rates are available in the banks that exchange money, and are also published daily in the newspapers.

The French post office offers most of the same facilities as banks, including online accounts.

BANKING TERMS

amount	**le montant**	*luh moh<u>n</u>-tahn*
ATM	**le guichet automatique**	*luh gee-sheh oh-toh mah-teek*
bad check	**le chèque sans provision**	*luh shehk sah<u>n</u> proh-vee-zyoh<u>n</u>*
bank	**la banque**	*lah bah<u>n</u>k*
banker	**le banquier**	*luh bah<u>n</u>-kyay*

bill	**le billet**	*luh bee-yeh*
borrow (to)	**emprunter**	*ah<u>n</u>-pruh<u>n</u>-tay*
cash advance	**l'avance de crédit**	*lah-vah<u>n</u>ss duh kray-dee*
cashier	**le caissier**	*luh kehss-yay*
check	**le chèque**	*luh shehk*
checkbook	**le carnet de chèques**	*luh kahr-neh duh shehk*
credit card	**la carte de crédit**	*la kahrt duh kray-dee*
debit card	**la carte de débit**	*lah kahrt duh day-bee*
endorse (to)	**endosser**	*ah<u>n</u>-doh-ssay*
exchange rate	**le cours du change**	*luh koor-dew shah<u>n</u>zh*
interest rate	**le taux d'intérêt**	*luh toh da<u>n</u>-tay-reh*
investment	**le placement**	*luh plahss-mah<u>n</u>*
lend (to)	**prêter**	*preh-tay*
make change (to)	**faire de la monnaie**	*fehr duh la moh-neh*
money	**l'argent (m.)**	*lahr-zhah<u>n</u>*
open an account (to)	**ouvrir un compte**	*oo-vreer uh<u>n</u> koh<u>n</u>t*
profit	**le bénéfice**	*luh bay-nay-feess*
safe	**le coffre-fort**	*luh koh-fruh fohr*
signature	**la signature**	*lah see-nyah-tewr*
window	**le guichet**	*luh gee-sheh*

The franc, the old unit of French currency, has been replaced by the **euro**, the approximate equivalent of one U.S. dollar, which is used throughout Europe.

The euro is the official monetary currency not only of France but of the entire European Union, which means that you can use the same currency throughout Western Europe. The euro is issued in the following denominations: notes—5, 10, 20, 50, 100, 200, and 500; coins—1, 2, 5, 10, 20, 50 cents, 1 and 2 euros.

EXCHANGING MONEY

Where is ____?	**Où se trouve ____ ?** *oo suh troov*
■ an automatic teller machine	**un guichet automatique** *uhn gee-sheh oh-toh-mah-teek*
■ a bank	**une banque** *ewn bahnk*
■ a money exchange	**un bureau de change** *uhn bew-roh duh shahnzh*
At what time do they open (close)?	**On ouvre (ferme) à quelle heure?** *ohn noo-vruh (fehrm) ah kehl uhr*
I would like to ____.	**Je voudrais ___.** *zhuh voo-dreh*
■ arrange a transfer	**faire un virement** *fehr uhn veer-mahn*
■ cash a check	**encaisser un chèque** *ahn-keh-ssay uhn shehk*
■ change money	**changer de l'argent** *shahn-zhay duh lahr-zhahn*
■ change travelers' checks	**changer des chèques de voyage** *shahn-zhay day shehk duh vwah-yahzh*
■ have large bills	**avoir de grosses coupures** *ah-vwahr duh grohss kew-pewr*
■ get a cash advance	**obtenir une avance de crédit** *ohp-tuh-neer uhn ah-vahnss duh kray-dee*
■ withdraw money	**retirer de l'argent** *ruh-tee-ray duh lahr-zhahn*
What's the current exchange rate?	**Quel est le cours (du change) le plus récent?** *kehl eh luh koor (dew shahnzh) luh plew ray-sahn?*

Do you have an ATM machine?	**Avez-vous un guichet automatique?** *ah-vay voo zuhn gee-sheh oh-toh-mah-teek*
Where is your ATM?	**Où est votre guichet automatique?** *oo eh voh-truh gee-sheh oh-toh-mah-teek*
I forgot my PIN.	**J'ai oublié mon code confidentiel.** *zhay oo-blee-ay mohn kohd kohn-fee-dahn-ssyehl*
How can I retrieve it?	**Comment puis-je le retrouver?** *koh-mahn pweezh luh ruh-troo-vay*
I'd like the money ____.	**Je voudrais l'argent ____.** *zhuh voo-dreh lahr-zhahn*
▨ in (large) bills	**en (grosses) coupures** *ahn (grohss) koo-pewr*
▨ in small change	**en petite monnaie** *ahn puh-teet moh-nay*
The ATM ____.	**Le guichet automatique ____.** *luh gee-sheh oh-toh-mah-teek*
▨ took my card	**a avalé ma carte** *ah ah-vah-lay mah kahrt*
▨ gave me too much money	**m'a donné trop d'argent** *mah doh-nay troh dahr-zahn*
▨ didn't give me enough money	**ne m'a pas donné assez d'argent** *nuh mah pah doh-nay ah-ssay dahr-zhahn*

TIPPING

In many instances, service charges are included in the price of the service rendered. These generally amount to 15% and should be indicated on the bill. For example, French law dictates that a 15% gratuity is to be added to every restaurant, bar, and café check, whether you can see the amount on the bill or not. If you want to tip, leave one euro for every 20–25 euros of the total. Do not leave the tip on your credit card bill because your server may not receive it. In general, leave nothing in bars or, if you feel compelled to do so, leave .15 euro for a 3-euro glass of wine.

The following table is merely a suggested guide. Tips will vary from time to time due to inflation and other factors. It is therefore advisable to ask some knowledgeable person such as the hotel concierge or tour director, once you get to the country, for proper tipping information, or you should check the rate of exchange.

SERVICE	TIP
waiter	10–15%
bellboy, porter	1 euro per bag
housekeeping	1 euro per person per day
room service	1 euro
concierge	10 euros for good service
	15 euros for excellent service
coat check	1 euro per item
usher	.5–1 euro per person
taxi driver	10% of fare (if helped with luggage)
guide	10%
barber, hairdresser	10–15%
bathroom attendant	small change
gas station attendant	1 euro, if he did more than pump gas

TIPPING AT HOTELS

Check to see whether the service charge (usually 15%) is included in the room price. The words **service compris** or **toutes taxes comprises** indicate that your tipping obligations have been fulfilled except for the bellboy carrying your luggage and the concierge, who may perform special services for you. Should any other employee go out of his/her way to help you, then a small additional tip would be in order.

AT THE HOTEL

LODGING

Accommodations are varied and plentiful, and are available in different price ranges. If you have not made a reservation and are looking for a place to stay, it is best to go to a tourist information center called **le Syndicat d'Initiative (SI)** or **Office du Tourisme (OT).** Someone there will gladly help you find a room to suit your needs and your budget. You will find yourself staying at one of the following.

HOTEL

Although there are hotel rooms in every price range, it is best to make an advance reservation. Festivals, exhibitions, shows, and trade fairs attract many visitors and rooms are quickly filled. The French government rates hotels by using a star system ranging from one star to four stars (indicated by a red star) or 5 stars (luxury—*luxe*) (indicated by a gold star). Prices displayed outside hotels are all-inclusive. Because hotel rates are unregulated, there may be a charge for breakfast or an extra bed. A hotel receives its rating based on room price and the conveniences its provides: size of room, telephone availability, bathroom facilities. A continental breakfast, consisting of rolls, butter and jam, and coffee or tea is often included in the price of the room. English is spoken in the larger, more exclusive hotels, and American-style breakfasts are usually available there.

CHÂTEAU-HOTEL

Running the gamut from a simple bed-and-breakfast to the most luxurious accommodations available, these once privately-owned aristocratic mansions, castles, estates, and country manors offer an interesting change from the typical hotel setting.

MOTEL

Motels have recently appeared in France. They are located near main roads outside towns and cities and at the airport.

PENSION

Pensions resemble rooming houses where the visitor pays for a room and all or part of his meals.

AUBERGE (LOGIS)

This is usually a small, modest, and inexpensive country inn found off the main roads in rural areas. An **auberge de jeunesse** is a relatively inexpensive youth hostel that is set up dormitory fashion.

CHAMBRES D'HÔTE

In towns or villages rooms are made available in the homes of local families, who will supply bed and breakfast for a fee.

GÎTES RURAUX

If you visit the countryside, you may rent a gîte, a private residence—house or apartment.

You should be aware that in France, especially outside of Paris, it is customary and expected that a guest eat dinner at his hotel. Many smaller hotels will charge you for dinner whether you eat it or not, or refuse to rent the room unless you eat in the hotel. You may inquire about this at the desk.

Travel Tips Touring on a budget? Then it pays to do your homework. Look for hotels or bed-and-breakfast establishments that include a morning meal in the price of a room. Carry nutrition bars from home in your tote bag for snacking when only expensive airport or restaurant food is available. Use public transportation whenever possible. Rail and air passes are sold for Europe and other regions but often can only be purchased in the United States before departure. If you must rent a car and have booked one from home, double-check local prices. Sometimes better deals can be arranged on the spot. When you first arrive in a country, check with a visitors' bureau. Agents there will explain discount cards or money-saving packets offered by local governments or merchants. The discount plans often cover transportation, food, lodging, museums, concerts, and other entertainment.

GETTING TO YOUR HOTEL

I'd like to go to the _____ Hotel.	**Je voudrais aller à l'hôtel _____.** *zhuh voo-dreh zah-lay ah loh-tel*
Is it near (far)?	**C'est près (loin) d'ici?** *seh preh (lwan) dee-ssee*
Where can I get a taxi?	**Où puis-je trouver un taxi?** *oo pweezh troo-vay uhn tahk-see*
Where is the nearest bus (métro) stop?	**Où est l'arrêt de bus (métro) le plus proche?** *oo eh lah-reh duh bews (duh may-troh) luh plew prohsh*
How much is the fare?	**Quel est le tarif?** *kehl eh luh tah-reef*

CHECKING IN

When you register, it will be necessary to fill out a form (*une fiche*) with your name, address, and passport number at the registration desk of any establishment.

I'd like a single (double) room for tonight _____.	**Je voudrais une chambre à un lit (à deux lits) pour ce soir _____.** *zhuh voo-dreh zewn shahn-bruh ah uhn lee (ah duh lee) poor suh swahr*	
■ 3 days	**trois jours** *trawh zhoor*	
■ a week	**une semaine** *ewn suh-mehn*	
■ with a balcony	**avec balcon** *ah-vehk bahl-kohn*	
■ facing the ocean	**qui donne sur l'océan** *kee dohn sewr loh-ssay-ahn*	
■ facing the street	**qui donne sur la rue** *kee dohn sewr lah rew*	
■ facing the courtyard	**qui donne sur la cour** *kee dohn sewr lah koor*	
Does it have _____?	**Il y a _____?** *eel yah*	
■ air conditioning	**la climatisation** *lah klee-mah-tee-zah-ssyohn*	
■ a hair dryer	**un sèche-cheveux** *uhn sehsh-shuh-vuh*	
■ a television	**une télévision** *ewn tay-lay-vee-zyohn*	
■ a safe	**un coffre-fort** *uhn kohfr-fohr*	
■ a private bathroom	**une salle de bain particulaire** *ewn sahl duh ban pahr-tee-kew-lehr*	
■ a mini-bar	**un mini-bar** *uhn mee-nee bahr*	
I (don't) have a reservation.	**J'ai une (Je n'ai pas de) réservation.** *zhay ewn (zhuh nay pah duh) ray-zehr-vah-ssyohn*	

I don't like the room.	**La chambre ne me plaît pas.**	*lah shahn-bruh nuh muh pleh pah*
Do you have something _____?	**Avez-vous quelque chose _____?**	*Ah-vay voo kehl-kuh shohz*
▪ better	**de meilleur**	*duh meh-yuhr*
▪ larger	**de plus grand**	*duh plew grahn*
▪ smaller	**de plus petit**	*duh plew puh-tee*
▪ cheaper	**de meilleur marché**	*duh meh-yuhr mahr-shay*
On what floor is it?	**C'est à quel étage?**	*seh tah kehl ay-tahzh*
Where are the elevators?	**Où sont les ascenseurs?**	*oo sohn lay zah-sahn-suhr*
How much do you charge for _____?	**Quel est le tarif _____?**	*kehl eh luh tah-reef*
▪ the American plan	**pension complète**	*pahn-ssyohn kohn-pleht*
▪ bed and breakfast	**petit déjeuner compris**	*puh-tee day-zhuh-nay kohn-pree*
▪ breakfast and dinner	**en demi-pension**	*ahn duh-mee pahn-ssyohn*
▪ the room without meals	**pour la chambre sans repas**	*poor lah shahn-bruh sahn ruh-pah*
Do we have to eat here?	**Doit-on manger ici?**	*dwah-tohn mahn-zhay ee-see*
Is breakfast included?	**Le petit déjeuner est compris?**	*luh puh-tee day-zhuh-nay eh kohn-pree*
What is my room number?	**Quel est le numéro de ma chambre?**	*kehl eh luh new-may-roh duh mah shahn-bruh*

Is there Internet service in the room (hotel)?	**Il y a le service à Internet dans la chambre (l'hôtel)?** *eel yah luh sehr-veess ah an-tehr-neht dahn lah shahn-bruh (loh-tehl)*
Is there on demand wireless (WiFi) service?	**Il y a accès sans fil (WiFi) à Internet sur demande?** *eel yah ahk-seh sahn feel (wi-fi) ah an-tehr-neht sewr duh-mahnd*
Is it free?	**C'est gratuit?** *seh grah-twee*
Is there a discount for children (seniors)?	**Il y a une réduction pour les enfants (personnes du troisième âge)?** *eel yah ewn ray-dewk-ssyohn poor lay zahn-fahn (pehr-sohn dew trwah-zyehm ahzh)*
Could you put another bed (a crib) in the room?	**Pourriez-vous mettre un autre lit (un berceau) dans la chambre?** *poo-ree-yay voo meh-truh uhn noh-truh lee (uhn behr-soh) dahn lah shahn-bruh*

Is there a charge? How much?	**Faut-il payer cela? Combien?** *foh teel peh-yay suh-lah? kohn-byan*

OTHER ACCOMMODATIONS

I'm looking for _____.	**Je cherche _____.** *zhuh shehrsh*
■ a boarding house	**une pension** *ewn pahn-ssyohn*
■ a private house	**une maison particulière** *ewn meh-zohn pahr-tee-kew-lyehr*
I want to rent an apartment.	**Je voudrais louer un appartement.** *zhuh voo-dreh loo-ay uhn nah-pahr-tuh-mahn*
I would like one (two) bedrooms.	**Je voudrais une (deux) chambre(s) à coucher.** *zhuh voo-dreh zewn (duh) shahn-bruh ah koo-shay*
Do you have a furnished room?	**Avez-vous une chambre meublée? (garnie?)** *ah-vay voo zewn shahn-bruh muh-blay (gahr-nee)*
How much is the rent?	**C'est combien le loyer?** *seh kohn-byan luh lwah-yay*
I'll be staying here for _____.	**Je resterai ici _____.** *zhuh rehss-tray ee-ssee*
■ one week	**une semaine** *ewn suh-mehn*
■ two weeks	**quinze jours** *kahnz zhoor*
■ one month	**un mois** *uhn mwah*
■ the whole summer	**tout l'été** *too lay-tay*

| I would like a place that's near public transportation. | **Je voudrais une résidence près des transports publics.** *zhuh voo-dreh zewn ray-zee-dahnss preh day trahnss-pohr pew-bleek* |
| Is there a youth hostel around here? | **Il y a une auberge de jeunesse par ici?** *eel yah ewn oh-behrzh duh zhuh-nehss preh dee-ssee* |

ORDERING BREAKFAST

The French or continental breakfast is usually simple—coffee or hot chocolate and a croissant or brioche with jam or marmalade. At the larger hotels you will be able to order an English-style breakfast (juice, eggs, bacon, toast). You may enjoy having breakfast in your room.

| We'll have breakfast in the room. | **Nous prendrons le petit déjeuner dans la chambre.** *noo prahn-drohn luh puh-tee day-zhuh-nay dahn lah shahn-bruh* |

Please send up _____.	**Faites monter _____, s'il vous plaît.** *feht mohn-tay _____ seel voo pleh*
We'd like _____.	**Nous voudrions _____.** *noo voo-dree-yohn*
▇ one (two) coffee(s)	**un (deux) café(s)** *uhn (duh) kah-fay*
▇ tea	**un thé** *uhn tay*
▇ hot chocolate	**un chocolat** *uhn shoh-koh-lah*
▇ a (some) croissant(s)	**un (des) croissant(s)** *uhn (day) krwah-ssahn*
▇ fruit	**des fruits** *day frwee*
▇ fruit juice	**du jus de fruit** *dew zhew duh frwee*
▇ scrambled (fried) (boiled) eggs	**des oeufs brouillés (au plat) (à la coque)** *day zuh broo-yay (oh plah) (ah lah kohk)*
▇ toast	**du pain grillé** *dew pan gree-yay*
▇ jam	**de la confiture** *duh lah kohn-fee-tewr*
▇ butter	**du beurre** *dew buhr*
We'll eat breakfast downstairs.	**On descend prendre le petit déjeuner.** *ohn day-sahn prahn-druh luh puh-tee day-zhuh-nay*

NOTE: See Food section (page 113) for more phrases for ordering meals.

HOTEL SERVICES

Where is (are) _____?	**Où est (sont) _____?** *oo eh (sohn)*
▇ the dining room	**la salle à manger** *lah sahl ah mahn-zhay*
▇ the restrooms	**les toilettes** *lay twah-leht*
▇ the elevator	**l'ascenseur** *lah-ssahn-ssuhr*

Please send up ____.	**Faites monter ____ s'il vous plaît.**	
	feht mohn-tay ____ seel voo pleh	
■ a bellboy	**un chasseur** *uhn shah-ssuhr*	
■ housekeeping	**une femme de chambre** *ewn fahm duh shahn-bruh*	
Please give me ____.	**Donnez-moi ____ s'il vous plait.**	
	doh-nay mwah ____ seel voo pleh	
■ a towel	**une serviette** *ewn sehr-vyeht*	
■ a bar of soap	**une savonnette** *ewn sah-voh-neht*	
■ some hangers	**des cintres** *day san-truh*	
■ a pillow	**un oreiller** *uhn noh-reh-yay*	
■ a blanket	**une couverture** *ewn koo-vehr-tewr*	
■ some ice	**de la glace** *duh lah glahss*	
■ ice cubes	**des glaçons** *day glah-ssohn*	
■ an ashtray	**un cendrier** *uhn sahn-dree-yay*	
■ toilet paper	**un rouleau de papier hygiénique** *uhn roo-loh duh pah-pyay ee-zhyay-neek*	
■ a bottle of mineral water	**une bouteille d'eau minérale** *ewn boo-tehy doh mee-nay-rahl*	
■ an electric adaptor	**un transformateur** *uhn trahnss-fohr-mah-tuhr*	
■ some tissues	**des mouchoirs en papier** *day moo-shwahr ahn pah-pyay*	

NOTE: Electric current is usually 220 volts. A European-style adaptor plug or an adaptable appliance is necessary for electric hair dryers or clocks. Large international hotels may have an adaptor plug at the reception desk, but smaller hotels or pensions are unlikely to be able to provide one.

Just a minute.	**Un moment.** *uhn moh-mahn*
Come in.	**Entrez.** *ahn-tray*
Put that on the table, please.	**Mettez ça sur la table, s'il vous plaît.** *meh-tay sah sewr lah tah-bluh seel voo pleh*
Please wake me tomorrow at ____.	**Réveillez-moi demain matin à ____, s'il vous plaît.** *ray-vay-yay mwah duh-man mah-tan ah ____ seel voo pleh*
There is no ____.	**Il n'y a pas ____.** *eel nyah pah*
running water	**d'eau courante** *doh koo-rahnt*
hot water	**d'eau chaude** *doh shohd*
electricity	**d'électricité** *day-lehk-tree-ssee-tay*
The ____ doesn't work.	**____ ne fonctionne pas.** *____ nuh fohnk-ssyohn pah*
air conditioner	**le climatiseur** *luh klee-mah-tee-zuhr*
fan	**le ventilateur** *luh vahn-tee-lah-tuhr*
faucet	**le robinet** *luh roh-bee-neh*
lamp	**la lampe** *lah lahnp*
radio	**la radio** *lah rah-dyoh*
socket	**la prise de courant** *lah preez duh koo-rahn*
switch	**le commutateur** *luh koh-mew-tah-tuhr*
television	**la télévision** *lah tay-lay-vee-zyohn*
Can you fix it?	**Pouvez-vous la réparer?** *poo-vay voo lah ray-pah-ray*
now	**maintenant** *mant-nahn*
as soon as possible	**aussitôt que possible** *oh-ssee-toh kuh poh-ssee-bluh*
The room is dirty.	**La chambre est sale.** *lah shahn-bruh eh sahl*

Are there any ____ for me?	**Il y a ____ pour moi?** *eel yah ____ poor mwah*
■ letters	**des lettres** *day leh-truh*
■ messages	**des messages** *day meh-ssahzh*
■ packages	**des colis** *day koh-lee*
■ postcards	**des cartes postales** *day kahrt pohss-tahl*

Can you make a phone call for me?	**Pouvez-vous faire un coup de téléphone pour moi?** *poo-vay voo fehr uhn koo duh tay-lay-fohn poor mwah*

I'd like to put this in the hotel safe.	**Je voudrais mettre ceci dans le coffre-fort de l'hôtel.** *zhuh voo-dreh meh-truh ssuh-ssee dahn luh koh-fruh-fohr duh loh-tehl*

CHECKING OUT

I'd like the bill, please.	**Je voudrais la note, s'il vous plaît.** *zhuh voo-dreh lah noht seel voo pleh*
I'm leaving today (tomorrow).	**Je pars aujourd'hui (demain).** *zhuh pahr oh-zhoor-dwee (duh-man)*
Please send someone up for the baggage.	**Faites monter quelqu'un pour les valises, s'il vous plaît.** *feht mohn-tay kehl-kuhn poor lay vah-leez seel voo pleh*
Will you please call me a taxi?	**Voudriez-vous appeler un taxi pour moi?** *voo-dree-yay voos ah-play uhn tak-ssee poor mwah*
Where is the stop for the bus to the airport?	**Où est l'arrêt du bus qui va à l'aéroport?** *oo eh lah-reh dew bewss kee vah ah lah-ee-roh-pohr*

GETTING AROUND TOWN

In villages or out in the country you may want to stroll around to do your sightseeing. Although walking in the city is also rewarding, you'll want to be familiar with the types of public transportation available.

For information on plane, train, or boat travel, see pages 62–68.

The **R.A.T.P.** (**Régie Autonome des Transports Parisiens**) directs the entire Parisian bus and subway system. In addition to the **métropolitain** (subway), commonly referred to as the **métro**, the R.A.T.P. also provides service on the **R.E.R.** (**Réseau Express Régional**), the local suburban system, which covers eight zones within the Paris region. R.E.R. lines are identified by letters and by the end-of-the-line name of the station.

THE SUBWAY (UNDERGROUND)

Le métro (the subway) is the clean, inexpensive, and efficient underground train system in Paris. Above ground, a big yellow **M** within a circle, or easily recognizable curly, green railings and an archway indicate the métro, which can take you within walking distance of almost any tourist attraction in the city. Trains run very frequently—about every five minutes.

There are 16 numbered subway lines (numbered 1–14, with two minor lines: 3ibis and 7ibis), indicated by different numbers and by different colors on the free subway maps available in most stations, hotel lobbies, and department stores. Each métro station also displays a map with a **plan du quartier**, a detailed map of the surrounding area. The métro is easy to navigate if you know the name of the last station, in both directions, on the line you plan to take, since all subway lines are identified on signs by their final destination.

Transfers from one line to another are free within 1½ hours from the first validation point, and connections are indicated by orange correspondance signs. You may transfer as often as you like on one ticket, provided that you do not exit to the street. Exits are clearly marked by blue **SORTIE** signs.

A ticket may be purchased at any métro station, R.E.R., or tramway station or upon boarding a bus. Note that in the métro, tickets are sold only through self-service machines (which can be programmed for English instructions). Tickets may also be bought at many newsstands or **tabacs** (tobacco stores) around the city. A transfer may be used on the entire métro network, on buses, trams, and in Zone 1 of the R.E.R.

Each metro ride costs one ticket (a standard **T+ métro** ticket). For convenience and economy, a book of 10 tickets (**un carnet**) is available for regular riders. Frequent riders may wish to purchase an orange card (**une carte orange**), which permits unlimited rides for a month. To obtain this card you will need a small photo. **Paris Visites** one-, two-, three-, or five-day tourist tickets (valid for the consecutive number of days purchased) are available in advance from U.S. travel agents and are valid for unlimited travel on the bus, métro, R.E.R., tramway, and nationwide S.N.C.F. trains. They also give discounts on certain sightseeing trips and at some museums, attractions, and restaurants.

Entrance to the French métro is by automated gate, opened by smart cards and simple tickets.

Métro tickets are a little tricky to use. Slide the ticket into the automatic ticket machine and then wait for it to quickly pop up. It is essential that you keep your ticket until you reach the point that says **Limite de Validité des Billets** for two reasons: An inspector may ask to see your ticket at any time and you risk a fine if you cannot furnish it, and you will need the ticket in the event that you would like to transfer to the R.E.R. within Paris. For trips to the suburbs, a special R.E.R. ticket will have to be purchased.

The Parisian subways are open Monday–Thursday and Sunday from 5:30 A.M. to 1:15 A.M. and Friday and Saturday from 5:30 A.M. to 2:15 A.M.

IMPORTANT SIGNS

Attention: Danger de mort	Attention: Danger of Death
Contrôle des billets	Ticket Verification (by métro officials)
En travaux	Under Construction
En cas d'affluence, ne pas utiliser les strapontins	In case of overcrowding, please don't use the fold-down seats (in subways)
La correspondance n'est pas assure	A transfer is not available
Places prioritaires	Reserved Seats (for the elderly, pregnant women, passengers with young children, or disabled passengers)

I'm looking for a métro station.	**Je cherche un station de métro.** *zhuh shehrsh ewn stah-ssyohn duh may-troh*
Where is the nearest subway station?	**Où se trouve la station de métro la plus proche?** *oo suh troov lah stah-ssyohn duh may-troh lah plew prohsh*
One ticket, please.	**Un billet, s'il vous plaît.** *uhn bee-yeh seel voo pleh*
A book of tickets, please.	**Un carnet, s'il vous plaît.** *uhn kahr-neh seel voo pleh*
How much is the fare?	**Quel est le prix du trajet?** *kehl eh luh pree dew trah-zheh*
How do I get to the station?	**Comment aller à la station?** *koh-mahn tah-lay ah lah stah-ssyohn*
Where can I buy a ticket?	**Où puis-je acheter un billet?** *oo pweezh ahsh-tay uhn bee-yeh*
Which line goes to _____?	**Quelle ligne va à _____?** *kehl lee-nyuh vah ah*

Does this train go to _____?	**Çe train va à _____?** *suh tran vah ah*	
How many more stops are there?	**Il reste combien d'arrêts?** *eel rehsst kohn-byan dah-reh*	
What's the next station?	**Quelle est la prochaine station?** *kehl eh lah proh-shehn stah-ssyohn*	
Where should I get off to go to _____?	**Où dois-je descendre pour aller à _____?** *oo dwahzh day-sahn-druh poor ah-lay ah*	
Do I have to change trains?	**Faut-il prendre une correspondance?** *foh teel prahn-druh ewn koh-rehss-pohn-dahnss*	
Please tell me when we get there.	**S'il vous plaît, dites-moi quand nous y arrivons.** *seel voo pleh, deet mwah kahn noo zee ah-ree-vohn*	
Where is the exit, please?	**S'il vous plaît, où est la sortie?** *seel voo pleh, oo eh lah sohr-tee*	

In the trains, buses, and métro, certain seats with numbers are reserved. You may sit in one of those seats if there are enough seats vacant. A war veteran may come up to you and show you his ID card, and in that case, you have to give him your seat. You may see the following notices posted:

LES PLACES NUMÉROTÉES SONT RÉSERVÉES:	NUMBERED SEATS ARE RESERVED FOR:
1. Aux invalides de guerre	Disabled veterans
2. Aux invalides civils	Handicapped persons
3. Aux femmes enceintes	Pregnant women
4. Aux personnes accompagnées d'enfants de moins de 4 ans	Persons with children under 4 years of age

THE BUS (STREETCAR, TRAM)

Green Parisian buses post their route and destination in the front of the bus and their major stops on the sides of the bus. The routes of each line are indicated on a sign at each stop. A free bus map **Autobus Paris—Plan du Réseau** is available at tourist offices and some métro information booths.

The same ticket is used for buses as for the métro. Regular tickets are validated by inserting them into a canceling machine at the driver's seat. A **carte orange**, on the other hand, is merely shown to the driver. Once again, it is important to keep your ticket until the end of the ride.

Bus hours vary, but major lines run from about 5:30 A.M. to midnight. Night buses run throughout the night. Many bus stops are equipped with electronic information systems that indicate when the next bus will arrive.

European Express and Europabus serve major European cities. They are less expensive, but slower, than trains. If you plan to travel around the city by bus, you can purchase a discount book of tickets (**un carnet**).

The tramway, with its one T3 line, runs within the city limits of Paris, mainly through the southern districts.

Where is the bus stop? (bus terminal?)	**Où est l'arrêt de bus? (le terminus?)** *oo eh lah-reh duh bewss (luh tehr-mee-newss)*
How often do the buses run?	**Quelle est la fréquence des bus?** *kehl eh lah fray-kah<u>n</u>ss day bewss*
I want to go to _____.	**Je voudrais aller à _____.** *zhuh voo-dreh zah-lay ah*
In which direction do I have to go?	**Dans quel sens dois-je aller?** *dah<u>n</u> kehl sah<u>n</u>ss dwahzh ah-lay*
Which bus do I take to get to _____?	**Quel bus faut-il prendre pour aller à _____?** *kehl bewss foh teel prah<u>n</u>-druh poor ah-lay ah*

Is it far from here?	**C'est loin d'ici?** *seh lwan dee-ssee*
How many stops are there?	**Il y a combien d'arrêts?** *eel yah kohn-byan dah-reh*
Do I have to change?	**Faut-il changer de bus?** *foh teel shahn-zhay duh bewss*
Do you go to ____?	**Vous allez à ____?** *voo zah-lay ah*
Where do I get off?	**Où dois-je descendre?** *oo dwahzh day-sahn-druh*
Could you tell me when to get off?	**Pourriez-vous me dire quand je dois descendre?** *poo-ree-yay voo muh deer kahn zhuh dwah day-sahn-druh*

TAXIS

Taxis, except for certain ones that make trips to and from the airport and give a flat rate, are metered. Taxi rates vary according to time of day and geographical area. A 10% tip is customary if the driver helped you with your luggage. Taxis may refuse to accept more than three passengers. Look for the sign **Stationnement de Taxis** indicating a taxi stand. You cannot hail a taxi on the street within 100 meters of a stand. There is a supplement (indicated on the meter) after 11:00 P.M.

Is there a taxi stand around here?	**Il y a une station de taxis près d'ici?** *eel yah ewn stah-ssyohn duh tahk-ssee preh dee-ssee*
Where can I get a taxi?	**Où puis-je trouver un taxi?** *oo pweezh troo-vay uhn tahk-ssee*
Taxi! Are you free?	**Taxi! Êtes-vous libre?** *tahk-ssee eht voo lee-bruh*

I would like to go _____.	**Je voudrais aller_____.** *zhuh voo-dreh zah-lay*	
■ to the airport	**à l'aéroport** *ah lahy-roh-pohr*	
■ to this address	**à cette adresse** *ah seht ah-drehss*	
■ to the hotel _____	**à l'hôtel ___** *ah loh-tehl*	
■ to the train station	**à la gare** *ah lah gahr*	
■ to _____ Street	**à la rue _____** *ah lah rew*	
■ to _____ Avenue	**à l'avenue _____** *ah lahv-new*	
■ to _____ Boulevard	**au boulevard _____** *oh bool-vahr*	

Do you know where it is? **Savez-vous où ça se trouve?** *sah-vay voo oo sah suh troov*

How much is it to _____? **C'est combien pour aller à _____?** *seh koh<u>n</u>-bya<u>n</u> poor ah-lay ah*

I'm in a hurry. **Je suis pressé(e)!** *zhuh swee preh-ssay*

Don't go so fast. **Ne conduisez pas si vite, s'il vous plaît.** *nuh koh<u>n</u>-dwee-zay pah see veet seel voo pleh*

Stop here at the corner.

Arrêtez-vous ici, à l'angle.
ah-ray-tay voo zee-ssee ah lah<u>n</u>gl

Stop at the next block.

Arrêtez-vous à la prochaine rue.
ah-ray-tay voo ah lah proh-shehn rew

Wait for me. I'll be right back.

Attendez-moi, s'il vous plaît. Je reviens tout de suite. *ah-tah<u>n</u>-day mwah seel voo pleh zhuh ruh-vya<u>n</u> toot sweet*

How much do I owe you?

Je vous dois combien? *zhuh voo dwah koh<u>n</u>-bya<u>n</u>*

This is for you.

Voilà pour vous. *vwah-lah poor voo*

PLACES TO GO/SIGHTSEEING

Where is the Tourist Office?

Où est le Syndicat d'Initiative?
oo eh luh sa<u>n</u>-dee-kah dee-nee-ssyah-teev

I need a (an English-speaking) guide.

J'ai besoin d'un guide (qui parle anglais). *zhay buh-zwa<u>n</u> duh<u>n</u> geed (kee pahrl ah<u>n</u>-gleh)*

How much is it?

C'est combien _____? *seh koh<u>n</u> bya<u>n</u>*

■ per hour

à l'heure *ah luhr*

■ per day

à la journée *ah lah zhoor-nay*

There are two (four, six) of us.

Nous sommes deux (quatre, six).
noo sohm duh (kah-truh, seess)

Where can I buy a guidebook? (a map?) (a street map?)

Où puis-je acheter un guide touristique? (une carte?) (un plan de la ville?) *oo pweezh ahsh-tay uh<u>n</u> geed too-reess-teek (ewn kahrt) (uh<u>n</u> plah<u>n</u> duh lah veel)*

What are the main attractions?	**Qu'est-ce qu'il y a de plus intéressant à voir?** *kehss keel yah duh plew zan-tay-reh-ssahn ah vwahr*
Are there tours of the city?	**Il y a des tours de la ville?** *eel yah day toor duh lah veel*
Where do they leave from?	**D'où partent-elles?** *doo pahr tehl*
We want to see _____.	**Nous voudrions voir _____.** *noo vood-ree-yohn vwahr*

- the botanical garden **le jardin botanique** *luh zhahr-dan boh-tah-neek*
- the castle **le château** *luh shah-toh*
- the cathedral **la cathédrale** *lah kah-tay-drahl*
- the church **l'église** *lay-gleez*
- the concert hall **la salle de concert** *lah sahl duh kohn-ssehr*
- the downtown area **le centre ville** *luh sahn-truh veel*
- the fountains **les fontaines** *lay fohn-tehn*
- the library **la bibliothèque** *lah bee-blee-oh-tehk*
- the main square **la place principale** *lah plahss pran-ssee-pahl*
- the market **le marché** *luh mahr-shay*
- the mosque **la mosquée** *lah mohss-kay*
- the museum (of fine arts) **le musée (des beaux arts)** *luh mew-zay (day boh zahr)*
- a nightclub **une boîte de nuit** *ewn bwaht duh nwee*
- the old part of town **la vieille ville** *lah vyehy veel*
- the opera **l'opéra** *loh-pay-rah*
- the palace **le palais** *luh pah-leh*
- the park **le parc** *luh pahrk*
- the stadium **le stade** *luh stahd*

■ the synagogue	**la synagogue**	*lah see-nah-gohg*
■ the university	**l'université**	*lew-nee-vehr-ssee-tay*
■ the zoo	**le zoo**	*luh zoh*

Is it open?	**C'est ouvert?**	*seh too-vehr*
Is it closed?	**C'est fermé?**	*seh fehr-may*
At what time does it open?	**Ça ouvre à quelle heure?** *sah oo-vruh ah kehl uhr*	
At what time does it close?	**Ça ferme à quelle heure?** *sah fehrm ah kehl uhr*	
What's the admission price?	**Combien coûte un billet d'entrée?** *kohn-byan koot uhn-bee-yeh dahn-tray*	
How much do children (seniors) pay?	**C'est combien pour les enfants? (personnes du troisième âge)** *seh kohn-byan poor lay zahn-fahn (pehr-sohn dew trwah-zyehm ahzh)*	
Can they go in free?	**Est-ce gratuit pour les enfants?** *ehss grah-twee poor lay zahn-fahn.*	
Until what age?	**Jusqu'à quel âge?** *zhewss-kah kehl ahzh*	
Is it all right to take pictures?	**Peut-on prendre des photos?** *puh tohn prahn-druh day foh-toh*	

A SIGHTSEEING ITINERARY

France is a country overwhelmingly rich in places and things to be seen. Its cities and countryside overflow with sites and institutions filled with historic, intellectual, and artistic tradition. Few indeed are the areas not commemorated by a general's triumph, a king's passage, an artist's inspiration, or a philosopher's thoughts. To attempt an exhaustive tour in the usual short vacation span would be foolhardy. We try here simply to suggest, in broad outline, some of the highlights, the best-known and most popular attractions to which visitors are drawn. Modern France has an extensive and sophisticated system of public transportation, enabling the traveler to get quickly to whatever area most interests him.

PARIS

Paris is the cultural, economic, political, and social center of France. Among its museums are: The *Louvre*, which contains the Venus de Milo and the Mona Lisa, with Leoh Ming Pei's controversial Pyramid in front, as well as art and antiquities from all over Europe; the *Army Museum* at the Invalides in which stands the tomb of Napoleon; the *Musée d'Orsay* (located in the old Gare d'Orsay, one of Paris's first railroad stations), which, in addition to housing some of the vast collection of Impressionist paintings formerly displayed in the Jeu de Paume Museum, traces the development of contrasting artistic styles at the end of the nineteenth and beginning of the twentieth centuries; the *Jeu de Paume Museum*, which now exhibits contemporary art, sculpture, and photography; the *Panthéon*, commemorating illustrious French men and women; the *Cluny Museum* with beautiful medieval art and a superb tapestry collection; the *Musée Grévin*, which displays delightful wax replicas of the rich and famous; the *Orangerie*, which contains modern art and early twentieth-century Impressionist paintings by, among others, Monet and Renoir; the *Picasso Museum*, which traces the development of the artist's work and where each room depicts a certain stage in his career; the *Rodin Museum*, in which sculptures are displayed in a lovely house and magnificent garden, the perfect setting for a typical French picnic; the *Musée National d'Art Moderne*, located within the Pompidou Center, which contains a large selection of very avant-garde paintings and sculptures; the *Muséum national d'histoire naturelle*, which houses a spectacular Great Gallery of Evolution; the *Maison de Victor Hugo*, located at 6 Place des Vosges, which displays memorabilia from the artist's life; the *Cité des sciences et de l'industrie*, located in a lovely park with gardens in northern Paris, with its geodesic dome and giant-screen science movies, which is a masterwork of modern architecture; and the *Musée du Quai Branly*, built in 2006 by Jean Nouvel, which houses a permanent collection of artifacts from all over the world and hosts a variety of shows, concerts, films, and cultural activities.

Those with an interest in church sculpture and architecture will be particularly interested in the Cathedral of *Notre-Dame*. Its spires, portals, stained glass windows, and flying buttresses make it an outstanding example of Gothic architecture. Vividly colored stained glass windows dating back to the thirteenth century and portraying over 1,000 biblical scenes make the *Sainte-Chapelle* church unique. *Sacré-Coeur*, the domed white church dominating Montmartre, resembles a mosque and is decorated on the interior with mosaics. The eighteenth–nineteenth-century church of the *Madeleine* with its colonnade is also of interest. The *Église St-Germain*, Paris's oldest church and one of the few remaining examples of the Romanesque style, certainly warrants a visit.

Noted public squares frequented by tourists include: the *Place de la Concorde*, where many historical figures, including Louis XVI and Marie Antoinette, were guillotined during the French Revolution. The obelisk in the middle of the square comes from the ruins of the Temple of Luxor in Egypt and is covered with hieroglyphics. The *Place Vendôme* is the site of the

Vendôme column, which has scenes depicting Napoleon's military campaigns at its center. On top of the column is a statue of the emperor. *The Place de l'Opéra*, dominated by the Opéra (renovated in 1995), is the home of the national opera and ballet companies and is renowned for its architecture and décor. Its Gobelin tapestries, gilded mosaics, Chagall ceiling, and 6-ton chandelier attract many tourists. The *Place de la Bastille* is the site of the once famous prison, since destroyed, where the first shots of the French Revolution are commemorated every July 14. The *Place Charles de Gaulle*, upon which stands the Arc de Triomphe, is one of France's best known landmarks. Under the arch is the Tomb of the Unknown Soldier. Twelve avenues fan out from the arch, creating the pattern of a star. Leading to the arch, the Champs-Elysées is lined with trees, cafés, and luxurious shops. The *Place des Vosges*, an example of seventeenth-century secular architecture, is noted for its grassy enclosure containing a children's playground.

The *Centre National d'Art et de Culture Georges Pompidou*, on the site of the old Les Halles market, is a national museum with frequent expositions and a voluminous research library. From the observation deck on the roof you can see all of Paris.

Since almost one-half of the area of the site is open, spontaneous public spectacles and unprogrammed outdoor events hosted by jugglers, artists, acrobats, mimes, musicians, and fire-eaters are not uncommon, and attract large crowds.

The center is easily recognizable because of its network of boldly colored pipes and tubes of all sizes adorning the outside walls. The exterior, glass-enclosed tubular escalators also give a panoramic view of Paris.

With a focus on contemporary art, the center offers numerous exhibits and activities, a huge library, a museum of modern art, a movie library (**la cinémathèque**), and an institute for acoustic and musical research and coordination.

The *Eiffel Tower* stands over 1,000 feet tall and acts as a radio and television transmitter. From any of its three different levels one gets a panoramic view of Paris. At its base there is a popular restaurant. Walking along the *quais* of the *Seine* you will find the parapets lined with quaint bookshops. *Montmartre*, or the "Butte," as it is commonly known, is a center of artistic life where bohemianism may be said to have its roots. The *Latin Quarter* is the home of the Sorbonne University and an intellectual hub.

At the *Palais de Justice*, the seat of the courts and all the judicial system, you will see the *Conciergerie*, which served as a prison during the Revolution. A guillotine remains in the chapel where prisoners were led before their executions. Also not to be missed are *La Bourse* or Stock Exchange, *Le Marché aux puces*, the Paris flea market, and the *Comédie Française*, the theater that houses France's leading dramatic groups.

When your feet hurt and you want to take a break, relax in the *Tuileries* gardens, beside the Seine. Statues, figures, and decorative vases line these formal French gardens. The *Bois de Boulogne* is a vast park containing ornamental lakes, flower gardens, cafés, restaurants, two racetracks, and a children's amusement park. Best, however, not to frequent it at night. The *Bois de Vincennes* contains museums and a zoo. The *Luxembourg* gardens, on the left bank, are often used by students.

The *Cimetière Père-Lachaise* (Père-Lachaise Cemetery) would interest those who want to see the graves of renowned French personages such as Balzac, Colette, Delacroix, Molière, Édith Piaf, and Seurat, as well as foreigners Chopin, Oscar Wilde, Gertrude Stein, and James Douglas "Jim" Morrison.

Two areas of particular interest within Paris are *La Défense*, where modern sculpture created by celebrated artists from around the world adorns the streets and buildings, and *Le Marais*, where small streets, gothic churches, and old-fashioned houses lend a flavor of the Middle Ages to the neighborhood.

Just outside Paris is *Versailles*, the luxurious palace known for its architecture, style, and gardens. Not to be missed is the fabulous *Galerie des Glaces* (Hall of Mirrors), where the Treaty of Versailles was signed in 1919. A bus tour from Paris to Versailles might also include side trips to *Fontainebleau* and *Chantilly* castles. The *Basilica de Saint Denis*, and the small city of *Sèvres*, known for its multicolored porcelain, are also not far from the capital. Many tourists are attracted to Monet's house at *Giverny*, where the rooms have been restored according to the artist's original designs, and one can enjoy the luxurious garden and a water garden with lilies and bridges.

Travel Tips   A two-, four-, or six-day (consecutive days) museum pass may be purchased from your travel agent within the United States or at various locations throughout Paris. For a very reasonable fee, the pass entitles the bearer to free admission to over 60 museums, castles, gardens, cathedrals, and monuments throughout Paris. This includes multiple visits at no extra charge. Groups of 10 or more receive a 5% discount. A major plus is that one does not have to wait to enter and immediately passes to the front of the line. The only drawback to the pass is that it must be used on consecutive days.

FARTHER AFIELD

A bus tour of the Loire Valley allows you to visit many splendid castles:

Amboise—a castle that offers a beautiful view across the river.

Angers—a castle and two museums, one famous for medieval tapestry and the other for its nineteenth-century sculpture.

Azay-le-Rideau—a castle with romantic appeal and charm.

Blois—a castle whose architecture represents many styles.

Chambord—the largest of all the châteaux, surrounded by a vast forest.

Chaumont—a castle offering a fantastic view across the river.

Chenonceau—a castle in a truly magnificent setting.

Cheverny—one of the last castles to be built.

Chinon—a truly authentic castle.

Villandry—a castle with formal, Renaissance gardens.

A tour of medieval French Gothic churches would certainly prove worthwhile. Among the most popular are:

Amiens—the largest completed Gothic cathedral.

Beauvais—the highest cathedral in France; its nave was never built.

Chartres—a cathedral containing sculptures representing biblical personages. The stained glass windows of the cathedral are exquisite and unique.

Reims—the cathedral where the kings of France were crowned.

Rouen—a cathedral that incorporates almost all intermediate styles of Gothic architecture.

The beaches of *Normandy*, where the Allies landed in 1944, will be of special interest to history buffs.

Mont-Saint-Michel, a monastery surrounded by a medieval fortress, is situated on a small island in the English Channel, between Normandy and Brittany. Tourists must beware of the surrounding quicksand that reaches the island only during high tide.

Carcassonne, in southern France, is one of the finest examples of a medieval, fortified European city.

Every year Catholics make a pilgrimage to *Lourdes*, a city at the foot of the Pyrénées, the mountains that separate France from Spain. It is believed that here, in 1858, the Virgin Mary appeared to Bernadette. For this reason, many people bathe in the sacred waters of the grotto where the vision appeared, hoping to find a miracle that will restore their health.

The seaside resort of *Deauville*, in Normandy, comes alive in the summer when casinos, horse racing, and an exciting nightlife attract the rich and famous.

Biarritz, in the Pays Basque, near Spain, is a popular summer resort city. Here you can enjoy watching pelote, the regional sport known as jai alai in the United States.

Strasbourg, an industrial city, has a cathedral famous for its astronomical clock. It also contains the offices of the EEC, the European Economic Community, previously known as the European Common Market.

The cities of *Chamonix* and *Grenoble*, and the *French Alps*, are extremely popular and offer a wide variety of winter activities.

Nice, capital of the *Côte d'Azur (Riviera)*, vacation spot of the jet set and refuge from the ravages of winter, has pebble beaches and a casino. If you prefer a sand beach, *Cannes*, also on the *Côte d'Azur*, is a pleasant alternative.

A visit to the *wine country*, the regions of Bordeaux, Champagne, and Languedoc, will be interesting and informative.

Corsica, birthplace of Napoleon, is a French island in the Mediterranean Sea, 200 kilometers from Nice. This island boasts beautiful scenery and tiny villages that maintain their medieval charm.

On a side trip to *Monaco*, a visit to Prince Rainier's palace provides a view of the harbor and the yachts moored there. The casino at *Monte Carlo* is its principal attraction.

In *Avignon* there is the *Palace of the Popes* and the *Bridge of St. Bénezet*. *Nîmes* and *Arles*, quaint cities noted for their Roman ruins, have amphitheaters still in their original form.

OUTSIDE FRANCE

For a glimpse of France closer to the United States, visit *Québec* with its magnificent beaches, parks, mountains, forests, and lakes. Participate in your favorite summer or winter sport. See the old and the new cities and visit the charming castles.

If you prefer a tranquil vacation, visit a tropical island. Rest in the shade of the palm and coconut trees of *Martinique* or *Guadeloupe* in the Lesser Antilles. Enjoy the beaches, the languorous lifestyle, and the fruit-flavored daiquiris. In Martinique, tour the capital, *Fort-de-France*, see the ruins of *Saint-Pierre* and *Mt. Pelée*, and the luxuriant rain forest. In Guadeloupe, the town of *Gosier* is the heart of vacation life. At *Le Moule*, the horseshoe beach is one of the island's most popular attractions. Or visit *Haiti*, on the island of Hispaniola, in the Greater Antilles. Horseback ride to the famed *Citadelle*, tour *Port-au-Prince*, the capital, relax by the *waterfalls of Cayes*, and lie on the beautiful beaches of *Port Salut*.

A trip to the French side of *Saint-Martin*, and to its quaint village of *Grand Case*, famous for its beautiful beaches, exquisite restaurants, and fabulous duty-free French stores, is a must.

A most exotic vacation might lead you to Western Africa, where French is spoken in *Senegal*, *Mali*, *Guinea*, *Niger*, and *the Ivory Coast*.

AMUSEMENT PARKS

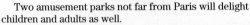

Two amusement parks not far from Paris will delight children and adults as well.

Just 20 miles east of Paris is *Disneyland Paris*, complete with Mickey Mouse, Donald Duck, and their friends. Its two theme parks contain retail stores, dining and entertainment districts, and seven hotels, six associated hotels, a golf course, and a railway station for a new town, *Val d'Europe*. The park is serviced by the **R.E.R.** (**Réseau Express Régional**), the suburban railroad line that makes Paris a mere 35 minutes away. The **TGV** (**train à grande vitesse**), the high-speed French train, also includes a stop on its lines to accommodate tourists.

But if it's typical French amusement, fantastic roller-coaster rides, and adventures based on historic cultures that you seek, try *Parc Astérix*, 20 miles north of Paris. The theme of the park is based on the exploits of Astérix le Gaulois, the famous and much-loved comic-book character, whose fictional exploits took place 2,000 years ago during the Roman invasion of France. North of Metz, in the region of Alsace-Lorraine, children can enjoy the *Walygator Parc*, another fine French amusement park.

PLANNING A TRIP

During your stay, you may want to plan some longer excursions. In France you can get around by moped (**mobylette**), bicycle, or even hiking. For more extensive trips, boats, planes, and trains are all readily available, as are rental cars (see Driving a Car). You may even rent a barge to travel through France on an elaborate canal system.

Travel Tips Most airlines allow passengers to select a seat location and the type of meal preferred at the time reservations are made.Especially on overseas flights, good choices mean the difference between a pleasant or a miserable trip. To get some sleep, choose a window seat well away from the galley (kitchen area). If you like to walk around, request an aisle seat. To watch the movie, avoid the row facing the bulkhead. The reservations agent will know the aircraft being used and can help you pick the best location. Among the meal options are vegetarian, kosher, and low-fat menus. If you have other special dietary needs, ask the reservations agent if those can be met. Be sure to confirm your seat assignment and meal choice when checking in for the flight.

AIR SERVICE

The major airline that services France is Air France. Although very time-efficient, air travel is an expensive option.

When is there a flight to (from) ___?	**Quand y a-t-il un vol à (de) _____?** *kahn tee ah-teel uhn vohl ah (duh)*
I would like a ___ ticket	**Je voudrais ___.** *zhuh voo-dreh*
■ round-trip	**un aller et retour** *zuhn ah-lay ay ruh-toor*

■ one-way	**un aller simple** *zuhn nah-lay san-pluh*
■ tourist class	**un billet en seconde classe** *zuhn bee-yeh ahn suh-gohnde klahss*
■ first class	**un billet en première classe** *zuhn bee-yeh ahn pruh-myehr klahss*
■ child's ticket	**un billet au tarif enfant** *zuhn bee-yeh oh tah-reef ahn-fahn*
■ student's ticket	**un billet au tarif étudiant** *zuhn bee-yeh oh tah-reef ay-tew-dyahn*
I'd like a ___ seat.	**Je voudrais une place ___.** *zhuh voo-dreh zewn plahss*
■ window	**à côté de la fenêtre** *ah koh-tay duh lah fuh-neh-truh*
■ on the aisle	**côté couloir** *koh-tay koo-lwahr*
How much is it?	**C'est combien?** *seh kohn-byan*
Are meals served?	**Sert-on des repas?** *sehr-tohn day ruh-pah*
At what time does the plane leave (arrive)?	**L'avion part (arrive) à quelle heure?** *l'ah-vyohn pahr (ah-reev)ah kehl uhr*
What is the flight number?	**Quel est le numéro de mon vol?** *kehl eh luh new-may-roh duh mohn vohl*
What gate do we leave from?	**De quelle porte partons-nous?** *duh kehl pohr parh-tohn-noo*
I want to confirm (cancel) (change) my reservation for flight ___.	**Je voudrais confirmer (annuler) (changer) ma réservation pour le vol numéro___.** *zhuh voo-dreh kohn-feer-may (ah-new-lay) (shahn-zhay) mah ray-zehr-vah-ssyohn poor luh vohl new-may-roh*

How long is the trip?	**Le trajet dure combien de temps?** *luh trah-zheh dewr koh<u>n</u>-bya<u>n</u> duh tah<u>n</u>*
Is it a direct flight?	**C'est direct?** *seh dee-rehkt*
Is there a stopover?	**Il y a une escale?** *eel yah ewn ehs-kahl*
What time do I have to check in?	**À quelle heure faut-il se presenter à l'enregistrement?** *ah kehl uhr foh-teel suh pray-zah<u>n</u>-tay ah lah<u>n</u>-ruh-zhee-sstruh-mah<u>n</u>*
I'd like to check my bags.	**Je voudrais enregistrer mes bagages.** *zhuh voo-dreh zah<u>n</u>-ruh-zheess-tray may bah-gahzh*
I have only carry-on baggage.	**J'ai seulement des bagages à main.** *zhay suhl-mah<u>n</u> day bah-gahzh ah ma<u>n</u>*
Where is the luggage claim?	**Où sont les bagages?** *oo soh<u>n</u> ley bah-gahzh*
My baggage is lost.	**Mes bagages sont perdus.** *mey bah-gahzh soh<u>n</u> pehr-dew*
My baggage is damaged.	**Mes bagages sont endommagés.** *mey bah-gahzh soh<u>n</u> ah<u>n</u>-doh-mah-zhay*
I am missing a suitcase.	**Il me manque une valise.** *eel muh mah<u>n</u>k ewn vah-leez*

SHIPBOARD TRAVEL

If you plan to travel by boat, a **Tourisme Fluvial** brochure may be obtained from a travel agent or tourist office.

Where is the dock?	**Où est le dock?** *oo eh luh dohk*

When does the next boat leave for _____? **Quand part le prochain bateau pour _____?** *kahn pahr luh proh-shan bah-toh poor*

How long does the crossing take? **La traversée dure combien de temps?** *lah trah-vehr-ssay dewr kohn-byan duh tahn*

At what ports do we stop? **Dans quels ports est-ce qu'on fait escale?** *dahn kehl pohr ehss kohn feh ehss-kahl*

How long is the stopover? **L'escale dure combien de temps?** *lehss-kahl dewr kohn-byan duh tahn*

When do we dock? **Quand est-ce qu'on y arrive?** *kahn tehss kohn nee ah-reev*

At what time do we have to be back on board? **À quelle heure faut-il retourner au bateau?** *ah kehl uhr foh teel ruh-toor-nay oh bah-toh*

I'd like a _____ ticket.	**Je voudrais un billet _____.** *zhuh voo-dreh zuhn bee-yeh*
■ first-class	**de première classe** *duh pruh-myehr klahss*
■ tourist-class	**de deuxième classe** *duh duh-zyehm klahss*
■ cabin	**de cabine** *duh kah-been*
I'm seasick.	**J'ai le mal de mer.** *Zhay luh mahl duh mehr*
Can you give me something for seasickness?	**Pouvez-vous me donner quelque chose contre le mal de mer?** *poo-vay voo muh doh-nay kehl-kuh shohz kohn-truh luh mahl duh mehr*

TRAIN SERVICE

The French railway system is extensive, serving small as well as large cities. Known to be fast, punctual, and comfortable, the **S.N.C.F.** (Société Nationale des Chemins de fer Français) is considered Europe's most efficient train service.

Train schedules may be obtained in every major railroad station and a complete S.N.C.F. timetable may be purchased at newsstands in the stations. Seat reservations are rarely necessary, except when traveling on a **TGV** (**train à grande vitesse**) or on longer international trips. Tickets must be validated before boarding the train. Due to the efficiency of the French train service, long-distance buses are rare.

The TGV makes the regions of Rhône-Alps, Savoy, Rhône Valley, Provence, Languedoc, and even western Switzerland only a few hours' journey from Paris. There are also special tourist trains (**CEVENOL**) running from Paris to Marseilles.

Eurostar is a high-speed passenger train service connecting London with Paris and Brussels.

If you have to sleep on a train you will find that you may purchase a **couchette** (a berth) in one of the first-class four-berth compartments or in one of the second-class six-berth compartments. A first-class compartment may be purchased for single or double occupancy.

If you want an international train, the **Elipsos Train Hotels** are night trains with accommodations that can compete with a contemporary hotel.

Most trains have only non-smoking (**non-fumeur**, *nohn few-muhr*) cars.

EATING ON A TRAIN

You can get anything from a light snack and drinks to a full meal on the train. Use the **wagon-restaurant** (dining car). Also, when the train pulls into a large station, call out the window to the vendors of sandwiches, cheese, and drinks. You may, if you prefer, carry on your own meals and refreshments, as the dining car can be very expensive.

STATION

Where is the train station? (the ticket office)	**Où est la gare? (le guichet)** *oo eh lah gahr (luh gee-sheh)*
I'd like to see the schedule.	**Je voudrais voir l'horaire.** *zhuh voo-dreh vwahr loh-rehr*
■ A first-class (second-class) ticket to _____, please.	**Un billet de première classe (seconde classe) à _____, s'il vous plaît.** *uhn bee-yeh duh pruh-myehr klahss (suh-gohnd klahss) a _____ seel voo pleh*
■ a one-way (round-trip) ticket	**un aller simple (un aller et retour)** *uhn nah-lay san-pluh (uhn nah-lay ay ruh-toor)*
Do you have smoking compartments?	**Avez-vous des compartiments fumeur?** *ah-vay voo day kohn-pahr-tee-mahn few-muhr*

Is it necessary to make a reservation?	**Faut-il réserver?** *foh-teel ray-zehr-vay*
At what time does the train arrive (leave)?	**Le train arrive (part) à quelle heure?** *luh tran ah-reev (pahr) ah kehl uhr*
From what platform does it leave?	**Il part de quel quai (de quelle voie)?** *eel pahr duh kehl kay (duh kehl vwah)*
At what platform does it arrive?	**Il arrive à quel quai (à quelle voie)?** *eel ah-reev ah kehl kay (ah kehl vwah)*
Does this train stop at ____?	**Est-ce que ce train s'arrête à ____?** *ehss kuh suh tran sah-reht ah*
Is the train on time?	**Le train est à l'heure?** *luh tran eh tah luhr*
How long does it stop?	**Il s'arrête pendant combien de temps?** *eel sah-reht pan-dan kohn-byan duh tahn*
Is there a dining car?	**Il y a un wagon restaurant?** *eel yah uhn vah-gohn rehss-toh-rahn*
Do I have to change trains? Where?	**Faut-il changer de train? Où?** *foh-teel shahn-zhay duh tran oo*
Where are we now?	**Où sommes-nous maintenant?** *oo sohm noo mant-nahn*
Is this seat taken?	**Est-ce que cette place est occupée?** *ehss kuh seht plahss eh toh-kew-pay*
Will we arrive on time? (late?)	**On arrive à l'heure? (en retard?)** *ohn ah-reev ah luhr (ahn ruh-tahr)*
What is the next station?	**Quelle est la prochaine gare?** *kehl eh lah proh-shehn gahr*

DRIVING A CAR

ROAD SYSTEM

You may choose to drive on one of the following kinds of roads:

Autoroute	a high-speed superfreeway for long-distance trips. These are toll roads.
Route nationale	a main highway used by cars going from one small town to another
Route départementale	a minor highway
Chemin communal	a local road
Chemin rural	a scenic country road

In order to escape the horrendous traffic jams, the fearless European drivers, and the impossibility of finding a legal parking spot, avoid driving in Paris at all costs.

To rent a car, a passport and major credit card are generally required. It is not necessary to obtain an international license, since U.S. and Canadian drivers' licenses are valid in France.

A good idea would be to purchase a French **Code de la Route**, which explains driving rules and regulations. The French Government Tourist Office issues free road maps. Speed limits are high and it will take some time getting used to the French way of driving. Remember to buckle up.

PARKING

During the day, you may park at parking meters located in metropolitan areas, or you may find a spot in a "Blue Zone." To park there you must use a special parking disk (**disque**), which can be obtained free of charge at auto clubs, garages, gas stations, hotels, police stations, bookstores, driving schools, car accessory shops, insurance agencies, or tourist offices. When you set the time of your arrival, the departure time will show automatically on the disk. The disk should be displayed on your windshield. Be careful: If you are caught cheating, you risk a fine. Parking at night may be free.

SIGNS

Familiarize yourself with the traffic signs listed below:

Accotement non stabilisé	Soft shoulder
Allumez vos phares	Put on headlights
Arrêt interdit	No stopping
Attention	Caution
Cédez la priorité	Yield
Chaussée déformée	Poor roadway
Chute de pierres	Falling rocks
Circulation interdite	No thoroughfare
Descente (Pente) dangereuse	Steep slope (hill)
Déviation	Detour
Douane	Customs
École	School
Entrée interdite	No entrance
Fin d'interdiction de ____	End of ____ zone
Interdiction de doubler	No Passing
Interdiction de stationner	No Parking
Interdit aux piétons	No Pedestrians
Péage	Toll

Piste réservée aux transports publics	Lane for Public Transportation
Ralentir (Ralentissez)	Slow
Réservé aux piétons	Pedestrians only
Sens interdit	Wrong way
Sens unique	One Way
Serrez à gauche (à droite)	Keep left (right)
Sortie d'autoroute	Freeway (throughway) Exit
Sortie de véhicules	Vehicle Exit
Stationnement autorisé	Parking Permitted
Stationnement interdit	No Parking
Tenez la droite (gauche)	Keep to the right (left)
Verglas	Icy Road
Virage dangereux	Dangerous Curve
Voie de dégagement	Private Entrance
Zone Bleue	Blue Zone (parking)

Guarded railroad crossing

Yield

Stop

Right of way

Dangerous intersection ahead

Gasoline (petrol) ahead

Parking

No vehicles allowed

Dangerous curve

Pedestrian crossing

Oncoming traffic has right of way

No bicycles allowed

No parking allowed

No entry

No left turn

No U-turn

No passing

Border crossing

Traffic signal ahead

Speed limit

Traffic circle (roundabout) ahead

Minimum speed limit

All traffic turns left

End of no passing zone

One-way street

Detour

Danger ahead

Entrance to expressway

Expressway ends

CAR RENTALS

You may use your driver's license to drive in France. Cars may be rented or leased at airports or major railroad stations. This can be quite costly since the price of gasoline abroad is prohibitive. The most economical method of renting a car is to reserve it with one of the rental agencies before you leave home.

I would like to rent _____.	**Je voudrais louer _____.**	*zhuh voo-dreh loo-ay*
■ a car	**une voiture**	*ewn vwah-tewr*
■ a 4x4	**un quatre-quatre**	*uhn kah-truh kah-truh*
■ a motorcycle	**une motocyclette**	*ewn moh-toh-see-kleht*
■ a bicycle	**une bicyclette**	*ewn bee-ssee-kleht*
■ a scooter	**un scooter**	*uhn skoo-tehr*
■ a moped	**une mobylette**	*ewn moh-bee-leht*
■ an SUV	**un VUS (un véhicule utilitaire sport)**	*uhn vay-ew-ess (uhn vay-ee-kewl ew-tee-lee-tehr spohr)*
I want _____.	**Je voudrais _____.**	*zhuh voo-dreh*
■ a small car	**une petite voiture**	*zewn puh-teet vwah-tewr*
■ a large car	**une grande voiture**	*zewn grahnd vwah-tewr*
■ a sports car	**une voiture de sport**	*zewn vwah-tewr duh spohr*
Does it have an automatic (a manual) transmission?	**Est-ce une automatique (une manuel)?**	*ehss ewn oh-toh-mah-teek (ewn mah-new-ehl)*

How much does it cost _____?	**C'est combien _____?**	*seh kohn-byan*
per day	**à la journée**	*ah lah zhoor-nay*
per hour	**à l'heure**	*ah luhr*
per week	**à la semaine**	*ah la suh-mehn*
per kilometer	**au kilomètre**	*oh kee-loh-meh-truh*

How much is the insurance?

Quel est le montant de l'assurance? *kehl eh luh mohn-tahn duh lah-ssew-rahnss*

Does it have a GPS?

Elle a un système de navigation (par GPS)? *ehl ah uhn seess-tehm duh nah-vee-gah-ssyohn pahr zhay-pay-ehss*

Does it have Bluetooth?

Elle a Bluetooth? *ehl ah blew-tooth*

Is gas included?

L'essence est comprise? *leh-ssahnss eh kohn-preez*

Is mileage included?

Le kilométrage est compris? *luh kee-loh-may-trahzh eh kohn-pree*

What kind of gas does it take?

Quelle essence emploie-t-elle? *kehl eh-ssahnss ahn-plwah-tehl*

Do you accept credit cards?

Acceptez vous des cartes de crédit? *ahk-ssehp-tay voo day kahrt duh kray-dee*

Which ones?

Lesquelles? *lay-kehl*

Here's my driver's license.

Voici mon permis de conduire. *vwah-ssee mohn pehr-mee duh kohn-dweer*

Do I have to leave a deposit?

Dois-je verser des arrhes? *dwahzh vehr-ssay day zahr*

I want to rent the car here and leave it in _____ (name of city).	**Je veux louer la voiture ici et la laisser à _____.** *zhuh vuh loo-ay lah vwah-tewr ee-ssee ay lah leh-ssay ah*
Can I return it in another city?	**Je peux la rendre dans une autre ville?** *zhuh puh lah rahn-druh dahn zewn oh-truh veel*
Is there a drop-off charge?	**Faut-il payer plus en cas de non-retour ici?** *foh-teel peh-yay plews ahn kah duh nohn-ruh-toor ee-ssee*

ON THE ROAD

Excuse me.	**Excusez-moi.** *ehkss-kew-zay mwah* **Pardon** *pahr-dohn*
Can you tell me _____?	**Pouvez-vous me dire _____?** *poo-vay voo muh deer*
How do I get to _____?	**Comment va-t-on à _____?** *koh-mahn vah-tohn ah*
I think we're lost.	**Nous sommes sur la mauvaise route.** *noo sohm sewr lah moh-vehz root*
Is this the road (way) to _____?	**Est-ce la route pour _____?** *ehss lah root poor*
Do I go straight?	**Est-ce que je vais tout droit?** *ehss kuh zhuh veh too drwah*
Do I turn to the right (to the left)?	**Est-ce que je tourne à droite (à gauche)?** *ehss kuh zhuh toorn ah drwaht (ah gohsh)*
Where does this road go?	**Où mène cette route?** *oo mehn seht root*

How far is it from here to the next town?	**À quelle distance sommes-nous de la prochaine ville?** *ah kehl deess-tah<u>n</u>ss sohm noo duh lah proh-sheh<u>n</u> veel*
How far away is _____?	**À quelle distance est _____?** *ah kehl deess-tah<u>n</u>ss eh*
Is the next town far?	**La prochaine ville, est-elle loin?** *lah proh-sheh<u>n</u> veel eh-tehl lwa<u>n</u>*
What's the next town called?	**Comment s'appelle la prochaine ville?** *koh-mah<u>n</u> sah-pehl lah proh-sheh<u>n</u> veel*
Do you have a road map?	**Avez-vous une carte routière?** *ah-vay voo zewn kahrt roo-tyehr*
Do you have a map of the city?	**Avez-vous un plan de la ville?** *ah-vay voo uh<u>n</u> plah<u>n</u> duh lah veel*
Can you show it to me on the map?	**Pourriez-vous me l'indiquer sur la carte?** *poo-ree-yay voo muh la<u>n</u>-dee-kay sewr lah kahrt*

Is the road in good condition?	**Est-ce que la route est en bon état?** *ehss kuh lah root eh tahn bohn nay-tah*
Is this the most direct way?	**Est-ce le chemin le plus direct?** *ehss luh shuh-man luh plew dee-rehkt*
Is it a toll road?	**Est-ce une autoroute à péage?** *ehss ewn oh-toh-root ah pay-ahzh*
What's the speed limit?	**Quelle est la vitesse maximum?** *kehl eh lah vee-tehss mahk-ssee-muhm*
(How long) Can I park here?	**(Combien de temps) Puis-je me garer ici?** *(kohn-byan duh tahn) pweezh muh gah-ray ee-ssee*

AT THE SERVICE STATION

Gasoline is sold by the liter in Europe; for the traveler accustomed to gallons, it may seem confusing, especially if you want to calculate your mileage per gallon (kilometer per liter). Here are some tips on making those conversions.

LIQUID MEASURES			
LITERS	GALLONS	LITERS	GALLONS
1	0.26	50	13.0
5	1.3	60	15.6
10	2.6	70	18.2
20	5.2	80	20.8
30	7.8	90	23.4
40	10.4	100	26.0

DISTANCE MEASURES			
KILOMETERS	MILES	KILOMETERS	MILES
1	0.62	30	18.6
5	3.1	35	21.7
10	6.2	40	24.8
15	9.3	45	27.9
20	12.4	50	31.1
25	15.5	100	62.1

Where is a gas station?	**Où se trouve une station-service?** *oo suh troov ewn stah-ssyohn sehr-veess*
Fill'er up with _____, please.	**Le plein, s'il vous plaît _____.** *luh plan seel voo pleh*
■ diesel	**du diesel** *dew dyay-zehl*
■ regular	**de l'ordinaire** *duh lohr-dee-nehr*
■ super	**du super** *dew sew-pehr*
I would like _____ liters, please.	**Je voudrais ___ litres, s'il vous plaît.** *zhuh voo-dreh ___ lee-truh seel voo pleh*
Please check _____.	**Veuillez vérifier _____.** *vuh-yay vay-ree-fyay*
■ the battery	**la batterie** *lah bah-tree*
■ the brakes	**les freins** *lay fran*
■ the carburetor	**le carburateur** *luh kahr-bew-rah-tuhr*
■ the oil	**le niveau de l'huile** *luh nee-voh duh lweel*
■ the spark plugs	**les bougies (f.)** *lay boo-zhee*
■ the tires	**les pneus** *lay pnuh*
■ the water	**le niveau de l'eau** *luh nee-voh duh loh*

le carburateur
CARBURETOR

le radiateur
RADIATOR

la batterie
BATTERY

le phare
HEADLIGHT

l'aile
FENDER

le capot
HOOD

le pneu
TIRE

l'essuie-glace
WINDSHIELD WIPER

la poignée de porte
DOOR HANDLE

le coffre
TRUNK

le feu arrière
TAILLIGHT

le pare-chocs
BUMPER

I think there's something wrong with _____.	**Je crois que _____ ne fonctionne pas.** *zhuh krwah kuh _____ nuh fohnk-ssyohn pas*
■ the brakes	**les freins** *lay fran*
■ the bumper	**le pare-choc** *luh pahr-shohk*
■ the directional signal	**le clignotant** *luh klee-nyoh-tahn*
■ the door handle	**la poignée** *lah pwah-nyay*
■ the electrical system	**l'installation électrique** *lan-stah-lah-ssyohn ay-lehk-treek*
■ the exhaust	**l'échappement (m.)** *lay-shahp-mahn*
■ the fan	**le ventilateur** *luh vahn-tee-lah-tuhr*
■ the fan belt	**la courroie de ventilateur** *lah koor-wah duh vahn-tee-lah-tuhr*
■ the fender	**l'aile (f.)** *lehl*
■ the fuel pump	**la pompe à essence** *lah pohnp ah eh-ssahnss*
■ the gas tank	**le réservoir à essence** *luh ray-zehr-vwahr ah eh-ssahnss*
■ the gears	**l'engrenage (m.)** *lahn-gruh-nahzh*
■ the gearshift	**le changement de vitesses** *luh shahnzh-mahn duh vee-tehss*
■ the headlight	**le phare** *luh fahr*
■ the hood	**le capot** *luh kah-poh*
■ the horn	**le klaxon** *luh klahk-ssohn*
■ the ignition	**l'allumage (m.)** *lah-lew-mahzh*
■ the radio	**la radio** *lah rah-dyoh*
■ the starter	**le démarreur** *luh day-mah-ruhr*
■ the steering wheel	**le volant** *luh voh-lahn*
■ the taillight	**le feu arrière** *luh fuh ah-ryehr*
■ the tire pressure	**la pression des pneus** *lah preh-ssyohn day pnuh*

■ the transmission	**la transmission**	*lah trah__nz__-mee-ssyoh__n__*
■ the trunk	**le coffre**	*luh koh-fruh*
■ the water pump	**la pompe à eau**	*lah poh__np__ ah oh*
■ the windshield wipers	**les essuie-glaces**	*lay zeh-sswee glahss*

What's the matter? **Qu'est-ce qui ne va pas?** *kehss kee nuh vah pah*

Can you fix my car today? **Pouvez-vous réparer ma voiture aujourd'hui?** *poo-vay voo ray-pah-ray mah vwah-tewr oh-zhoor-dwee*

Can you repair it temporarily? **Pouvez-vous la réparer provisoirement?** *poo-vay voo lah ray-pah-ray proh-vee-zwahr-mah__n__*

Do you have the part? **Avez-vous la pièce de rechange?** *ah-vay voo lah pyehss duh ruh-shah__nzh__*

How long will it take? **Ça va prendre combien de temps?** *sah vah prah__n__-druh koh__n__-bya__n__ duh tah__n__*

Is everything fixed now? **Tout est réparé maintenant?** *too teh ray-pah-ray ma__n__t-nah__n__*

How much do I owe you? **Combien vous dois-je?** *koh__n__-bya__n__ voo dwahzh*

Where do I pay? **Où est-ce que je paie?** *oo ehss-kuh zhuh pay*

Do you accept credit cards? **Acceptez-vous des cartes de crédit?** *ahk-ssehp-tay voo day kahrt duh kray-dee*

Change the oil. **Changez l'huile, s'il vous plaît.** *shah__n__-zhay lweel seel voo pleh*

Grease the car.	**Faites un graissage complet de la voiture, s'il vous plaît.** *feht zuhn greh-ssahzh kohn-pleh duh lah vwah-tewr seel voo pleh*
Charge the battery.	**Rechargez la batterie, s'il vous plaît.** *ruh-shahr-zhay lah bah-tree seel voo pleh*
Change this tire.	**Changez ce pneu.** *shahn-zhay suh pnuh*
Do you have rest-rooms?	**Avez-vous des toilettes?** *ah-vay voo day twah-leht*
Where are they?	**Où sont-elles?** *oo sohn-tehl*

TIRE PRESSURES			
Kg/Sq.Cm	Lb/Sq.In	Kg/Sq.Cm	Lb/Sq.In
1.2	17	2.1	30
1.3	18	2.2	31
1.4	20	2.3	33
1.5	21	2.4	34
1.6	23	2.5	36
1.7	24	2.6	37
1.8	26	2.7	38
1.9	27	2.8	40
2.0	28	2.9	41

ACCIDENTS, REPAIRS

The car overheats.	**La voiture chauffe.** *lah vwah-tewr shohf*
It doesn't start.	**Elle ne démarre pas.** *ehl nuh day-mahr pah*

I have a flat tire.	**J'ai un pneu crevé.** *zhay-uhn pnuh kruh-vay*
My car has broken down.	**Ma voiture est en panne.** *mah vwah-tewr eh tahn pahn*
The radiator is leaking.	**Le radiateur coule.** *luh rah-dee-ah-tuhr kool*
The battery is dead.	**La batterie est morte.** *lah bah-tree eh mohrt*
Do you have jumper cables?	**Avez-vous des cables de démarrage?** *ah-vay voo day kah-bluh duh day-mah-rahzh*
The car won't start.	**La voiture ne veut pas démarrer.** *lah vwah-tewr nuh vuh pah day-mah-ray*
The keys are locked inside.	**Les clés sont enfermées à l'intérieur.** *lay klay sohn tahn-fehr-may ah lan-tay-ree-yuhr*
I had an accident.	**J'ai eu un accident.** *zhay ew uhn ahk-see-dahn*
I need a mechanic (tow truck).	**Il me faut un mécanicien (une dépanneuse).** *eel muh foh tuhn may-kah-nee-ssyan (ewn day-pah-nuhz)*
Could you _____?	**Pourriez-vous _____?** *poo-ryay voo*
■ give me a hand	**me donner un coup de main** *muh doh-nay uhn koo duh man*
■ help me	**m'aider** *meh-day*
■ push me	**me pousser** *muh poo-ssay*
■ tow me	**me remorquer** *muh ruh-mohr-kay*

le volant
STEERING WHEEL

le changement de vitesse
GEARSHIFT

le clignotant
DIRECTIONAL SIGNAL

la radio
RADIO

le frein à main
PARKING BRAKE
HAND BRAKE

la pédale d'embayage
CLUTCH PEDAL

la pédale de frein
BRAKE PEDAL

la pédale d'accélérateur (l'accélérateur)
GAS PEDAL

I don't have tools.	**Je n'ai pas d'outils.**	*zhuh nay pah doo-tee*
Do you have _____?	**Avez-vous _____?**	*ah-vay voo*
■ a flashlight	**une lampe de poche**	*ewn lahnp duh pohsh*
■ a hammer	**un marteau**	*uhn mahr-toh*
■ a jack	**un cric**	*uhn kreek*
■ a monkey wrench	**une clé anglaise**	*ewn klay ahn-glehz*
■ pliers	**des pinces**	*day pansss*
■ a screwdriver	**un tournevis**	*uhn toorn-veess*
I need _____.	**J'ai besoin _____.**	*zhay buh zwan*
■ a bolt	**d'un boulon**	*duhn boo-lohn*
■ a bulb	**d'une ampoule**	*dewn ahn-pool*
■ a filter	**d'un filtre**	*duhn feel-truh*
■ a nut	**d'un écrou**	*duhn nay-kroo*

ENTERTAINMENT AND DIVERSION

MOVIES

Movies are generally shown from 2:00 P.M. to 10:00 P.M., with late night schedules on Saturday. *Pariscope* and *L'Officiel des Spectacles* are two guides to the movies in Paris, indicating the time and place of the film showing. The abbreviation **V.O. (version originale)** means that the original version of the movie in the language in which it was made is being shown. **V.F. (version française)** means that the movie is dubbed in French. In the movies or theater it is customary to tip the usher or usherette. Movies generally change on Wednesday. The bigger, more expensive, more comfortable movie houses are on the Champs-Elysées in Paris.

What's there to do at night?	**Qu'est-ce qu'on peut faire le soir?** *kehss kohn puh fehr luh swahr*	
Let's go to the _____.	**Allons au _____.** *ah-lohn zoh*	
■ movies	**cinéma** *see-nay-mah*	
■ museum	**musée** *mew-zay*	
■ theater	**théâtre** *tay-ah-truh*	
Is there an entertainment guide?	**Il y a un programme des spectacles?** *eel yah uhn proh-grahm day spehk-tah-kluh*	
Where could I get a movie listing?	**Où pourrais-je trouver un programme de cinéma?** *oo poo-rehzh troo-vay uhn proh-grahm duh see-nay-mah*	
What's playing?	**Qu'est-ce qu'on passe?** *kehss kohn pahss*	

Who's in the movie?	**Qui joue dans le film?** *kee zhoo dahn luh feelm*
It's____.	**C'est ____.** *seh*
■ an action movie	**un film d'action** *tuhn feelm dahk-ssyohn*
■ a mystery	**un mystère** *tuhn mee-sstehr*
■ a comedy	**une comédie** *tewn koh-may-dee*
■ a drama	**un drame** *tuhn drahm*
■ a musical	**une comédie musicale** *tewn koh-may-dee mew-zee-kahl*
■ a romance	**une histoire d'amour** *tewn eess-twahr dah-moor*
■ a Western	**un western** *tuhn wehss-tehrn*
■ a war film	**un film de guerre** *tuhn feelm duh gehr*
■ a science fiction film	**un film de science fiction** *tuhn feelm duh see-yahnss feek-ssyohn*
Is it in English?	**C'est en anglais?** *seh tahn ahn-gleh*
Are there English subtitles?	**Il y a des sous-titres en anglais?** *eel yah day soo-tee-truh ahn nahn-gleh*
Where is the box office (time schedule)?	**Où est le bureau de location (l'horaire)?** *oo eh luh bew-roh duh loh-kah-ssyohn (loh-rehr)*
What time does the show begin?	**À quelle heure commence le spectacle?** *ah kehl uhr koh-mahnss luh spehk-tah-kluh*
What time does the show end?	**À quelle heure se termine le spectacle?** *ah kehl uhr suh tehr-meen luh spehk-tah-kluh*
Where can I get a movie listing?	**Où pourrais-je trouver un programme de cinéma?** *Oo poo-rehzh troo-vay uhn proh-grahm duh see-nay-mah*

THEATER

France has several national theaters such as the **Comédie Française** and the **Théatre National de l'Odéon**. There are also about 50 private playhouses. Theaters are closed one day a week. The day is listed in the newspapers. Box offices are generally open from 11:00 A.M. to 6:00 P.M. Most of the theaters are closed one month in the summer, usually August.

For entertainment information in Paris consult *Pariscope*, the weekly entertainment magazine that is widely distributed free of charge.

I would like tickets for tonight.	**Je voudrais des billets pour ce soir.**	*zhuh voo-dreh day bee-yeh poor suh swahr*
Two _____ seats.	**Deux places _____.**	*duh plahss*
▦ orchestra	**à l'orchestre**	*ah lohr-kehss-truh*
▦ balcony	**au balcon**	*oh bahl-kohn*
▦ first balcony	**au premier balcon**	*oh pruh-myay bahl-kohn*
▦ mezzanine	**au parterre**	*oh pahr-tehr*

OPERA—BALLET—CONCERTS

We would like to go to _____.	**Nous voudrions aller à _____.**	*noo voo-dree-yohn zah-lay ah*
▦ a ballet	**un ballet**	*uhn bah-leh*
▦ a concert	**un concert**	*uhn kohn-ssehr*
▦ an opera	**un opéra**	*uhn noh-pay-rah*
Is there a _____ nearby?	**Il y a _____ par ici?**	*eel yah _____ pahr ee-ssee*
▦ concert hall	**une salle de concert**	*ewn sahl duh kohn-ssehr*

■ opera house

un opéra *uhn noh-pay-rah*

What are they playing?

Qu'est-ce qu'on joue? *kehss kohn zhoo*

Who is the conductor?

Qui est le chef d'orchestre? *kee eh luh shehf d'ohr-kehss-truh*

I prefer _____.

Je préfère _____. *zhuh pray-fehr*

■ classical music

la musique classique *lah mew-zeek klah-sseek*

■ modern music

la musique moderne *lah mew-zeek moh-dehrn*

Are there any seats for tonight's performance?

Il y a des places pour ce soir? *eel yah day plahss poor suh swahr*

When does the season end?

Quand se termine la saison? *kahn suh tehr-meen lah seh-zohn*

Is it necessary to get the tickets in advance?

Faut-il acheter les billets d'avance? *foh teel ahsh-tay lay bee-yeh dah-vahnss*

Do I have to dress formally?	**La tenue de soirée est de rigueur?** *lah tuh-new duh swah-ray eh duh ree-guhr*
What are the least (most) expensive seats?	**Quelles sont les places les moins (les plus) chères?** *kehl sohn lay plahss lay mwan (lay plew) shehr*
How much are the tickets?	**Combien coûtent les billets?** *kohn-byan koot lay bee-yeh*
May I have a program?	**Un programme, s'il vous plaît.** *uhn proh-grahm seel voo pleh*

NIGHTCLUBS

If it's lively entertainment you want, try the bars, nightclubs, and discos in the major cities. Paris, of course, offers the widest selection of things to do. Nightclubs, providing dinner and a show, are very expensive. A late night drink at a jazz spot or bar might interest you. Discos abound with the latest in music and special lighting effects.

Let's go to a nightclub!	**Allons dans une boîte de nuit!** *ah-lohn dahn zewn bwaht duh nwee*
Is a reservation necessary?	**Faut-il réserver?** *foh teel ray-zehr-vay*
I feel like dancing.	**J'ai envie de danser.** *zhay ahn-vee duh dahn-ssay*
Where are the___?	**Où sont les___?** *oo sohn lay*
■ bars (karaoke)	**bars (karaoké)** *bahr (kah-rah-oh-kay)*
■ clubs	**clubs** *kluhb*
■ discos	**discothèques** *deess-koh-tehk*

Is there a minimum (cover charge)?	**Il y a un prix d'entrée?** *eel yah uh<u>n</u> pree dah<u>n</u>-tray*
Where is the checkroom?	**Où est le vestiaire?** *oo eh luh vehss-tyehr*
At what time does the show begin?	**À quelle heure commence le spectacle?** *ah kehl uhr koh-mah<u>n</u>ss luh spehk-tah-kluh*

CASINOS

While on the Côte d'Azur you must visit the world-famous Casino of Monte Carlo in Monaco. There are other casinos throughout France, all of which are licensed, regulated, and monitored by the French government. A passport is needed to enter. Admission is restricted to adults (over 18 years of age).

QUIET RELAXATION

I would like to play cards.	**Je voudrais jouer aux cartes.** *zhuh voo-dreh zhoo-ay oh kahrt*
■ bridge	**au bridge** *oh breedzh*
■ black jack	**au black-jack** *oh blahk-zhahk*
■ poker	**au poker** *oh poh-kehr*
Where can I get a deck of cards?	**Où puis-je obtenir des cartes à jouer?** *oo pweezh ohp-tuh-neer day kahrt ah zhoo-ay*
Do you want to play _____?	**Voulez-vous jouer _____?** *voo-lay voo zhoo-ay*
■ checkers	**aux dames** *oh dahm*
■ dominoes	**aux dominos** *oh doh-mee-noh*
■ chess	**aux échecs** *oh zay-shehk*

SPORTS

Golf, tennis, swimming, cycling, skiing, basketball, ice-skating, fishing, hiking, and sailing are recreational activities in which you can participate throughout the country.

Boxing and wrestling matches, soccer, rugby, and pelote (jai alai) matches draw large crowds of spectators.

Two special events that attract natives and tourists alike are **Le Tour de France**, a three-week bicycle race across France (held each June) and **Le Mans**, a 24-hour Formula One auto race (also in June).

I like to play (do) ___.	**J'aime faire ____.** *zhehm fehr*
■ aerobics	**de l'aérobic** *duh lay-roh-beek*
■ baseball	**du base-ball** *dew behz-bohl*
■ basketball	**du basket-ball** *dew bahss-keht-bohl*
■ bicycling	**du vélo** *dew vay-loh*
■ boating	**du canotage** *dew kah-noh-tahzh*
■ bodybuilding	**de la musculation** *duh lah mew-sskew-lah-ssyohn*
■ bungee jumping	**du saut à l'élastique** *dew soh ah lay-lahss-teek*
■ canoeing	**du canoë** *dew kah-noh-ay*
■ cave exploring	**de la spéléologie** *duh lah spay-lay-oh-loh-zhee*
■ cycling	**du cyclisme** *dew see-kleez-muh*
■ diving	**du plongeon** *dew plohn-zhohn*
■ fishing	**de la pêche** *duh lah pehsh*
■ deep-sea fishing	**de la pêche sous-marine** *duh lah pehsh soo mah-reen*
■ football	**du football américain** *dew foot-bohl ah-may-ree-kan*
■ golf	**du golf** *dew gohlf*
■ hockey	**du hockey** *dew oh-kee*

▦ horseback riding	**de l'équitation (f.)**	*duh lay-kee-tah-ssyohn*
▦ hunting	**de la chasse**	*duh lah shahss*
▦ ice skating	**du patin à glace**	*dew pah-tan ah glahss*
▦ jogging	**du jogging**	*dew zhoh-geeng*
▦ mountain biking	**du vélo tout-terrain**	*dew vay-loh too-teh-ran*
▦ mountain climbing	**de l'alpinisme (m.)**	*duh lahl-pee-neez-muh*
▦ parasailing	**du parachutisme**	*dew pah-rah-shew-teez-muh*
▦ ping-pong	**du ping-pong**	*dew peeng-pohng*
▦ rock climbing	**de la varappe**	*duh lah vah-rahp*
▦ roller skating	**du patin à roulettes**	*dew pah-tan ah roo-leht*
▦ rugby	**du rugby**	*dew rewg-bee*
▦ sailing	**du bateau à voiles**	*dew bah-toh ah vwahl*
▦ scuba diving	**de la plongée sous-marine**	*duh lah plohn-zhay soo-mah-reen*
▦ skateboarding	**de la planche à roulettes**	*duh lah plahnsh ah roo-leht*
▦ skating	**du patin**	*dew pah-tan*
▦ skiing	**du ski**	*dew skee*
▦ skydiving	**du parachutisme**	*dew pah-rah-shew-teez-muh*
▦ soccer	**du football**	*dew foot-bohl*
▦ squash	**du squash**	*dew skwahsh*
▦ surfing	**du surf**	*dew sewrf*
▦ swimming	**de la natation**	*duh lah nah-tah-ssyohn*
▦ tennis	**du tennis**	*dew tay-neess*
▦ track and field	**de l'athlétisme**	*duh laht-lay-teez-muh*

■ volleyball	**du volley-ball**	*dew voh-lee-bohl*
■ waterskiing	**du ski nautique**	*dew skee noh-teek*
■ white-water rafting	**du rafting**	*dew rahf-teeng*
■ windsurfing	**de la planche à voiles**	*duh lah plahnsh ah vwahl*

How about a game of golf?
On fait une partie de golf?
ohn feh tewn parh-tee duh gohlf

How about a game of tennis?
On fait un match de tennis?
ohn feh tuhn mahtch duh teh-neess

PLAYING FIELDS

Shall we go (to the) _____?
On va _____? *ohn vah*

Let's go (to the) _____.
Allons _____. *ah-lohnz*

■ beach	**à la plage**	*ah lah plahzh*
■ course (golf)	**au parcours**	*oh pahr-koor*
■ court	**au court**	*oh koohr*
■ field	**au terrain**	*oh teh-ran*
■ gymnasium	**au gymnase**	*oh zheem-nahz*
■ mountain	**à la montagne**	*ah lah mohn-tah-nyuh*
■ ocean	**à l'océan (m.)**	*ah loh-say-ahn*
■ park	**au parc**	*oh pahrk*
■ path	**au sentier**	*oh sahn-tyay*
■ pool	**à la piscine**	*ah lah pee-sseen*
■ rink	**à la patinoire**	*ah lah pah-tee-nwahr*
■ sea	**à la mer**	*ah lah mehr*
■ slope	**à la piste**	*ah lah peesst*
■ stadium	**au stade**	*oh stahd*
■ track	**à la piste**	*ah lah peesst*

SPORTS EQUIPMENT

Could you lend (rent)(give) me ___?

Pourriez-vous me prêter (louer) (donner)___? *poor-yay voo muh preh-tay (loo-ay) (doh-nay)*

■ a ball (football, soccer)

un ballon *uhn bah-lohn*

■ a ball (baseball, tennis)

une balle *ewn bahl*

■ a bat

une batte *ewn baht*

■ a bicycle

un vélo *uhn vay-loh*
une bicyclette *ewn bee-ssee-kleht*

■ a boat

un bateau *uhn bah-toh*

■ a boots (ski)

des chaussures de ski (f.) *day shoh-sewr duh skee*

■ a canoe

un canoë *uhn kah-noh-ay*

■ a diving suit

un scaphandre *uhn skah-fahn-druh*

■ a fishing rod

une canne à pêche *ewn kahn ah pehsh*

■ flippers

des nageoires (f.) *day nahzh-wahr*

■ goggles

des lunettes protectrices (f.) *day lew-neht proh-tehk-treess*

■ golf clubs

des club de golf (m.) *day klewb duh gohlf*

■ a helmet (diver's)

un casque de scaphandre *uhn kahsk duh skah-fahn-druh*

■ jogging shoes

des joggers *day zhohg-gehr*

■ a jogging suit

un survêt *uhn sewr-veh*

■ kneepads

des genouillères (f.) *day zhuh-noo-yehr*

■ a mitt

un gant *uhn gahn*

■ a net

un filet *uhn fee-leh*

■ poles (ski)	**des bâtons** (m.)	*day bah-tohn*
■ a puck (hockey)	**une rondelle** *ewn rohn-dehl* (Canada) **un palet** *uhn pah-leh* (France)	
■ a racquet	**une raquette**	*ewn rah-keht*
■ a sailboard	**une planche à voile** *ewn plahnsh ah vwahl*	
■ a skateboard	**une planche à roulettes** *ewn plahnsh ah roo-leht*	
■ skates	**des patins** (m.)	*day pah-tan*
roller	**à roulettes**	*ah roo-leht*
ice	**à glace**	*ah glahss*
■ ski bindings	**des fixations de ski** *day feek-sah-ssyohn duh skee*	
■ skis	**des skis** (m.)	*day skee*
■ a stick (hockey)	**une crosse**	*ewn krohss*
■ a surfboard	**une planche de surf** *ewn plahnsh duh sewrf*	
■ water skis	**des skis nautiques** (m.) *day skee noh-teek*	
■ weights	**des haltères** (m.)	*day zahl-tehr*
■ a wet suit	**une combinaison de plongée** *ewn kohn-bee-neh-zohn duh plohn-zhay*	

SPECTATOR SPORTS

SOCCER

I'd like to see a soccer match.	**Je voudrais voir un match de football.** *zhuh voo-dreh vwahr uhn mahtch duh foot-bohl*
Where's the stadium?	**Où est le stade?** *oo eh luh stahd*

At what time does the match begin?	**Le match commence à quelle heure?** *luh mahtch koh-mah<u>n</u>ss ah kehl uhr*
When are they going to kick off?	**Quand vont-ils donner le coup d'envoi?** *kah<u>n</u> voh<u>n</u> teel doh-nay luh koo dah<u>n</u>-vwah*
What teams are playing?	**Quelles équipes jouent?** *kehl zay-keep zhoo*
Who scored to goal?	**Qui a marqué le but?** *kee ah mahr-kay luh bew*

HORSE RACING

Is there a racetrack here?	**Il y a un champ de courses par ici?** *eel yah uh<u>n</u> shah<u>n</u> duh koorss pahr ee-ssee*
I want to see the horse races.	**Je voudrais voir les courses de chevaux.** *zhuh voo-dreh vwahr lay koorss duh shuh-voh*

ACTIVE SPORT

TENNIS

Do you play tennis?	**Jouez-vous au tennis?** *zhoo-ay-voo oh tay-neess*
I'd like to play tennis.	**Je voudrais jouer au tennis.** *zhuh voo-dreh zhoo-ay oh tay-neess*
I (don't) play very well.	**Je (ne) joue (pas) bien.** *zhuh (nuh) zhoo (pah) bya<u>n</u>*
Do you know where there is a (good) court?	**Savez-vous où se trouve un (bon) court de tennis?** *sah-vay voo oo suh troov uh<u>n</u> boh<u>n</u> koohr duh tay-neess*

Can I rent a racquet?	**Puis-je louer une raquette?** *pweezh loo-ay ewn rah-keht*
Where can I reserve a court?	**Où puis-je réserver un court?** *oo pweezh ray-zehr-vay ewn koor*
How much is it per hour?	**C'est combien à l'heure?** *seh kohn-byan ah luhr*
love	**zero** *zay-roh*
match point	**balle de match** *bahl duh mahtsh*

BEACH/POOL

I'd like to go to the (public) (nude) beach (to the pool).	**J'ai envie d'aller à la plage (publique) (naturiste) (à la piscine).** *zhay ahn-vee dah-lay ah lah plahzh (pew-bleek) (nah-tew-reesst) (ah lah pee-seen)*
Is there a beach nearby?	**Il y a une plage tout près?** *eel yah ewn plahzh too preh*
How do you get there?	**On y va comment?** *ohn nee vah koh-mahn*
Which bus will take us to the beach?	**Quel bus faut-il prendre pour aller à la plage?** *kehl bewss foh teel prahn-druh poor ah-lay ah lah plahzh*
Is there a pool in the hotel?	**Il y a une piscine à l'hôtel?** *eel yah ewn pee-sseen ah loh-tehl*
Is it an indoor (outdoor) pool?	**Est-ce une piscine couverte (en plein air)?** *ehss ewn pee-sseen koo-vehrt (ahn pleh nehr)*

I (don't) know how to swim well.	**Je (ne) sais (pas) bien nager.** *zhuh (nuh) seh (pah) byan nah-zhay*	

Is it safe to swim (dive) here? **Peut-on nager (plonger) ici sans danger?** *puh-tohn nah-zhay (plohn-zhay)ee-ssee sahn dahn-zhay*

Is there any danger for children? **Il y a du danger pour les enfants?** *eel yah dew dahn-zhay poor lay zahn-fahn*

Is there a dangerous undertow? **Il y a un courant sous-marin dangereux?** *eel yah uhn koo-rahn soo mah-ran dahn-zhuh-ruh*

Is there a lifeguard? **Il y a un maître-nageur?** *eel yah uhn meh-truh nah-zhuhr*

Where can I get _____? **Où puis-je obtenir _____?** *oo pweezh ohp-tuh-neer*

■ an air mattress **un matelas pneumatique** *uhn maht-lah pnuh-mah-teek*

■ a bathing suit **un maillot de bain** *uhn mah-yoh duh ban*

■ a beach ball **un ballon de plage** *uhn bah-lohn duh plahzh*

■ a beach chair **une chaise longue** *ewn shehz lohng*

■ a beach towel **une serviette de plage** *ewn sehr-vyeht duh plahzh*

■ a cabana **une cabine de plage** *ewn kah-been duh plahzh*

■ a chaise lounge **une chaise longue** *ewn shehz lohng*

■ sunglasses **des lunettes de soleil** *day lew-neht duh soh-lehy*

■ suntan lotion **la lotion pour bronzer** *lah loh-ssyohn poor brohn-zay*

■ a surfboard **une planche de surf** *ewn plahnsh duh sewrf*

■ an umbrella **un parasol** *uhn pah-rah-sohl*

■ water skis **des skis nautiques** *day skee noh-teek*

ON THE SLOPES

Which ski area do you recommend? **Quelle station de ski recommandez-vous?** *kehl stah-ssyohn duh skee ruh-koh-mahn-day voo*

I am a ____ skier. **Je suis ___.** *zhuh swee*

■ beginner **un(e) débutant(e)** *zuhn (zewn) day-bew-tahn(t)*

■ intermediate **un skieur moyen (une skieuse moyenne)** *zuhn skee-uhr mwah-yan (ewn skee-uhz mwah-yehn)*

■ advanced **un skieur avancée (une skieuse avancée)** *uhn skee-uhr ah-vahn-ssay (ewn skee-uhz ah-vahn-ssay)*

How difficult is this slope? **Quelle est la difficulté de cette piste?** *keh eh lah dee-fee-kew-tay duh seht peesst*

What are the skiing conditions? **Quel est l'état des pistes?** *kehl eh lay-tah day peesst*

What kind of lifts are there? **Il y a genre de téléski?** *eel yah kehl zhahn-ruh duh tay-lay-sskee*

Is there _____?	**Il y a __?** *eel yah*
■ a cable car	**un téléphérique** *uhn tay-lay-fay-reek*
■ a chair lift	**un télésiège** *uhn tay-lay-syehzh*
■ alpine skiing	**le ski alpin** *luh skee ahl-pan*
■ an instructor	**un moniteur (une monitrice)** *uhn moh-nee-tuhr (ewn moh-nee-treess)*
■ cross-country skiing	**le ski du fond** *luh skee dew fohn*
■ snowboarding	**le surf de neige** *luh sewrf duh nehzh*
■ tobogganing	**le toboggan** *luh toh-boh-gahn*
How much does the lift cost?	**Combien coûte le forfait-skieurs?** *koh-byan koot luh fohr-feh skee-uhr*
Do they give lessons?	**On donne des leçons?** *ohn dohn day luh-ssohn*

Is there enough snow this time of year?	**Il y a assez de neige en ce moment?** *eel yah ah-ssay duh nehzh ahn suh moh-mahn*
How do I get there?	**On va comment à cet endroit-là?** *ohn vah koh-mahn ah seht ahn-drwah lah*
I would like to rent ____.	**Je voudrais louer ____.** *zhuh voo-dreh loo-ay*
goggles	**des lunettes protectrices** *day lew-neht proh-tehk-treess*
poles	**des batons de ski** *day bah-tohn duh skee*
skis	**des skis** *day skee*
ski bindings	**des fixations de ski** *day feek-ssah-syohn duh skee*
ski boots	**des chaussures de ski** *day shoh-ssewr duh skee*

ON THE LINKS

Is there a golf course here?	**Il y a un terrain de golf par ici?** *eel yah uhn teh-ran duh gohlf pahr ee-ssee*
Can one rent clubs?	**Peut-on louer des clubs?** *puh tohn loo-ay day kluhb*

CAMPING

   Campgrounds are located all over France. They are often crowded, especially in the month of August when most French families are on vacation. Arrive early to be sure of getting a spot. Campsites are rated by stars; the fewer the stars, the less desirable the site. Most sites have adequate facilities. Students are sometimes offered discounts. A camping permit is sometimes required. You may camp unofficially in a suitable place as long as you have permission from the landowner. Be sure to leave the property in the same condition as you found it.

Where is the nearest campsite?	**Où es le terrain de camping le plus proche?** *oo eh luh teh-ran duh kahn-peeng luh plew prohsh*
Can you show me how to get there?	**Pouvez-vous m'indiquer comment y aller?** *poo-vay voo man-dee-kay koh-mahn tee ah-lay*
Where is it on the map?	**Où se trouve-t-il sur la carte?** *oo suh troov teel sewr lah kahrt*
Where can we park our trailer?	**Où pouvons-nous garer notre caravane?** *oo poo-vohn noo gah-ray noh-truh kah-rah-vahn*
How much do they charge _____?	**Ça coûte combien _____?** *sah koot kohn-byan*
■ per person	**par personne** *pahr pehr-sohn*
■ per tent	**par tente** *pahr tahnt*
■ per vehicle	**par véhicule** *pahr vay-ee-kewl*
■ per trailer	**pour une caravane** *poor ewn kah-rah-vahn*
Can we camp for the night?	**Pouvons-nous camper cette nuit?** *poo-vohn noo kahn-pay seht nwee*
Is there _____?	**Il y a _____?** *eel yah*
■ drinking water	**de l'eau potable** *duh loh poh-tah-bluh*
■ running water	**de l'eau courante** *duh loh koo-rahnt*
■ gas	**du gaz** *dew gahz*

■ electricity	**de l'électricité**	*duh lay-lehk-tree-ssee-tay*
■ a children's playground	**un cour de récréation pour enfants**	*uhn koor duh ray-kray-ah-ssyohn poor ahn-fahn*
■ a grocery store	**une épicerie**	*ewn ay-peess-ree*
■ toilet facilities	**des toilettes sanitaires**	*day twah-leht sah-nee-tehr*
■ showers	**des douches**	*day doosh*
■ washrooms	**des lavabos**	*day lah-vah-boh*
■ tents	**des tentes**	*day tahnt*
■ cooking facilities	**des installations pour faire la cuisine**	*day zan-stah-lah-ssyohn poor fehr lah kwee-zeen*

We intend staying ____ days/weeks.

Nous comptons rester ____ jours/semaines. *noo kohn-tohn rehss-tay ____ zhoor/suh-mehn*

IN THE COUNTRYSIDE

I'd like to drive through the countryside.

Je voudrais conduire dans la campagne. *zhuh voo-dreh kohn-dweer dahn lah kahn-pah-nyuh*

Where can I rent a car for the day?

Où puis-je louer une voiture à la journée? *oo pweezh loo-ay ewn vwah-tewr ah lah zhoor-nay*

Are there tours to the country?

Il y a des excursions à la campagne? *eel yah day zehkss-kewr-zyohn ah lah kahn-pah-nyuh*

When do they leave?

Quand sont les départs? *kahn ssohn lay day-pahr*

From where do they leave?	**D'où partent-elles?** *doo pahrt-ehl*
Is there anyone who can drive me?	**Il y a quelqu'un qui puisse me conduire?** *eel yah kehl-kuhn kee pweess muh kohn-dweer*

Look at _____.	**Regardez _____.** *ruh-gahr-day*
▦ the barn	**la grange** *lah grahnzh*
▦ the bridge	**le pont** *luh pohn*
▦ the farm	**la ferme** *lah fehrm*
▦ the fields	**les champs** *lay shahn*
▦ the flowers	**les fleurs** *lay fluhr*
▦ the forest	**la forêt** *lah foh-reh*
▦ the hill	**la colline** *lah koh-leen*
▦ the lake	**le lac** *luh lahk*
▦ the mountains	**les montagnes** *lay mohn-tah-nyuh*
▦ the ocean	**l'océan** *loh-ssay-ahn*
▦ the plants	**les plantes** *lay plahnt*
▦ the pond	**l'étang** *lay-tahn*
▦ the river	**la rivière** *lah ree-vyehr*
▦ the stream	**le ruisseau** *luh rwee-ssoh*
▦ the trees	**les arbres** *lay zahr-bruh*
▦ the valley	**la vallée** *lah vah-lay*
▦ the village	**le village** *luh vee-lahzh*
▦ the waterfall	**la cascade** *lah kahss-kahd*

Where does this _____ lead to?	**Où mène _____?** *oo mehn*
▦ path	**ce sentier** *suh sahn-tyay*
▦ road	**ce chemin** *suh shuh-man*

How long does it take to get to ____?	**Combien de temps faut-il pour aller à ____?** *kohn-byan duh tahn foh teel poor ah-lay ah*
I'm lost.	**J'ai perdu mon chemin.** *zhay pehr-dew mohn shuh-man*
What is the way to ____?	**Quelle est la route pour ____?** *kehl eh lah root poor*
I'd like to take a hike.	**Je voudrais faire une randonnée.** *zhuh voo-dreh fehr ewn rahn-doh-nay*
Where can I get information about hiking trails?	**Où puis-je me renseigner sur les sentiers?** *oo pweezh muh rahn-seh-nyay sewr lay sahn-tyay*

AT THE GYM

Where's a nearby gym?	**Où y a-t-il un gymnase par ici?** *oo ee-ah-teel uhn zheem-nahz pahr ee-ssee*
Do you have to be a member?	**Faut-il être membre?** *foh-teel eh-truh mahn-bruh*
Can I rent a locker?	**Puis-je louer un casier?** *pweezh loo-ay uhn kahz-yay*
Can I see (have) a list of (aerobic) classes?	**Puis-je voir (avoir) une liste de classes (aérobic)?** *pweezh vwahr (ah-vwahr) ewn leest duh klahss (ah-ay-roh-beek)*
Can I see the gym?	**Puis-je voir le gymnase?** *pweezh vwahr luh zheem-nahz*

Is there ____?	**Il y a ____?** *eel yah*
■ a jacuzzi	**un Jacuzzi** *uhn zhah-koo-zee*
■ a pool	**une piscine** *ewn pee-seen*
■ a sauna	**un sauna** *uhn soh-nah*
■ a steam room	**un hammam** *uhn ahm-ahm*
■ a track	**une piste** *ewn peesst*

What is the price ____?	**Quel est le prix ____?** *kehl eh luh pree*
■ daily	**par jour** *pahr zhoor*
■ weekly	**par semaine** *pahr suh-mehn*

Where are the changing rooms?	**Où sont les vestiaries?** *oo sohn lay vehss-tyehr*

FOOD AND DRINK

The world has only a few truly great cuisines, and French is one of them. Respected for its extensive selection of dishes, its inventive uses of ingredients, and its exactness in preparation, French food is always reliably appetizing. French people are inherently great cooks, for they have been developing the elements of good taste since childhood. Wherever you eat in France, whether in Paris or Lyons, in the country or in the city, the food you will be offered will be carefully and lovingly prepared.

The past masters—notably Carême and Escoffier—defined and codified French food, so that you will not find the variations in ingredients or preparations that you notice in most other foods; a hollandaise sauce, for example, will always be made with egg yolks, into which are whisked butter and a dash of vinegar or lemon juice. It will be the same sauce, whether you are enjoying it in a Paris bistro or a country inn. What will vary will be the particularly regional dishes—dishes from the provinces of France that are made chiefly by the cooks in small restaurants and inns.

France's restaurants are famous, and they alone are worth a trip to that country. The most celebrated ones are those graded with one, two, or three stars in the *Michelin Guide*. There are other ratings, too, especially from the Gault-Millau guide, which tends to favor restaurants whose chefs prepare the **nouvelle cuisine** dishes. The three-star restaurants are also among the most expensive and the most formal; these are the towers of **haute cuisine,** and all other restaurants strive to be in that category some day.

Eating in France is a somewhat structured affair. To make your stay enjoyable and to gather a bit of the French flavor, we suggest you follow the French manner of eating. First, here are the types of restaurants you are likely to encounter.

Auberge, Relais, Hostellerie	a country inn.
Bistro	a small neighborhood restaurant in town, similar to a pub or tavern and usually very informal.

Brasserie	a large café that serves quick meals throughout the day or evening; most meals involve only the entrée, such as a steak or chop.
Cabaret	a nightclub where you may also eat a meal.
Café	a neighborhood spot to socialize, either indoors or out, where you can linger over coffee or a glass of wine or beer and perhaps have a little snack. Cafés also serve breakfast (usually a **croissant** and **café au lait**) and later in the day serve soft drinks and ice cream.
Casse-croûte	a restaurant specializing in sandwiches.

Crêperie	a small stand specializing in the preparation of crêpes—thin pancakes dusted with sugar or covered with jam and rolled up.
Fast-food	a small place to eat an American-style snack, mostly hamburgers and French fries; most are in Paris along the Champs-Elysée, and many are American chains such as McDonald's and Burger King.
Restaurant	an establishment that can range from a small, family-owned inn, where mom seats you, dad cooks the meal, and the children serve you, to a formal, three-star palace where you receive the most elegant service and most beautifully garnished foods.
Self	a cafeteria, popular with students and usually located near a university.
Troquet	a wine shop where you can also have a snack.

By law, all establishments serving food must post a menu showing the prices. Most often, you will see two menus posted, one that lists the *à la carte* offerings, and the other that has one, two, or three different *prix fixe* meals. You can, of course, order the dishes you wish following the *à la carte* menu, but the resulting cost will be higher than if you choose one of the menus. The menus are a good choice since they always feature a freshly prepared entrée and usually reflect the specialty of the chef. When there is more than one menu from which to choose, they will differ depending upon the number of courses or the relative value of the entrée; lower-priced menus usually include a grilled steak or chicken dish as entrée, while the higher-priced one might feature an additional cheese course or perhaps both fish and meat courses. In some regions, especially those that receive a number of tourists, you'll often see a special "tourist" menu, which will feature a specialty of the region—cassoulet in Languedoc or truffles in Perigord, for example. Wherever you eat, look for the **plat du jour** (day's specialty) or the **spécialités de la maison** (chef's specialties).

Most menus include a line at the bottom stating that the service charge is included in the price of the meal; it is usually about 15%. It is also customary to leave some small change on the table for the waiter, usually what would round off your bill. If you order a wine other than the house wine, you should also tip the steward, although the service for wine is sometimes also included in the bill. Often, especially in very casual restaurants, the wine is included in the menu (**boisson comprise**). If you want a simple, inexpensive wine, select the house wine, which will usually be a regional wine; if you want advice in a casual restaurant, ask the waiter—as a Frenchman, he will have been brought up to know wines and will recommend one that you will enjoy drinking with what you are eating (see also pages on wine, 144–147).

MEALS OF THE DAY

Most tourists will have their breakfast in the hotel, so much of the information that follows applies to lunch and dinner. Breakfast, **le petit déjeuner**, is usually small, consisting of a croissant or part of a loaf of French bread, with butter and jam. It is usually served with **café au lait**—a large cup or bowl of hot coffee mixed half-and-half with steamed milk; this breakfast is called **café complet** and it is what you will most often be served, especially if breakfast is included in the cost of your room. You may also order hot tea or hot chocolate for breakfast.

Lunch and dinner in France are about the same in character and courses. Lunch, referred to as **le déjeuner**, is usually served between 12:30 and 3:00 P.M. Especially in smaller towns or on the road, be sure to stop early—by 12:15 to secure a table for lunch; many local spots have reserved tables for residents; you'll even see their napkins saved from the previous day.

In warm weather, do what many French people do for lunch—picnic. Especially if you are sightseeing and don't want to take the time for a lengthy lunch, buy some French bread in a **boulangerie**, then go next door to the **charcuterie** for 100 grams of **pâté de campagne**, stop in an **épicerie** for salads or sliced tomatoes and some cheese, and also pick up a bottle of wine or mineral water. Take the food to a park or stop along the road in a field and enjoy your lunch. In France, you'll find the roads are vacated by 12:30, and everyone has pulled over, set up tables, and begun to eat. In Paris, they will go to the **Jardin des Plantes** or **Bois de Boulogne**.

Dinner (**le dîner**) is a bit more formal than lunch and usually served more graciously. In Paris, people eat late—8:00 P.M. is the earliest—while in the country, you can properly begin by 7:30. It is a time for the enjoyment of food and wine, and a meal can carry on for at least two hours. Most French people do not begin their meal with a cocktail, but sometimes will have an apéritif. The meal consists of the following courses, in this order: cold or hot hors d'oeuvres, soup, fish, meat or poultry with accompanying vegetables, cheese, dessert. In recent years, lighter eating patterns have cut down on the number of courses, and you can of course decline a particular course.

In the specialty restaurants—those particularly noted for their food—you will often see a **menu dégustation** (tasting menu) or a **menu gastronomique**. The former is a dinner in which you receive a sampling of a large number of items on the menu, so as to try many of the chef's dishes—this is most popular in **nouvelle cuisine** restaurants. The latter is a special menu for food lovers that features rare items or dishes that are difficult to prepare.

TYPES OF FRENCH COOKING

The basics of French food were established centuries ago, but there have been developments in recent years that have released this food from its straitjacket. The following is a breakdown of the types of food you are likely to encounter.

Haute Cuisine   This is classic French cooking, offered in the top restaurants. The food is refined and exquisitely presented.

Cuisine Bourgeoise	This is the country food of France, made for centuries in everyday kitchens; it is from this cuisine that **haute cuisine** was developed. This is the food you'll have in most bistros and small restaurants.
Nouvelle Cuisine	Developed in the 1970s and now less popular, this food represented a break from traditional flour-based sauces and rigid rules. Fruits were combined with meats and fish, sauces were reduced until thickened, and salads with elaborate arrangements were developed. This cuisine was promoted by such leaders as Paul Bocuse, Roger Vergé, and the Troisgros brothers; its influences are still apparent in most restaurants.
Cuisine Minceur	A special diet-conscious cuisine developed by Michel Guérard.

Nowadays, you'll find that menus will include a mixture of dishes—some considered **nouvelle cuisine** and others more along the line of traditional provincial food.

EATING OUT

Do you know a good restaurant (café), (bar)?	**Connaissez-vous un bon restaurant (café), (bar)?** *koh-neh-ssay voo zuhn bohn rehss-toh-rah (kah-fay)(bahr)*
It is very expensive?	**C'est très cher?** *seh treh shehr*

Do you know a restaurant that serves regional dishes?	**Connaissez-vous un restaurant de de cuisine régionale?** *koh-neh-ssay voo uhn rehss-toh-rahn duh kwee-zeen ray-zhyoh-nahl*
I'd like to make a reservation _____.	**Je voudrais réserver une table _____.** *zhuh voo-dreh ray-zehr-vay ewn tah-bluh*
▓ for tonight	**pour ce soir** *poor suh swahr*
▓ for tomorrow evening	**pour demain soir** *poor duh-man swahr*
▓ for two (four) persons	**pour deux (quatre) personnes** *poor duh (kah-truh) pehr-ssohn*
▓ at 8 (8:30) P.M.	**à vingt heures (vingt heures trente)** *ah van-tuhr (van-tuhr trahnt)*
Waiter!	**Monsieur!** *muh-ssyuh*
Miss!	**Mademoiselle!** *mahd-mwah-zehl*
A table for two in the corner (near the window).	**Une table pour deux dans un coin (près de la fenêtre).** *ewn tah-bluh poor duh dahn zuhn kwan (preh duh lah fuh-neh-truh)*
How long would we have to wait?	**Combien de temps faut-il attendre?** *kohn-byan duh tahn foh-teel ah-tahn-druh*
The menu, please.	**La carte, s'il vous plaît.** *lah kahrt seel voo pleh*
Do you have a menu in English?	**Avez-vous une carte en anglais?** *ah-vay voo ewn kahrt ahn ahn-gleh*
I'd like the price-fixed menu.	**Je voudrais le menu prix-fixe.** *zhuh voo-dreh luh muh-new pree feekss*

What's today's special?	**Quel est le plat du jour?** *kehl eh luh plah dew zhoor*
What's the house specialty?	**Quelle est la spécialité de la maison?** *kehl eh lah spay-ssyah-lee-tay duh lah meh-zohn*
What do you recommend?	**Qu'est-ce que vous conseillez?** *kehss kuh voo kohn-say-yay*
Do you have a children's menu?	**Avez-vous un menu enfant?** *ah-vay voo uhn muh-new ahn-fahn*
I'm (not) very hungry.	**J'ai (Je n'ai pas) très faim.** *zhay (zhuh nay pah) treh fan*
We're in a hurry.	**Nous sommes pressés.** *noo sohm preh-ssay*
Will it take long?	**Il faudra longtemps?** *eel foh-drah lohn-tahn*
To begin, bring _____.	**Pour commencer, apportez _____.** *poor koh-mahn-ssay, ah-pohr-tay*
▩ an apéritif	**un apéritif** *uhn nah-pay-ree-teef*
▩ some white (red, rosé) wine	**du vin blanc (rouge, rosé)** *dew van blahn (roozh, roh-zay)*
▩ some water	**de l'eau** *duh loh*
▩ a bottle of mineral water, with (without) carbonation	**une bouteille d'eau minérale gazeuse (plate)** *ewn boo-tehy doh mee-nay-rahl gah-zuhz (plaht)*
▩ a beer	**une bière** *ewn byehr*
We'd like to order now.	**Nous voudrions commander maintenant.** *noo voo-dree-yohn koh-mahn-day mant-nahn*

I'd like ___.	**Je voudrais ___.** *zhuh voo-dreh*

(See the listings that follow for individual dishes, and also the regional specialties noted on pages 142–143.)

Do you have a wine list?	**Avez-vous une carte des vins?** *ah-vay voo ewn kahrt day van*
Is it dry (mellow, sweet)?	**Est-ce sec (moelleux, doux)?** *ehss sehk (mwah-luh, doo)*
Please bring us ___.	**Apportez-nous s'il vous plaît ___.** *ah-pohr-tay noo seel voo pleh*

■ rolls **des petits pains** *day puh-tee pan*

■ bread **du pain** *dew pan*

■ butter **du beurre** *dew buhr*

■ a bowl **un bol** *uhn bohl*

■ a carafe **un carafe** *uhn kah-rahf*

■ a cup **une tasse** *ewn tahss*

■ a dinner plate **une assiette** *ewn nah-syeht*

■ a fork **une fourchette** *ewn foor-sheht*

■ a glass **un verre** *uhn vehr*

■ a knife **un couteau** *uhn koo-toh*

■ a menu **une carte (un menu)** *ewn kahrt (uhn muh-new)*

■ a napkin **une serviette** *ewn sehr-vyeht*

■ a place setting **un couvert** *uhn koo-vehr*

■ a saucer **une soucoupe** *ewn soo-koop*

■ a soup dish **une assiette à soupe** *ewn nah-syeht ah soop*

■ a tablecloth **une nappe** *ewn nahp*

■ a teaspoon **une cuiller** *ewn kwee-yehr*

■ a wineglass **un verre à vin** *uhn vehr ah van*

APPETIZERS (STARTERS)

Appetizers can be either hot or cold; if you order both, have the cold one first. The term **amuse gueule** (*ah-mewz guhl*) refers to appetizers. The following are among the most common items you'll see on a menu.

- **Artichauts à la vinaigrette:** Artichokes in a vinaigrette dressing.

- **Crudités variées:** Assorted vegetables—sliced tomatoes, shredded carrots, sliced cooked beets—in a vinaigrette dressing.

- **Escargots à la bourguignonne:** Snails cooked and served in the shell, seasoned with a garlic, shallot, and parsley butter.

- **Foie gras:** Fresh, often uncooked liver of a force-fed goose; sliced and served with toasted French bread slices.

- **Pâté:** Any of a number of meat loaves, made from puréed liver and usually also with meat—pork, veal, or chicken. **Pâté de foie gras** is made with goose liver; **pâté de campagne** is "of the country" and is a coarser mixed meat pâté; **pâté en croute** is a liver pâté encased in pastry.

● **Quiche lorraine:** An egg custard tart, sometimes with bacon strips or bits; some versions now also made with Gruyère cheese.

● **Quenelles:** Light dumplings, usually made from **brochet** (pike) but also from shellfish; served in a white sauce.

● **Rillettes:** A pork mixture that has been potted, then served as a spread, usually with French bread.

● **Terrine:** A type of pâté, usually served from a deep pot rather than sliced as pâté would be. Terrines can be made from pork, poultry, game, or fish.

SOUPS

Some of those that appear on menus are the following.

● **Bisque d'écrevisses:** A creamy soup made with crawfish; other bisques are made with lobster, shrimp, or oysters.

● **Bouillabaisse:** A seafood stew, made with a variety of fish and shellfish depending on the region, seasoned with saffron and fennel or pernod.

● **Consommé:** A clear broth, made usually from chicken or beef and flavored with herbs; **en gelée** is consommé that has been jelled and sliced; **madrilène** is with tomatoes; **printanier** has a variety of vegetables.

● **Crème:** A creamy soup, made from any of a number of vegetables and usually enriched with egg yolks. **D'Argenteuil** is cream of asparagus soup; **de volaille** is a creamy chicken soup.

● **Petite marmite:** A rich consommé served with meat and vegetables.

- **Potage:** A coarser soup, usually made with a purée of vegetables; some varieties of potage are **parmentier** (leeks and potatoes), **au cresson** (watercress), and **julienne** (shredded vegetables).

- **Soupe à l'oignon:** Famous French onion soup, served over French bread and covered with cheese.

- **Velouté:** A creamy soup, most common of which are **de volaille** (cream of chicken) and **de tomate** (tomato).

EGG DISHES

As is true for most of the continent, eggs are not eaten for breakfast but rather are served as a beginning course in a variety of preparations.

- **Œufs bercy:** Eggs baked with sausages in a tomato sauce.

- **Œufs en cocotte:** Eggs gently baked in individual cups until softly cooked, sometimes with cream, then eaten with a spoon.

- **Œufs en gelée:** Poached eggs that are set into jelled consommé and served chilled as a salad.

- **Omelette:** A French omelette is puffy and contains a variety of fillings—**aux fines herbes** is with a mixture of parsley, chives, and tarragon.

- **Piperade:** Scrambled eggs mixed with tomatoes, onions, and sweet peppers.

- **Soufflé:** Soufflés can be made with almost any ingredients—vegetables, chicken livers, cheese, ham, and so on; they are always light and puffy.

FISH COURSE

The French often eat a fish course preceding meat or poultry. You can also order the fish course as your main selection. Here are some of the names for fish and shellfish you'll find on menus; for the names of preparations, see pages 127–129. When there is no price on the menu, the abbreviation s.g. (*selon grosseur*) refers to a dish that is sold by weight.

les anchois	*lay zahn-shwah*	anchovies
les anguilles	*lay zahn-gee*	eel
le bar	*luh bahr*	bass (hake)
la barbue	*lah bahr-bew*	brill
la baudroie	*lah boh-drwah*	monkfish
le brochet	*luh broh-sheh*	pike
le cabillaud	*luh kah-bee-yoh*	cod
le calmar	*luh kahl-mahr*	squid
la carpe	*lah kahrp*	carp
le carrelet	*luh kahr-leh*	flounder
le congre	*luh kohn-gruh*	conger eel
les crevettes	*lay kruh-veht*	shrimp
la daurade	*lah doh-rahd*	porgy
les écrevisses	*lay zay-kruh-veess*	crawfish
les escargots	*lay zehss-kahr-goh*	snails

les harengs (fumés)	*lay ah-rah<u>n</u> (few-may)*	herring (smoked)
le homard	*luh oh-mahr*	lobster
les huîtres	*lay zwee-truh*	oysters
la lamproie	*lah lah<u>n</u>-prwah*	lamprey
la langouste	*lah lah<u>n</u>-goosst*	spiny lobster
les langoustines	*lay lah<u>n</u>-goo-ssteen*	large shrimp
la lotte	*lah loht*	monkfish
le loup de mer	*luh loo duh mehr*	sea bass
le maquereau	*luh mah-kroh*	mackerel
le merlan	*luh mehr-lah<u>n</u>*	whiting
la morue	*lah moh-rew*	cod
les moules	*lay mool*	mussels
les palourdes	*lay pah-loord*	clams
la perche	*lah pehrsh*	perch
les poulpes	*lay poolp*	octopus
la rascasse	*lah rahss-kahss*	scorpionfish
les sardines	*lay sahr-deen*	sardines
le saumon	*luh soh-moh<u>n</u>*	salmon
les scampi	*lay skah<u>n</u>-pee*	large shrimp
le thon	*luh toh<u>n</u>*	tuna
la truite	*lah trweet*	trout
le turbot	*luh tewr-boh*	European turbot

POULTRY AND GAME

The French have several names for chicken, depending on its size or age. They also have varying names for duck and some game. Below are some of the more common terms you'll see on menus:

la caille	*lah kahy*	quail
le cerf	*luh sehr*	venison
le canard, **le caneton**	*luh kah-nahr,* *luh kahn-tohn*	duckling
le chapon	*luh shah-pohn*	capon
le chevreuil	*luh shuh-vruhy*	venison
le cochon de lait	*luh koh-shohn* *duh leh*	suckling pig
la dinde	*lah dand*	turkey
le faisan	*luh feh-zahn*	pheasant
le lapin	*luh lah-pan*	rabbit
le lièvre	*luh lyeh-vruh*	hare
l'oie (f.)	*lwah*	goose
le perdreau, **la perdrix**	*luh pehr-droh, lah* *pehr-dree*	partridge
le pigeon, **le pigeonneau**	*luh pee-zhohn,* *luh pee-zhoh-noh*	squab
la pintade, **le pintadeau**	*lah pan-tahd, luh* *pan-tah-doh*	guinea fowl

la poule	*lah pool*	stewing fowl
le poulet,	*luh poo-leh, luh*	chicken
le poussin	*poo-ssan*	

Suprême de volaille is the fillet from a young chicken breast, usually served with a sauce or garnish.

MEATS

Here are some basic terms for different kinds of meat, followed by a listing of some common cuts of meat and other terms you'll find on a menu.

l'agneau (m.)	*lah-nyoh*	lamb
le boeuf	*luh buhf*	beef
la chèvre	*lah sheh-vruh*	goat
le jambon	*luh zhahn-bohn*	ham
le mouton	*luh moo-tohn*	mutton
le porc	*luh pohr*	pork
le veau	*luh voh*	veal
les andouilles	*lay zahn-dooy*	pork sausages
le bifteck	*luh beef-tehk*	steak
le boudin	*luh boo-dan*	blood sausage
le carré d'agneau	*luh kah-ray dah-nyoh*	rack of lamb

le cervelas	*luh sehr-vuh-lah*	garlicky pork sausage
la cervelle	*lah sehr-vehl*	brains
la charcuterie	*lah shahr-kew-tree*	assorted sausages, pâtés, and terrines
le chateaubriand	*luh shah-toh-bree-ah<u>n</u>*	porterhouse steak
la côte de boeuf	*lah koht duh buhf*	ribs of beef
les côtelettes	*lay koht-leht*	cutlets
les côtes de porc, de veau	*lay koht duh pohr, duh voh*	chops, pork or veal
les crépinettes	*lay kray-pee-neht*	small sausages
l'entrecôte (f.)	*lah<u>n</u>-truh-koht*	sirloin steak
l'escalope (f.)	*lehss-kah-lohp*	cutlet
le filet de boeuf	*luh fee-leh duh buhf*	fillet of beef
le foie	*luh fwah*	liver
le gigot d'agneau	*luh zhee-goh dah-nyoh*	leg of lamb
la langue	*lah lah<u>ng</u>*	tongue
le lard	*luh lahr*	bacon
les médaillons de veau	*lay may-dah-yoh<u>n</u> duh voh*	medallions of veal
les noisettes	*lay nwah-zeht*	small fillets
les pieds de porc	*lay pyay duh pohr*	pig's feet
le ris de veau	*luh ree duh voh*	veal sweetbreads

les rognons d'ag-neau	*lay roh-nyohn dah-nyoh*	lamb kidneys
le rosbif	*luh rohss-beef*	roast beef
les saucisses	*lay soh-sseess*	sausages
la selle d'agneau	*lah sehl dah-nyoh*	saddle of lamb
le steak	*luh stehk*	steak
le tournedos	*luh toor-nuh-doh*	small fillets of beef
les tripes	*lay treep*	tripe
I prefer the dish ____.	**Je préfère le plat ____.**	*zhuh pray-fehr luh plah*
▪ baked	**cuit au four**	*kwee(t) o foor*
▪ boiled	**bouilli**	*boo-yee*
▪ braised (stewed)	**braisé**	*breh-zay*
▪ breaded	**au gratin, gratiné**	*o grah-tan, grah-tee-nay*
▪ broiled	**rôti**	*ro-tee*
▪ browned	**gratiné**	*grah-tee-nay*
▪ chopped	**hâché**	*ah-shay*
▪ fried	**frit**	*free*
▪ grilled	**grillé**	*gree-yay*
▪ in its natural juices	**au jus**	*o zhew*
▪ mashed, pureed	**en purée**	*ahn pew-ray*
▪ medium	**à point**	*ah pwan*
▪ medium rare	**mi-saignant**	*mee seh-nyahn*
▪ medium well	**bien cuit**	*byan kwee*
▪ poached	**poché**	*poh-shay*
▪ roasted	**rôti**	*ro-tee*

■ sautéed	**sauté**	*so-tay*
■ steamed	**à la vapeur**	*ah lah vah-puhr*
■ stewed	**en cocotte**	*ahn koh-koht*
■ rare	**saignant**	*seh-nyahn*
■ very rare	**bleu**	*bluh*
■ well-done	**très cuit**	*treh kwee*
■ with dressing (sauce) on the side	**avec la sauce à côté**	*ah-vehk lah sohss ah koh-tay*
■ with sauce	**en sauce**	*ahn sos*
■ without dressing (sauce)	**sans sauce**	*sahn sohss*

I prefer my eggs____.	**Je préfère mes œufs____.**	*zhuh pray-fehr may zuh*
■ fried	**au plat**	*o plah*
■ hard-boiled	**durs**	*dewr*
■ medium-boiled	**mollets**	*moh-leh*
■ poached	**pochés**	*poh-shay*
■ scrambled	**brouillés**	*broo-yay*
■ soft-boiled	**à la coque**	*ah lah kohk*

PROBLEMS

This ____.	**Ceci ____.**	*suh-ssee*
■ is bitter.	**est aigre.**	*eh teh-gruh*
■ is burned.	**est brûlé.**	*eh brew-lay*
■ is cold.	**est froid.**	*eh frwah*
■ is overcooked.	**est trop cuit.**	*eh troh kwee*
■ is spoiled.	**est tourné.**	*eh toor-nay*
■ is too salty.	**est trop salé.**	*eh troh sah-lay*

■ is too spicy.	**est trop épicé.**	*eh troh ay-pee-say*
■ is too sweet.	**est trop sucré.**	*eh troh sew-krey*
■ is tough.	**est dur.**	*eh dewr*
■ is undercooked.	**n'est pas assez cuit.**	*neh pah zah-say kwee*

PREPARATIONS AND SAUCES

Of necessity, these descriptions are very brief and generalized, but they should give you an impression of what to expect.

- **Aioli:** Mayonnaise heavily flavored with garlic.
- **Allemande:** A light (blond) sauce.
- **À la bonne femme:** White wine sauce with vegetables.
- **Alsacienne:** With sauerkraut.
- **Béarnaise:** A butter-egg sauce flavored with shallots, wine, and tarragon.
- **Bercy:** Basic meat or fish sauce.
- **Beurre blanc:** Butter sauce flavored with shallots and wine.
- **Beurre noir:** Browned butter sauce.
- **Blanquette:** An egg-enriched cream sauce, usually part of a stewed dish.
- **Bordelaise:** A dish prepared with Bordeaux wine.
- **Bourguignonne:** A dish prepared with Burgundy red wine.
- **Bretonne:** A dish that includes beans.
- **Caen:** A dish made with Calvados (apple brandy).
- **Chantilly:** A sauce of whipped cream and hollandaise; as a dessert, made with sweetened whipped cream.

- **Chasseur:** A sauce made with mushrooms, white wine, shallots, and parsley.
- **Choron:** A béarnaise sauce with tomatoes.
- **Coquilles:** A preparation served in a scallop shell.
- **Coulibiac:** A preparation served in a pastry shell.
- **Crécy:** A dish made with carrots.
- **Daube:** A stew, usually beef, made with red wine, onions, and garlic.
- **Demi-deuil:** When slices of truffles are inserted beneath the skin of a chicken.
- **Diable:** A spicy sauce, usually with chili or cayenne pepper.
- **Duxelles:** A mushroom mixture, usually as a stuffing or sauce base.
- **Estragon:** A dish made with tarragon.
- **Farce:** A stuffing, or forcemeat filling.
- **Fenouil:** A sauce made with fennel.
- **Financière:** Madeira sauce with truffles.
- **Fines herbes:** A dish made with a variety of chopped fresh herbs.
- **Florentine:** A dish that includes spinach.
- **Forestière:** A dish made with wild mushrooms.
- **Fricassée:** A stewed or potted dish, usually chicken.
- **Gratin:** A crusty baked dish, named for the dish in which it is cooked.
- **Hollandaise:** An egg yolk and butter sauce, with vinegar or lemon juice.
- **Jardinière:** A dish with fresh vegetables.
- **Lyonnaise:** A preparation made with onions.
- **Madère:** A dish made with madeira wine.

- **Maître d'hôtel:** A butter sauce with parsley and lemon juice.
- **Marchand de vin:** A sauce with a meat stock and red wine.
- **Meunière:** A simple dish lightly dusted with flour and sautéed, served in a lemon-butter sauce.
- **Mornay:** A simple white sauce with grated cheese, usually gruyère.
- **Mousseline:** A hollandaise sauce with whipped cream.
- **Moutarde:** With mustard.
- **Nantua:** A basic white sauce with cream and shellfish.
- **Normande:** Either a fish sauce with oysters or shrimp, or a sauce with apples.
- **Parmentier:** A dish with potatoes.
- **Périgourdine:** With truffles.
- **Poivrade:** A dark sauce, seasoned with pepper.
- **Provençale:** A vegetable garnish, usually with tomatoes, olives, anchovies, and garlic.
- **Quenelles:** Light-as-air dumplings made from fish or shellfish.
- **Ragoût:** A thick stew.
- **Rémoulade:** A mayonnaise flavored with mustard and sometimes capers.
- **Véronique:** A dish with grapes.
- **Verte:** A green mayonnaise, flavored with parsley and other herbs.
- **Vinaigrette:** An oil and vinegar dressing for salads.
- **Vol-au-vent:** A puff-pastry shell in which a creamed meat dish is usually served.

VEGETABLES

l'artichaut (m.)	*lahr-tee-shoh*	artichoke
les asperges	*lay zahss-pehrzh*	asparagus
l'aubergine (f.)	*loh-behr-zheen*	eggplant
la betterave	*lah beh-trahv*	beet
les carottes	*lay kah-roht*	carrots
le céleri	*luh sayl-ree*	celery
le maïs	*luh mah-yeess*	corn
le céleri rave	*luh sayl-ree rahv*	knob celery
les champignons	*lay shahn-pee-nyohn*	mushrooms
le chou	*luh shoo*	cabbage (green)
le chou-fleur	*luh shoo-fluhr*	cauliflower
la courgette	*lah koor-zheht*	zucchini
le cresson	*luh kreh-ssohn*	watercress
les épinards	*lay zay-pee-nahr*	spinach
les flageolets	*lay flah-zhoh-leh*	green shell beans
les haricots verts	*lay zah-ree-koh vehr*	green beans
les oignons	*lay zoh-nyohn*	onions
l'oseille (f.)	*loh-zehy*	sorrel
le piment	*luh pee-mahn*	green pepper
les pois	*lay pwah*	peas
le poireau	*luh pwah-roh*	leek
les pommes de terre	*lay pohm duh tehr*	potatoes
la tomate	*lah toh-maht*	tomato

SEASONINGS

Although French food is usually perfectly seasoned, personal preferences sometimes intercede. Here's how to ask for what you want.

I'd like _____.	**Je voudrais _____.**	*zhuh voo-dreh*
▥ artificial sweetener	**du sucre artificiel**	*dew sew-kruh ahr-tee-fee-syehl*
▥ butter	**du beurre**	*dew buhr*
▥ horseradish	**du raifort**	*dew reh-fohr*
▥ ketchup	**du ketchup**	*dew keht-chuhp*
▥ margarine	**de la margarine**	*duh lah mahr-gah-reen*
▥ mayonnaise	**de la mayonnaise**	*duh lah mah-yoh-nehz*
▥ mustard	**de la moutarde**	*duh lah moo-tahrd*
▥ olive oil	**de l'huile d'olive**	*duh lweel doh-leev*
▥ pepper (black)	**du poivre (noir)**	*dew pwah-vruh (nwahr)*
▥ pepper (red)	**du poivre (rouge)**	*dew pwah-vruh (roozh)*
▥ salt	**du sel**	*dew sehl*
▥ sugar	**du sucre**	*dew sew-kruh*
▥ vinegar	**du vinaigre**	*dew vee-neh-gruh*
▥ Worcestershire sauce	**de la sauce anglaise**	*du lah sohss ah<u>n</u>-glehz*

CHEESE COURSE

The cheese course is offered after the meat course and before the dessert. Most often, the restaurant will offer a tray of cheeses, from which you select two or three that balance one another. The cheese course is an opportunity to sample some cheeses that never get exported.

What is that cheese?	**Quel est ce fromage?**	*kehl eh suh froh-mahzh*
Is it _____?	**Est-il _____?**	*eh-teel*
■ mild	**maigre**	*meh-gruh*
■ sharp	**piquant**	*pee-kahn*
■ hard	**fermenté**	*fehr-mahn-tay*
■ soft	**à pâte molle**	*ah paht mohl*

Among the more popular cheeses are the following.

● **Banon:** Made from sheep's or goat's milk, a soft cheese with a natural rind; a mild cheese with a nutty flavor.

● **Bleu d'auvergne:** Made from cow's milk, this soft cheese has an internal mold and when cut, the veins are visible. Has a very sharp flavor.

● **Boursin:** A soft cow's milk cheese, with a mild flavor, sometimes enhanced with herbs.

● **Brie:** A variety of cheeses made from cow's milk and with a bloomy rind. Varieties range in flavor from mild to very pronounced, some with a fruity flavor.

● **Camembert:** Less delicate than brie, but also a cow's milk cheese with a thin white rind. Should be eaten firm.

- **Cantal:** A cow's milk cheese that varies with length of aging. Some varieties are softer and milder, while more aged ones are hard and with a more pronounced flavor.

- **Chèvre:** Any of an almost infinite variety of goat's milk cheeses, which vary from very soft to quite firm, and from mild and creamy to tart and crumbly. There will always be a few chèvres on the cheese tray.

- **Colombière:** This cow's milk cheese is soft and supple, with a mild flavor.

- **Munster:** A cow's milk cheese that is soft and spicy, with a tangy flavor. In Alsace, where the cheese comes from, it is eaten young.

- **Pont-l'evêque:** A cow's milk cheese that is very smooth and supple, with a pronounced flavor.

- **Port-salut:** The brand name for the Saint-Paulin from the monastery of Port-du-Salut.

- **Reblochon:** A soft cow's milk cheese with a mild and creamy flavor.

- **Roquefort:** A sheep's milk cheese that is soft and pungent. The cheese is cured in caves, an ancient process with rigid standards for production. Texture is very buttery.

- **Saint-Paulin:** Made from cow's milk, this is a velvety smooth cheese with a mild flavor.

- **Tomme de savoie:** A mild cow's milk cheese with a nutty flavor.

Petit Suisse is a fresh, unsalted cheese made from cow's milk and enriched with cream, then molded into heart shapes and sprinkled with sugar; it is a common dessert.

Fromage à la crème is *fromage blanc*, a rich, creamy white cheese made from unskimmed cow's milk. It is eaten topped with cream and sugar for breakfast.

Fondue is a specialty of Switzerland and parts of France that border on Switzerland. It is a large pot of bubbling melted cheese (usually Gruyère or Emmental), into which are dipped cubes of French bread. Fondue is served as a warming lunch or dinner course.

Raclette is a specialty of French-speaking Switzerland. It involves the slow melting of a hard cheese, usually alongside a roaring fire, during which the diners scrape off the cheese, as it melts, onto slices of French bread.

FRUITS AND NUTS

Here are the names of some common fruits, followed by nuts. Note that there is no generic term for nuts in French. Therefore, you must name the specific nut: I am allergic to almonds. **Je suis allergique aux amands**. (*zhuh swee zah-lehr-zheek oh zah-mahn*).

l'abricot	*lah-bree-koh*	apricot
l'ananas	*lah-nah-nah*	pineapple
la banane	*lah bah-nahn*	banana
les cassis	*lay kah-sseess*	black currants
la cerise	*lah suh-reez*	cherry
le citron	*luh see-trohn*	lemon
la datte	*lah daht*	date
la figue	*lah feeg*	fig
les fraises	*lay frehz*	strawberries
les fraises des bois	*lay frehz day bwah*	wild strawberries
les framboises	*lay frahn-bwahz*	raspberries
les groseilles	*lay groh-sehy*	red currants

la limette	*lah lee-meht*	lime
la mandarine	*lah mah<u>n</u>-dah-reen*	tangerine
le melon	*luh muh-loh<u>n</u>*	melon
les mûres	*lay mewr*	mulberries
les myrtilles	*lay meer-tee*	blueberries
l'orange	*loh-rah<u>n</u>zh*	orange
la noix de coco	*lah nwah duh koh-koh*	coconut
le pamplemousse	*luh pah<u>n</u>-pluh-mooss*	grapefruit
la pêche	*lah pehsh*	peach
la poire	*lah pwahr*	pear
la pomme	*lah pohm*	apple
la prune	*lah prewn*	plum
le pruneau	*luh prew-noh*	prune
le raisin	*luh reh-za<u>n</u>*	grape
le raisin sec	*luh reh-za<u>n</u> sehk*	raisin
l'amande (f.)	*lah-mah<u>n</u>d*	almond
le marron	*luh mah-roh<u>n</u>*	chestnut
la noisette	*lah nwah-zeht*	hazelnut
la noix	*lah nwah*	walnut
la cacahuète	*lah kah-kah-weht*	peanut
la pistache	*lah peess-tahsh*	pistachio

I am allergic to peanuts.	**Je suis allergique aux cacahuètes.** *zhuh swee zah-lehr-zheek oh kah-kah-weht*

DESSERTS—SWEETS

Often, a restaurant will display its desserts on a table in the dining room or the waiter will roll the cart to your table so you can make a selection. On the cart will be a variety of tarts, fruits in light syrup, and pastries. Here are some common items you might consider for dessert.

- **Bavaroise:** A bavarian cream; mont-blanc is a bavarian cream made with chestnuts.

- **Beignets:** Fritters, often made from fruit such as apple.

- **Bombe:** An ice cream construction, often with different flavors and sometimes also with sherbet.

- **Charlotte:** An assemblage of sponge fingers and pudding; usually the sponge cake is used to line the dish and the pudding is in the center.

- **Crème caramel:** An egg custard served with a caramel sauce.

- **Crêpes:** Dessert crêpes, the most famous of which are **Crêpes Suzette**, made with orange flavoring and served flaming with Grand Marnier.

- **Gâteau:** An elaborate layer cake, made with thin layers of sponge cake and pastry cream, and decorated.

- **Mousse au chocolat:** An airy pudding made with chocolate, cream, eggs, and brandy, garnished with whipped cream.

- **Macédoine de fruits:** A fresh fruit salad.

- **Œufs à la neige:** Soft meringue ovals served floating on a custard sauce.

- **Omelette norvégienne:** Baked Alaska.

- **Pâtisserie:** Pastry selection of any variety, including éclairs, millefeuilles, savarin, Saint-Honoré (creampuff cake).

- **Poires Belle-Hélène:** Poached pears, served with vanilla ice cream and chocolate sauce.

- **Profiteroles:** Cream puffs, served with chocolate sauce.

- **Soufflé:** There are an endless variety of sweet soufflés, the most famous one being the Grand Marnier soufflé.

- **Tarte:** An open-faced fruit pie, often made with apples or plums.

In addition, ice cream is a French favorite, as is sherbet and *granité* (fruit ice).

ice cream	**une glace**	*ewn glahss*
■ chocolate	**au chocolat**	*oh shoh-koh-lah*
■ vanilla	**à la vanille**	*ah lah vah-neey*
■ strawberry	**à la fraise**	*ah lah frehz*
sundae	**une coupe**	*ewn koop*
sherbet	**un sorbet**	*uhn sohr-beh*
fruit ice	**un granité**	*uhn grah-nee-tay*

SPECIAL CIRCUMSTANCES

Many travelers have special dietary requirements, so here are a few phrases that might help you get what you need or avoid what doesn't agree with you.

I'm on a special diet.	**Je suis un régime special.** *zhuh swee zuhn ray-zheem spay-ssyahl*
I'm a vegetarian.	**Je suis vegetarian (ne).** *zhuh swee vay-zhay-tah-ryan (ryen)*

Do you prepare vegetarian (kosher) meals?	**Vous préparez des repas vegetarians (casher)?** *voo pray-pah-ray day ruh-pah vay-zhay-tah-ryan (kah-shehr)*
I can't have____.	**Je ne peuz pas avoir ___.** *zhuh nuh puh pah zah-vwahr*
▇ alcohol	**l'alcool** *lahl-kohl*
▇ caffeine	**la caféine** *lah kah-fay-een*
▇ chocolate	**le chocolat** *luh shoh-koh-lah*
▇ dairy products	**les produits laitiers** *lay proh-dwee leh-tyay*
▇ gluten	**le gluten** *luh glew-tahn*
▇ MSG	**le glutamate de sodium** *luh glew-tah-maht duh soh-dyuhm*
▇ fish	**le poisson** *luh pwah-ssohn*
▇ salt	**le sel** *luh sehl*
▇ saturated fats	**la graisse saturée** *lah grehss sah-tew-ray*
▇ seafood	**les fruits de mer** *lay frwee duh mehr*
▇ shellfish	**les crustacés** *lay krew-stah-ssay*
▇ sugar	**le sucre** *luh sew-kruh*
▇ trans fat	**le gras trans** *luh grah trahnz*
I'm looking for a dish ____.	**Je cherche un plat____.** *zhuh shehrshh uhn plah*
▇ gluten free	**sans gluten** *sahn glew-tahn*
▇ high in fiber	**riche en fibre** *reesh ahn feebr*
▇ low in calories	**à basse calories** *ah bahss kah-loh-ree*
▇ low in cholesterol	**pauvre en cholestérol** *poh-vruh ahn koh-lehs-tay-rohl*

▦ low in fat	**pauvre en matières grasses**	*poh-vruh ahn mah-tyehr grahs*
▦ low in sodium	**pauvre en sodium**	*poh-vruh ahn sohd-yuhm*
▦ non-dairy	**non-laitier**	*nohn-leh-tyay*
▦ non-spicy	**non-épicé**	*nohn nay-pee-ssay*
▦ (extra) spicy	**(très) épicé**	*treh zay-pee-ssay*
▦ organic	**biologique**	*bee-oh-loh-zheek*
▦ salt-free	**sans sel**	*sahn sehl*
▦ sugar-free	**sans sucre**	*sahn sew-kruh*
▦ without artificial coloring	**sans colorant**	*sahn koh-loh-rahn*
▦ without butter	**sans beurre**	*sahn buhr*
▦ without eggs	**sans œufs**	*sahn zuh*
▦ without garlic	**sans ail**	*sahn zahy*
▦ without preservatives	**sans conservateurs**	*sahn kohn-sehr-vah-tuhr*
▦ without salt	**sahn sel**	*sahn sehl*

Is this dish made with ____?	**Ce plat est cuisine avec ____?** *suh plah eh kwee-zee-nay ah-vehk*	
▦ cheese	**du fromage**	*dew froh-mahzh*
▦ garlic	**de l'ail**	*duh lahy*
▦ meat	**de la viande**	*duh lah vee-yahnd*
▦ onions	**des oignons**	*day zoh-nyohn*

What are the ingredients?	**Quels sont les ingredients?** *kehl sohn lay zan-gray-dee-ahn*
Please ask the cook (chef).	**Demandez au cuisinier (au chef), s'il vous plait.** *duh-mahn-day oh kwee-zee-nyay (oh shehf) seel voo pleh*

BEVERAGES

See pages 143–147 for information on French apéritifs, wines, and brandies. As for other beverages, we give you the following phrases to help you ask for exactly what you wish.

Please bring me____.	**Apportez-moi____, s'il vous plait.** *ah-pohr-tay mwah ___ seel voo pleh*
coffee	**du café** *dew kah-fay*
■ coffee with milk (morning only)	**du café au lait** *dew kah-fay oh leh*
■ espresso	**du café-express** *dew kah-fay ehkss-prehss*
■ coffee with cream	**du café-crème** *dew kah-fay krehm*
■ black coffee	**du café noir** *dew kah-fay nwahr*
■ decaffeinated coffee	**du café decaféiné** *dew kah-fay day-kah-fay-ee-nay*
■ iced coffee	**du café glacé** *dew kah-fay glah-ssay*
cider (alcoholic)	**du cidre** *dew see-druh*
juice	**du jus de fruits** *dew zhew duh frwee*
lemonade	**de la citronnade** *duh lah see-troh-nahd*
milk	**du lait** *dew leh*
■ cold	**froid** *frwah*
■ hot	**chaud** *shoh*
■ milk shake	**un frappé** *uhn frah-pay*
orangeade	**une orangeade** *ewn oh-rahn-zhahd*
punch	**un punch** *uhn puhnsh*
soda	**un soda** *uhn soh-dah*

soft drink	**une boisson non-alcoolisée** *ewn bwah-sohn nohn-nahl-koh-lee-zay*
tea	**un thé** *uhn tay*
■ with milk	**au lait** *oh leh*
■ with lemon	**au citron** *oh see-trohn*
■ with sugar	**sucré** *sew-kray*
■ iced	**glacé** *glah-ssay*
water	**de l'eau (f.)** *duh loh*
■ cold	**fraîche** *frehsh*
■ ice	**glacée** *glah-ssay*
■ mineral	**minérale** *mee-nay-rahl*
■ sparkling	**gazeuse** *gah-zuhz*
■ non-carbonated	**plate** *plaht*

SETTLING UP

The bill normally includes a surcharge for service. In addition, most people leave the small change from the bill as a token of appreciation.

The check, please.	**L'addition, s'il vous plaît.** *lah-dee-ssyohn seel voo pleh*
Separate checks.	**Des additions séparées.** *day zah-dee-ssoyhn say-pah-ray*
Is the service (tip) included?	**Le service est compris?** *luh sehr-veess eh kohn-pree*
We didn't order this.	**On n'a pas commandé ceci.** *ohn nah pah koh-mahn-day suh-ssee*
I think there's a a mistake.	**Je crois qu'il y a une erreur.** *zhuh krwah keel yah ewn ehr-ruhr*
This is for you.	**Ceci est pour vous.** *suh-ssee eh poor voo*

REGIONAL FRENCH SPECIALTIES

French food is noted for its ingredients: wild mushrooms such as **chanterelles**, **cèpes**, and **morels**; truffles; fresh **foie gras**; chickens from Bresse; butter and cream from Normandy; cheese from all parts of France. Below we give you some of the notable dishes from some of the provinces of France, most of which are famous for their regional ingredients.

- **Alsace-Lorraine:** This region has a strong German influence in its food and the most famous dish is **choucroute garnie**, a sauerkraut, pork, and sausage mixture; also **pâté de foie gras**, **quiche lorraine**, and **chicken in Riesling wine**. The food is hearty, with much emphasis on fish, fruit, and pork.

- **Bordeaux:** Food from here is prepared simply, with Bordeaux wine, **cèpes**, and **confit d'oie**, a potted goose, preserved in its own fat. This is a noted wine-producing area.

- **Brittany:** **Crêpes** are the best-known food from here, with a variety of sweet and savory fillings. There is also much seafood and sausages. Cider is the popular beverage.

- **Burgundy:** With Lyons in the gastronomic center, this region has some of the best food in France. The chickens from Bresse are world famous, as is the beef; from Burgundy we also get the savory mustards, spiced gingerbread, and black-currant liqueur—cassis. This is also a major wine-producing region.

- **Normandy:** Foods from here are marked by a use of apples or apple **eau de vie** (brandy). The fish dishes in this region are noteworthy.

- **Provence:** This is a southern region that uses a lot of olive oil and garlic in its dishes. Fish and seafood predominate, with a generous use of vegetables and fruits. The most famous dish is **bouillabaisse**, a fish stew. **Salade niçoise**, with lettuce, tuna, hard-cooked eggs, olives, and anchovies, and **pissaladière**, a pizza made with anchovies, are also popular.

- **Paris:** Food from all parts of France influences the dishes that are served in Paris. Those especially Parisian are **boeuf à la mode** (boiled beef with vegetables) and brie cheese.

APÉRITIFS, WINES, AND AFTER-DINNER DRINKS

APÉRITIFS

Most French people prefer to drink an apéritif before a meal rather than a cocktail. An apéritif is an appetite stimulant, and can be a variety of drinks, ranging from a simple vermouth or vermouth mixed with a liqueur (such as cassis), to a distilled drink such as Cynar, made from artichoke hearts. Among the most popular are:

Byrrh **Dubonnet** **Saint-Raphaël**	wine- and brandy-based, flavored with herbs and bitters
Pernod **Ricard**	anise-based, licorice-flavored
Vermouth	fortified wine made from red or white grapes
Cynar	bitter tasting, distilled from artichoke hearts

WINE

The high quality of the soil and the moderate climate have given French vineyards their historically unique position among wine-producing countries. Wine served with meals follows a progression from the light white wines to richer, heartier reds. (One wouldn't drink a Mâcon after a Pommard, or a Bordeaux after a Burgundy.)

White wines and rosés are served very cold (52°F). Beaujolais, although red, should be lightly chilled. Bordeaux is served at room temperature (62°F), Burgundy just above room temperature. Sweet wines should be chilled, and Champagne iced. The chart below will help you select a wine to suit your tastes and your food.

wine	**le vin**	*luh va<u>n</u>*
■ red wine	**le vin rouge**	*luh va<u>n</u> roozh*
■ rosé	**le vin rosé**	*luh va<u>n</u> roh-zay*
■ sparkling wine	**le vin mousseux**	*luh va<u>n</u> moo-ssuh*
■ sherry	**un sherry**	*uh<u>n</u> sheh-ree*
■ white wine	**le vin blanc**	*luh va<u>n</u> blah<u>n</u>*

AFTER-DINNER DRINKS

Brandy is often enjoyed after a lengthy, especially fine meal. **Cognac**, the finest of brandies, is distilled from grapes grown in the Charente district, the principal city of which is Cognac. It is usually aged for 20 years in barrels made from Limousin oak trees. Four different types, which differ in character and taste, are Rémy-Martin, Martel, Courvoisier, and Hennessy. These cognacs are considerably less expensive in France than elsewhere.

Armagnac comes from the Basque region. It is often bottled straight, rather than blended as cognac is.

Eaux-de-vie are distilled fruit brandies. Unlike cognac and other brandies, they are aged in crockery, not wood, so their taste is harsher. Some eaux-de-vie are **kirsch** (black cherry), **framboise** (wild raspberries), **poire William** (Swiss William pears), **mirabelle** (yellow plum), **calvados** (apple), and **marc** (from stems, pits, and skins of certain grapes).

Some liqueurs to choose from are:

absinthe	light drink with a pronounced anise aroma.
anisette	clear, sweet aromatic liqueur made from aniseeds and herbs.
Bénédictine	a blend of 150 different herbs and plants.
B & B	a combination of Bénédictine and brandy.
Chambord	raspberry-flavored, combined with honey.
Chartreuse	a combination of 130 herbs, in green and yellow.
Cointreau	made from sweet and bitter tropical orange peels blended with cognac.
Crème de Cassis	made from black currants.
Grand Marnier	an orange-flavored liqueur made from the peel of bitter Curaçao oranges and blended with cognac.

WINE	REGION	DESCRIPTION	ORDER WITH
Anjou	Loire	semisweet rosé	fish, meat, game, poultry, esp. ham
Beaujolais	Burgundy	light, young, fruity red wine	meat, poultry, fowl, cheese
Chablis	Burgundy	dry white, flinty bouquet, nutty taste	fish, seafood, esp. lobster
Champagne	Champagne	delicate, sparkling white wine	
		Extra Dry (fruity)—medium dry	aperitif
		Brut—driest	aperitif
		Sec—least dry	dessert
Chardonnay	Burgundy	delicate, fruity, flinty wine	fish
Châteauneuf-du-Pape	Rhône	full-bodied red wine	game, poultry, meat
Côte de Beaune	Burgundy	very delicate light red wine	meat, esp. prime ribs, fowl, poultry
Côte de Bourg	Bordeaux	medium, full-bodied red wine	meat, poultry, fowl, cheese
Côtes du Rhône	Rhône	light fruity red wine full-bodied white wine	meat, poultry, fowl fish, poultry

Gewürztraminer	Alsace	light, crisp white wine	fish, poultry, some cheese
Graves (blanc)	Bordeaux	soft white wine	fish, poultry
Graves (rouge)	Bordeaux	robust red wine	meat, fowl, poultry, cheese
Mâconnais (Pouilly-Fuissé)	Burgundy	light, dry, white wine	fish, seafood, egg and cheese dishes
Médoc	Bordeaux	light red wine	meat, poultry, fowl, cheese
Merlot	Bordeaux	dry, fruity wine	roasted meat, poultry, cheese
Muscadet	Loire	light, dry white wine	fish, seafood, esp. scallops
Muscat	Alsace	sweet white wine (also sparkling)	fish, seafood, desserts
Pinot	Alsace	light, fruity, white wine	fish, shellfish, cold vegetable dishes, egg and cheese dishes
Pomerol	Bordeaux	mellow, full-bodied red wine	meat, fowl, poultry, cheese
Riesling	Alsace	light, fruity, white wine	fish, shellfish, cold vegetable dishes, egg and cheese dishes
Saumur	Loire	dry, white wine	fish, seafood, poultry
Sauternes (Barsac)	Bordeaux	honey-sweet white wine	desserts
St-Emilion	Bordeaux	full-bodied, dark red wine	meat, fowl, poultry, cheese, esp. ham
Vouvray	Loire	white or sparkling white	fish, seafood, meat

MEETING PEOPLE

Remember to shake hands when meeting people; a French person may feel offended if you do not. It is customary for the French to greet each other—men and women alike—by kissing on both cheeks.

In general, Europeans don't ask many personal questions at the beginning of an acquaintance. They make contact through a neutral topic such as the weather or the traffic.

The French café is the perfect neighborhood spot for young and old to go to socialize at any time of the day or evening. There one meets friends, watches passersby, reads a newspaper, or relaxes with a drink or a snack.

GREETINGS AND INTRODUCTIONS

Hello.	**Bonjour.**	*bohn-zhoor*
Hi.	**Salut.**	*sah-lew*
Good evening.	**Bonsoir.**	*bohn-swahr*
Good night.	**Bonne nuit.**	*bohn nwee*
How are you?	**Comment allez-vous?**	*koh-mahn tah-lay-voo*
I'm well.	**Je vais bien.**	*zhuh veh byan*
Where are you from?	**D'où êtes-vous?**	*doo eht voo*
I'm_____.	**Je suis ___.**	*zhuh swee*
▨ from England	**d'Angleterre**	*dahn-gluh-tehr*
▨ from Canada	**du Canada**	*dew kah-nah-dah*
▨ from the U.S.	**des États-Unis**	*day zay-tah zew-nee*

Let me introduce myself.	**Permettez-moi de me présenter.** *pehr-meh-tay-mwah duh muh pray-zahn-tay*
I'm pleased to meet you.	**Enchanté(e).** *ahn-shahn-tay*
The pleasure is mine.	**Moi de même.** *mwah duh mehm*
Let me introduce you to____?	**Je vous présente____?** *zhuh voo pray-zahnt*
▥ my family	**ma famille** *mah fah-meey*
▥ my brother	**mon frère** *mohn frehr*
▥ my father	**mon père** *mohn pehr*
▥ my friend	**mon ami(e)** *mohn nah-mee*
▥ my boyfriend	**mon petit ami** *mohn puh-tee tah-mee*
▥ my girlfriend	**ma petite amie** *mah puh-teet tah-mee*
▥ my husband	**mon mari** *mohn mah-ree*
▥ my mother	**ma mère** *mah mehr*
▥ my sister	**ma sœur** *mah suhr*
▥ my significant other	**mon (ma) partenaire** *mohn (mah) pahr-tuh-nehr*
▥ my sweetheart	**mon(ma) fiancé(e)** *mohn (mah) fee-yahn-ssay*
▥ my wife	**ma femme** *mah fahm*
My name is ____.	**Je m'appelle ____.** *zhuh mah-pehl*
I am a(an) ____.	**Je suis ____.** *zhuh swee*
▥ accountant	**comptable** *kohn-tah-bluh*
▥ businessperson	**homme (femme) d'affaires** *ohm (fahm) dah-fehr*

■ dentist	**dentiste**	*dahn-teesst*
■ doctor	**docteur**	*dohk-tuhr*
■ engineer	**ingénieur**	*an-zhay-nyuhr*
■ hairdresser	**coiffeur (-euse)**	*kwah-fuhr (fuhz)*
■ jeweler	**bijoutier (-ière)**	*bee-zhoo-tyay (tyehr)*
■ lawyer	**avocat(e)**	*ah-voh-kah(t)*
■ nurse	**infirmier (-ière)**	*an-feer-myay (myehr)*
■ police officer	**agent de police**	*ah-zhahn duh poh-leess*
■ secretary	**secrétaire (m. or f.)**	*suh-kray-tehr*
■ self-employed	**indépendant(e)**	*an-day-pahn-dahn(t)*
■ shopkeeper	**commerçant(e)**	*koh-mehr-ssahn(t)*

■ student	**étudiant(e)**	*ay-tew-dyah<u>n</u>(t)*
■ teacher	**professeur**	*proh-feh-suhr*

I am retired. **Je suis en retraite.** *zhuh sweez ah<u>n</u> ruh-treht*

I'm in sales and marketing. **Je travaille dans la vente et le marketing.** *zhuh trah-vahy dah<u>n</u> lah vah<u>n</u>t ay luh mahr-keh-teeng*

DATING AND SOCIALIZING

Do you speak English? **Tu parles anglais?** *tew pahrl ah<u>n</u>-gleh*

Can I be familiar? **Je peux vous tutoyer?** *zhuh puh voo tew-twah-yay*

Are you married? **Tu es marié(e)?** *tew eh mah-ree-yay*

I'm ____. **Je suis____.** *zhuh swee*

■ married	**marié(e)**	*mah-ree-yay*
■ single	**célibataire**	*say-lee-bah-tehr*
■ separated	**séparé(e)**	*say-pah-ray*
■ divorced	**divorcé(e)**	*dee-vohr-ssay*
■ a widower (widow)	**veuf (veuv)**	*vuhf (vuhv)*

Do you live nearby? **Tu habites par ici?** *tew ah-beet pahr ee-ssee*

Do you want to go out with me (us)? **Tu veux sortir avec moi (nous)?** *tew vuh sohr-teer ah-vehk mwah (noo)*

Do you want to go___?	**Tu veux aller___?** *tew vuh ah-lay*
▨ dancing	**danser** *dah<u>n</u>-ssay*
▨ for a drink	**prendre un verre** *prah<u>n</u>-druh uh<u>n</u> vehr*
▨ eat	**manger** *mah<u>n</u>-zhay*
▨ to dinner	**diner** *dee-nay*
▨ to a concert	**à un concert** *ah uh<u>n</u> koh<u>n</u>-seht*
▨ to the movies	**au cinéma** *oh see-nay-mah*
▨ to the theater	**au théâtre** *oh tay-ah-truh*
▨ to a nightclub	**en boîte** *ah<u>n</u> bwaht*
▨ to a party	**à une fête** *ah ewn feht*

Would you like to dance?	**Tu veux danser?** *tew vuh dahn-ssay*
Yes, all right. With pleasure.	**Oui, d'accord. Avec plaisir.** *Wee dah-kohr ah-vehk pleh-zeer*
Do you smoke?	**Tu fumes?** *tew fewm*
Would you like a cigarette?	**Voudrais-tu une cigarette?** *voo-dreh-tew ewn see-gah-reht?*
Do you have a light?	**Avez-vous du feu?** *ah-vay voo dew fuh*
Do you mind if I smoke?	**Ça vous dérange si je fume?** *sah voo day-rah<u>n</u>zh see zhuh fewm*
May I take you home?	**Puis-je vous raccompagner chez vous?** *pweezh voo rah-koh<u>n</u>-pay-nyah shay voo*
May I ___ you?	**Puis-je te _____?** *Pweezh tuh*
▨ call	**téléphoner** *tay-lay-foh-nay*

▓ e-mail	**t'envoyer un e-mail**	*tahn-vwah-yay uhn ee-mehl*
▓ text	**t'envoyer un message texte**	*tahn-vwah-yay uhn meh-sahzh tehksst*
▓ skype	**te skyper**	*tuh skahy-pay*

What is your _____?	**Quel est ton _____?**	*kehl eh tohn*
▓ telephone number	**numéro de téléphone**	*new-may-roh duh tay-lay-fohn*
▓ cell phone number	**numéro de portable**	*new-may-roh duh pohr-tah-bluh*
▓ e-mail address	**adresse e-mail**	*ah-drehss ee-mehl*

Are you on facebook (skype)?	**Tu es sur facebook (skype)?**	*tew eh sewr fayss-book (skahyp)*
May I add you as a friend?	**Puis-je t'ajouter comme ami(e)?**	*pweezh tah-zhoo-tay kohm ah-mee*
Here's my telephone number.	**Voici mon numéro de téléphone.**	*vwah-ssee mohn new-may-roh duh tay-lay-fohn*

Are you free ___?	**Es-tu libre ___.**	*eh tew lee-bruh*
▓ tomorrow	**demain**	*duh-man*
▓ this evening	**ce soir**	*suh swahr*
▓ this weekend	**ce week-end**	*suh week-ehnd*

I'll pick you up at ____ o'clock.	**Je viendrai te chercher à ____ heures.**	*zhuh vyan-dray tuh shehr-shay ah ____ uhr*
Nice to have met you.	**Enchanté(e).**	*ahn-shahn-tay*
See you soon.	**À bientôt.**	*ah byan-toh*

SHOPPING

SHOPS/STORES

It is best to start by shopping in the large department stores so that you can browse without feeling obligated to make a purchase. Most department stores are open Monday through Saturday, from 9:30 A.M. to 8 P.M. Most stores are closed on Sundays, with the exception of large stores on the Champs-Elysées (open 11 A.M. to 7 P.M.). Popular malls around Paris include **Le Carrousel du Louvre**, **Le Forum des Halles**, and **Les Quatre Temps**. These elegant, ultramodern shopping centers are open seven days a week and have hundreds of stores, fast-food restaurants, **bureaux de change**, and much more.

Large department stores line the boulevards of the Right Bank. The **Galeries Lafayette** and **Le Printemps** (two upscale rivals), and **Bazaar de l'Hôtel de Ville** (a more modestly priced establishment) offer a vast selection of items, cater to foreign visitors, employ multilingual sales personnel, and have bureaux de change on the premises. **Le Bon Marché** department store on the Left Bank is worth mentioning.

The huge **centres commerciaux** (malls) outside of Paris are dominated by the Auchan and Carrefour chain of stores, which are surrounded by walkways containing smaller boutiques and shops that cater to every taste, as well as banks and restaurants.

GOING SHOPPING

I'd like to do shopping chores (go shopping) today.

Je voudrais faire des courses (faire des achats) aujourd'hui.
zhuh voo-dreh fehr day koorss (fehr day zah-shah) oh-zhoord-wee

Where is ____?	**Où se trouve ____?** *oo suh troov*
■ a bakery	**une boulangerie** *ewn boo-lahnzh-ree*
■ a bookstore	**une librairie** *ewn lee-breh-ree*
■ a butcher	**une boucherie** *ewn boosh-ree*
■ a camera shop	**un magasin d'appareils-photo** *uhn mah-gah-zan dah-pah-rehy foh-toh*
■ a candy store	**une confiserie** *ewn kohn-feess-ree*
■ a clothing store	**un magasin de vêtements** *uhn mah-gah-zan duh veht-mahn*
for children's clothes	**pour enfants** *poor ahn-fahn*
men's store	**pour hommes** *poor ohm*
women's boutique	**pour femmes** *poor fahm*
■ a delicatessen	**une charcuterie** *ewn shahr-kew-tree*
■ a department store	**un grand magasin** *uhn grahn mah-gah-zan*
■ a drugstore	**une pharmacie** *ewn fahr-mah-ssee*
■ a florist	**un fleuriste** *uhn fluh-reesst*
■ a gift (souvenir) shop	**un magasin de souvenirs** *uhn mah-gah-zan duh soov-neer*
■ a grocery store	**une épicerie** *ewn ay-peess-ree*
■ a hardware store	**une quincaillerie** *ewn kan-kahy-ree*
■ a jewelry store	**une bijouterie** *ewn bee-zhoo-tree*
■ a liquor store	**un magasin de vins et spiritueux** *uhn mah-gah-zan duh van ay spee-ree-tew-uh*
■ a newsstand	**un kiosque à journaux** *uhn kee-ohsk ah zhoor-noh*
■ an optician	**un opticien** *uhn nohp-tee-ssyan*
■ a pastry shop	**une pâtisserie** *ewn pah-teess-ree*

Travel Tips A value-added tax (T.V.A.) of 19.6% is levied on all goods except medicine, food, and books. The T.V.A. in France is almost always included in the price indicated in shops. This money may, however, be refunded to you. A **détaxe** desk in most large department stores helps non-Europeans receive a discount on large purchases of luxury items. Spending over 175 euros in the same store on the same day entitles the buyer to this rebate. To avoid further inconvenience, have your export form stamped in the store on the day of your purchase. It is essential that you save all sales slips for the **détaxe**. Upon arriving at the airport for your trip home, an official will ask for your ticket, passport, and shopping forms before you proceed through customs.

▓ a record store	**un magasin de disques**	*uhn mah-gah-zan duh deessk*
▓ a shoemaker	**un cordonnier**	*uhn kohr-doh-nyay*
▓ a shoe store	**un magasin de chaussures**	*uhn mah-gah-zan duh shoh-ssewr*
▓ a supermarket	**un supermarché**	*uhn sew-pehr-mahr-shay*
▓ a tobacco shop	**un bureau de tabac**	*uhn bew-roh duh tah-bah*
▓ a toy store	**un magasin de jouets**	*uhn mah-gah-zan duh zhoo-eh*
▓ a wine merchant	**un négociant en vins**	*uhn nay-goh-ssee-yahn ahn van*
Can you help me?	**Pouvez-vous m'aider?**	*poo-vay voo meh-day*
I'm just looking.	**Je regard tout simplement.**	*zhuh ruh-gahrd too sam-pluh-mahn*
I'm looking for ____.	**Je cherche ____.**	*zhuh shehrsh*

Are there any sales?	**Il y a des soldes?**	*eel yah day sohld*
How much is it?	**C'est combien?**	*seh kohn-byan*
Do you accept ___?	**Acceptez-vous ___?**	*ahk-ssehp-tay voo*
credit cards	**les cartes de crédit**	*lay kahrt duh kray-dee*
debit cards	**les cartes de débit**	*lay kahrt duh day-bee*
Which ones?	**Lesquelles?**	*lay-kehl*
Could you please give me ___?	**Pourriez-vous me donner ___?**	*poo-ree-yay-voo muh doh-nay*
a bag	**un sac**	*uhn sahk*
a receipt	**un reçu**	*uhn ruh-sew*
Could you please gift wrap it for me?	**Pourriez-vous me faire un paquet-cadeau?**	*poo-ree-yay-voo muh fehr uhn pah-ket kah-doh*
Can you send it to the United States?	**Pouvez-vous l'envoyer aux États-Unis?**	*poo-vay-voo lahn-vwah-yay oh zay-tah zew-nee*
I'd like to return this.	**Je voudrais rapporter ceci.**	*zhuh voo-dreh rah-pohr-tay suh-ssee*
I'd like to exchange this.	**Je voudrais échanger ceci.**	*zhuh voo-dreh ay-shahn-zhay suh-ssee*
I'd like my money back.	**Je voudrais un remboursement.**	*zhuh voo-dreh zuhn rahn-boorss-mahn*
It's defective.	**C'est défectueux.**	*seh day-fehk-tew-uh*

It doesn't work. **Ça ne marche pas.** *sah nuh mahrsh pah*

There's a button missing. **Un bouton manque.** *uhn boo-tohn mahnk*

Can you fix this? **Pouvez-vous réparer ceci?** *poo-vay-voo ray-pah-ray suh-ssee*

When will it be ready? **Ça sera prêt quand?** *sah suh-rah preh kahn*

I need this ____. **J'en ai besoin ___.** *zhahn nay buh-zwan*

■ today **aujourd'hui** *oh-zhoord-wee*

■ tonight **ce soir** *suh swahr*

■ tomorrow **demain** *duh-man*

■ the day after tomorrow **après-demain** *ah-preh duh-man*

■ next week **la semaine prochaine** *lah suh-mehn proh-shehn*

■ as soon as possible **aussitôt que possible** *oh-see-toh kuh poh-ssee-bluh*

Where is the Lost and Found? **Où est le bureau des objets trouvés?** *oo eh luh bew-roh day zohb-zheh troo-vay*

I can't find what I'm looking for. **Je ne trouve pas ce que je cherche.** *zhuh nuh troov pah suh kuh zhuh shersh*

BOOKS

Where is the best (biggest) bookstore near here?	**Où se trouve la meilleure (la plus grande) librairie par ici?** *oo suh troov lah meh-yuhr (lah plew grahnd) lee-breh-ree pahr ee-ssee*
I would like _____.	**Je voudrais _____.** *zhuh voo-dreh*
■ a guidebook	**un guide touristique** *uhn geed too-reess-teek*
■ a map of the city	**un plan de la ville** *uhn plahn duh lah veel*
■ a newspaper	**un journal** *uhn zhoor-nahl*
■ a pocket dictionary	**un dictionnaire de poche** *uhn deek-ssyoh-nehr duh pohsh*
■ a French-English dictionary	**un dictionnaire français-anglais** *uhn deek-ssyoh-nehr frahn-sseh ahn-gleh*
Where can I find _____?	**Où puis-je trouver _____?** *oo pweezh troo-vay*
■ detective stories	**des romans policiers** *day roh-mahn poh-leess-yay*
■ history books	**des livres d'histoire** *day lee-vruh deess-twahr*
■ novels	**des romans** *day roh-mahn*
■ science fiction books	**des livres de science fiction** *day lee-vruh duh see-yahnss feek-syohn*
■ short story books	**des contes** *day kohnt*
I'll take this.	**Je vais prendre ceci.** *zhuh veh prahn-druh suh-ssee*

CLOTHING

Where is the _____ department?	**Où est le rayon des _____.**	*oo eh luh reh-yohn day*
Would you please show me _____.	**Veuillez me montrer _____.**	*vuh-yay muh mohn-tray*
▥ a bathing suit	**un maillot de bain**	*uhn mah-yoh duh ban*
▥ a belt	**une ceinture**	*ewn san-tewr*
▥ a blouse	**un chemisier**	*uhn shuh-mee-zyay*
▥ boots	**des bottes (f.)**	*day boht*
▥ a bra	**un soutien-gorge**	*uhn soo-tyan gohrzh*
▥ a dress	**une robe**	*ewn rohb*
▥ an evening gown	**une robe du soir**	*ewn rohb duh swahr*
▥ gloves	**des gants (m.)**	*day gahn*
▥ a hat	**un chapeau**	*uhn shah-poh*
▥ a jacket	**un veston**	*uhn vehss-tohn*
▥ jeans	**un jean**	*uhn zheen*
▥ a jogging suit	**un survêt, un jogging**	*uhn sewr-veh, uhn zhoh-geeng*
▥ an overcoat	**un manteau/pardessus**	*uhn mahn-toh/pahr-duh-ssew*
▥ pajamas	**un pyjama**	*uhn pee-zhah-mah*
▥ panties (women)	**un slip**	*uhn sleep*
▥ pants	**un pantalon**	*uhn pahn-tah-lohn*
▥ pantyhose	**des collants**	*day koh-lahn*
▥ a raincoat	**un imperméable**	*uhn nan-pehr-may-ah-bluh*
▥ a robe	**une robe de chambre**	*ewn rohb duh shahn-bruh*

▥ sandals	**des sandales (f.)**	*day sahn-dahl*
▥ scarf	**une écharpe**	*ewn ay-shahrp*
▥ a shirt	**une chemise**	*ewn shuh-meez*
▥ shoes	**des chaussures (f.)**	*day shoh-ssewr*
▥ shorts (briefs)	**un caleçon**	*uhn kahl-ssohn*
▥ a skirt	**une jupe**	*ewn zhewp*
▥ a slip	**un jupon**	*uhn zhew-pohn*
▥ slippers	**des pantoufles (f.)**	*day pahn-too-fluh*
▥ sneakers	**des baskets (f.)**	*day bahs-keht*
	des tennis (f.)	*day teh-nees*
▥ socks	**des chaussettes**	*day shoh-sseht*
▥ stockings	**des bas**	*day bah*
▥ a suit	**un complet** (for men)/**un tailleur** (for women)	*uhn kohn-pleh/uhn tah-yuhr*
▥ a sweater	**un chandail**	*uhn shahn-dahy*
	un pull	*uhn pewl*
▥ a T-shirt	**un tee-shirt**	*uhn tee-shehrt*

▥ a tie	**une cravate**	*ewn krah-vaht*
▥ an umbrella	**un parapluie**	*un̠n pah-rah-plwee*
▥ an undershirt (T-shirt)	**un sous-vêtement**	*uh̠n soo veht-mah̠n*
▥ a vest	**un gilet**	*uh̠n zhee-leh*
▥ a wallet	**un portefeuille**	*uh̠n pohr-tuh-fuhy*

I'd like short (long) sleeves. **Je voudrais les manches courtes (longues).** *zhuh voo-dreh lay mah̠nsh koort (loh̠ng)*

▥ sleeveless	**sans manches**	*sah̠n mah̠nsh*

Do you have anything _____? **Avez-vous quelque chose _____?** *ah-vay voo kehl-kuh shohz*

▥ else	**d'autre**	*doh-truh*
▥ larger	**de plus grand**	*duh plew grah̠n*
▥ smaller	**de plus petit**	*duh plew puh-tee*
▥ longer	**de plus long**	*duh plew loh̠n*
▥ shorter	**de plus court**	*duh plew koor*
▥ more (less) expensive	**de plus (moins) cher**	*duh plew (mwa̠n) shehr*
▥ of better quality	**de meilleure qualité**	*duh meh-yuhr kah-lee-tay*
▥ cheaper	**de moins cher**	*duh mwa̠n shehr*

I don't like the color. **Je n'aime pas la couleur.** *zhuh nehm pah lah koo-luhr*

Do you have it in _____? **L'avez-vous en _____?** *lah-vay voo zah̠n*

▥ beige	**beige**	*behzh*
▥ black	**noir**	*nwahr*
▥ blue	**bleu**	*bluh*
▥ brown	**brun/marron**	*bruh̠n/mah-roh̠n*

gray	**gris**	*gree*
green	**vert**	*vehr*
navy blue	**bleu marine**	*bluh mah-reen*
orange	**orange**	*oh-rah<u>n</u>zh*
pink	**rose**	*rohze*
purple	**mauve**	*mohv*
red	**rouge**	*roozh*
white	**blanc**	*blah<u>n</u>*
yellow	**jaune**	*zhohn*

I prefer a lighter (darker) color.	**Je préfère une couleur plus claire (foncée).** *zhuh pray-fehr ewn koo-luhr plew klehr (foh<u>n</u>-ssay)*

CHART OF MATERIALS

corduroy	**velours côtelé**	*vuh-loor koht-lay*
cotton	**coton**	*koh-toh<u>n</u>*
denim	**jean**	*zheen*
felt	**feutre**	*fuh-truh*
flannel	**flanelle**	*flah-nehl*
gabardine	**gabardine**	*gah-bahr-deen*
lace	**dentelle**	*dah<u>n</u>-tehl*
leather	**cuir**	*kweer*
linen	**lin**	*la<u>n</u>*
nylon	**nylon**	*nee-loh<u>n</u>*
permanent press	**infroissable**	*a<u>n</u>-frwah-ssah-bluh*
polyester	**polyester**	*poh-lee-ehss-tehr*
satin	**satin**	*sah-ta<u>n</u>*
silk	**soie**	*swah*

▪ suede	**daim** *dan*
▪ terrycloth	**tissu-éponge** *tee-ssew-ay-pohnzh*
▪ velvet	**velours** *vuh-loor*
▪ wool	**laine** *lehn*

Show me something _____.	**Montrez-moi quelque chose** _____. *mohn-tray mwah kehl-kuh-shohz*
▪ in a solid color	**d'uni** *dew-nee*
▪ with stripes	**à rayures** *ah rah-yewr*
▪ with polka dots	**à pois** *ah pwah*
▪ in plaid	**en tartan** *ahn tahr-tahn*
▪ in herringbone	**à chevrons** *ah shuh-vrohn*
▪ checked	**à carreaux** *ah kah-roh*

Please take my measurements.	**Veuillez prendre mes mesures.** *vuh-yay prahn-druh may muh-zewr*
I take size (My size is) _____.	**Je porte du (Ma taille est)** _____. *zhuh pohrt dew (mah tahy eh)*
▪ small	**petit (petite)** *puh-tee (puh-teet)*
▪ medium	**moyen (moyenne)** *mwah-yan (mwah-yehn)*
▪ large	**grand (grande)** *grahn (grahnd)*

I'd like to try this on.	**Je voudrais essayer ceci.** *zhuh voo-dreh ay-seh-yay suh-ssee*
Where are the dressing rooms?	**Où sont les vestiaires?** *oo sohn lay vehss-tee-yehr*
Can you alter this?	**Pouvez-vous retoucher ceci?** *poo-vay voo ruh-too-shay suh-ssee*
Can I return this?	**Puis-je rapporter ceci?** *pweezh rah-pohr-tay suh-ssee*

Is it handmade?	**C'est fait à la main?** *seh feh tah lah ma_n_*
The zipper doesn't work.	**La fermeture-éclair ne marche pas.** *lah fehr-muh-tewr ay-klehr nuh mahrsh pah*
It doesn't fit me.	**Cela ne me va pas.** *suh-lah nuh muh vah pah*
It fits very well.	**Ça va à la perfection.** *Sah vah ah lah pehr-fehk-ssyoh_n_*
I'll take this.	**Je prends ceci.** *zuh prah_n_ suh-ssee*
I'd like to see a pair of shoes (boots).	**Je voudrais voir une paire de chaussures (bottes).** *zhuh voo-dreh vwahr ewn pehr duh shoh-ssewr (boht)*
Show me that pair.	**Montrez-moi cette paire.** *moh_n_-tray mwah seht pehr*
I take size ____.	**Je chausse du ____.** *zhuh shohss dew*
These shoes are too narrow (wide).	**Ces chaussures sont trop étroites (larges).** *say shoh-ssewr soh_n_ troh pay-trwaht (lahrzh)*
They fit fine.	**Elles me vont très bien.** *ehl muh voh_n_ treh bya_n_*
I'll take them.	**Je les prends.** *zuh lay prah_n_*
I need shoelaces.	**J'ai besoin de lacets.** *zhay buh-zwa_n_ duh lah-sseh*
That's all for now.	**C'est tout pour le moment.** *seh too poor luh moh-mah_n_*

CONVERSION TABLES FOR CLOTHING SIZES

WOMEN												

SHOES

American	4	$4\frac{1}{2}$	5	$5\frac{1}{2}$	6	$6\frac{1}{2}$	7	$7\frac{1}{2}$	8	$8\frac{1}{2}$	9	$9\frac{1}{2}$	10
Continental	35	35	36	36	37	37	38	38	39	39	40	40	41

DRESSES, SUITS

American	8	10	12	14	16	18
Continental	36	38	40	42	44	46

BLOUSES, SWEATERS

American	32	34	36	38	40	42
Continental	40	42	44	46	48	50

MEN									

SHOES

American	7	$7\frac{1}{2}$	8	$8\frac{1}{2}$	9	$9\frac{1}{2}$	10	$10\frac{1}{2}$	11	$11\frac{1}{2}$
Continental	39	40	41	42	43	43	44	44	45	45

SUITS, COATS

American	34	36	38	40	42	44	46	48
Continental	44	46	48	50	52	54	56	58

SHIRTS

American	14	$14\frac{1}{2}$	15	$15\frac{1}{2}$	16	$16\frac{1}{2}$	17	$17\frac{1}{2}$
Continental	36	37	38	39	40	41	42	43

ELECTRIC APPLIANCES

Electric current in the U.S. is 110V AC, whereas in France it is 220V AC. Unless your electric shaver or alarm clock is able to handle both currents, you will need to purchase an adaptor. When making a purchase, please be aware that *some* French products are engineered to work with either system whereas others will require an adaptor. When making a purchase, be careful to check the warranty to ensure that the product is covered internationally.

FOOD AND HOUSEHOLD ITEMS

Don't forget to bring your own basket when you go to the food market. Large paper bags are not given out. The cashier does not load the basket for you; you must do that yourself. The French are more inclined than we are to shop in specialty stores, so you may want to follow their lead, buying bread in the **boulangerie**, pastries in a **pâtisserie**, or candy in a **confiserie**.

I'd like ____.	**Je voudrais ____.** *zhuh voo-dreh*
▣ a bar of soap	**une savonnette** *ewn sah-voh-neht*
▣ a bottle of juice	**une bouteille de jus de fruits** *ewn boo-tehy duh zhew duh frwee*
▣ a box of cereal	**une boîte de céréales** *ewn bwaht duh say-ray-ahl*
▣ a can of soup	**une boîte de soupe** *zewn bwaht duh soop*
▣ a dozen eggs	**une douzaine d'oeufs** *ewn doo-zehn duh*
▣ a jar of coffee	**un bocal de café** *uhn boh-kal duh kah-fay*
▣ a kilo (2.2 lbs.) of potatoes	**un kilo de pommes de terre** *uhn kee-loh duh pohm duh tehr*

▨ a half-kilo of butter	**un demi-kilo de beurre**	*uhn duh-mee kee-loh duh buhr*
▨ 200 grams (about ½ pound) of cookies	**deux cents grammes de biscuits**	*duh sahn grahm duh beess-kwee*
▨ a half-kilo (1.1 lbs.) of cherries	**un demi-kilo de cerises**	*uhn duh-mee kee-loh duh suh-reez*
▨ a liter (quart) of milk	**un litre de lait**	*uhn lee-truh duh leh*
▨ a package of candies	**un paquet de bonbons**	*uhn pah-keh duh bohn-bohn*
▨ a ¼ pound of cheese	**cent grammes de fromage**	*sahn grahm duh froh-mahzh*
▨ a quart of milk	**un litre de lait**	*uhn lee-truh duh leh*
▨ a roll of toilet paper	**un rouleau de papier hygiénique**	*uhn roo-loh duh pah-pyay ee-zhyay-neek*
▨ a kilo of oranges	**un kilo d'oranges**	*uhn kee-loh doh-rahnzh*

THE CHARCUTERIE

A **charcuterie** is a rather special type of French delicatessen where you can buy food to take out, including various sausages and smoked meats. You will often see ordinary butcher's meat being sold in the same case as the sausage. Besides smoked meats you can find simple items like salads or pâté. The **Rue de boucherie** in Paris is a street entirely filled with **charcuteries**, where you can go from one to another, selecting the items that appeal to you for your lunch or for a picnic.

METRIC WEIGHTS AND MEASURES

Solid Measures
(approximate measurements only)

OUNCES	GRAMS (GRAMMES)	GRAMS	OUNCES
$\frac{1}{4}$	7	10	$\frac{1}{3}$
$\frac{1}{2}$	14	100	$3\frac{1}{2}$
$\frac{3}{4}$	21	300	$10\frac{1}{2}$
1	28	500	18

POUNDS	KILOGRAMS (KILO)	KILOGRAMS	POUNDS
1	$\frac{1}{2}$	1	$2\frac{1}{4}$
5	$2\frac{1}{4}$	3	$6\frac{1}{2}$
10	$4\frac{1}{2}$	5	11
20	9	10	22
50	23	50	110
100	45	100	220

Liquid Measures
(approximate measurements only)

OUNCES	MILLILITERS (MILLILITRES)	MILLILITERS	OUNCES
1	30	10	$\frac{1}{3}$
6	175	50	$1\frac{1}{2}$
12	350	100	$3\frac{1}{2}$
16	475	150	5

GALLONS	LITERS (LITRES)	LITERS	GALLONS
1	$3\frac{3}{4}$	1	$\frac{1}{4}$ (1 quart)
5	19	5	$1\frac{1}{3}$
10	38	10	$2\frac{1}{2}$

Note: Common measurements for purchasing food are a kilo or fractions thereof: 100 (cent), 200 (deux cents), and 500 (cinq cents) grams (grammes). See also Numbers, pages 14–17.

JEWELRY

I'd like to see ____.	**Je voudrais voir ____.**	*zhuh voo-dreh vwahr*
a bracelet	**un bracelet**	*uhn brahss-leh*
a pin	**une broche**	*ewn brohsh*
a chain	**une chaînette**	*ewn sheh-neht*
a charm	**un porte-bonheur**	*uhn pohrt boh-nuhr*
earrings	**des boucles d'oreille**	*day boo-kluh doh-rehy*
clip-on earrings	**des clips**	*day kleep*
drop earrings	**des pendants d'oreille**	*day pahn-dahn doh-rehy*
hoop earrings	**des créoles**	*day kray-ohl*
a necklace	**un collier**	*uhn koh-lyay*
a ring	**une bague**	*ewn bahg*
an engagement ring	**une bague de fiançailles**	*ewn bahg duh fee-ahn-ssahy*
a wedding ring	**une alliance**	*ewn ah-lee-ahnss*
a watch (digital)	**une montre (digitale)**	*ewn mohn-truh (dee-zhee-tahl)*
Is this ____?	**Est-ce ____?**	*ehss*
gold	**en or**	*ahn nohr*
platinum	**en platine**	*ahn plah-teen*
silver	**en argent**	*ahn nahr-zhahn*
solid gold	**en or massif**	*ahn nohr mah-sseef*
How many carats is it?	**Combien de carats y a-t-il?**	*kohn byan duh kah-rah ee ah teel*
What is that stone?	**Quelle est cette pierre?**	*kehl eh seht pyehr*

I would like _____.	**Je voudrais _____.**	*zhuh voo-dreh*
▥ an amethyst	**une améthyste**	*zewn ah-may-teesst*
▥ an aquamarine	**une aigue-marine**	*zewn ehg mah-reen*
▥ a diamond	**un diamant**	*zuh<u>n</u> dee-ah-mah<u>n</u>*
▥ an emerald	**une émeraude**	*zewn aym-rohd*
▥ ivory	**un ivoire**	*zuh<u>n</u> nee-vwahr*
▥ jade	**un jade**	*zuh<u>n</u> zhahd*
▥ onyx	**un onyx**	*zuh<u>n</u> oh-neeks*
▥ pearls	**des perles**	*day pehrl*
▥ a ruby	**un rubis**	*zuh<u>n</u> rew-bee*
▥ a sapphire	**un saphir**	*zuh<u>n</u> sah-feer*
▥ a topaz	**une topaze**	*zewn toh-pahz*
▥ turquoise	**une turquoise**	*zewn tewr-kwahz*

How much is it?	**Cela coûte combien?**	*suh-lah koot koh<u>n</u>-bya<u>n</u>*
I'll take this.	**Je prends ceci.**	*zhuh prah<u>n</u> suh-ssee*
I need _____ for my watch.	**J'ai besoin_____.**	*zhay buh-zwa<u>n</u>*
▥ a battery	**d'une pile**	*dewn peel*
▥ a crystal	**d'un verre**	*duh<u>n</u> vehr*
▥ a watchband	**d'un bracelet**	*duh<u>n</u> brahss-lay*

Can you look at (fix) my watch?	**Pouvez-vous examiner (réparer) ma montre?** *poo-vay voo ehg-zah-mee-nay (ray-pah-ray) mah moh<u>n</u>-truh*
It's fast (slow).	**Elle avance (retarde).** *ehl ah-vah<u>n</u>ss (ruh-tahrd)*
It's stopped.	**Elle s'est arrêtée.** *ehl seh tah-reh-tay*

MULTIMEDIA EQUIPMENT

Be aware that Europe uses broadcasting and recording systems that are often incompatible with those of the U.S.

Is there a multimedia (CD) store around here?	**Il y a un magasin multimédia (de CD) par ici?** *eel yah uhn mah-gah-zan mool-tee-may-dee-ah (duh say-day) pahr ee-see*
Do you have the songs of ____?	**Avez-vous les chansons de ____?** *ah-vay voo lay shahn-sohn duh*
Do you have the latest hits of ____?	**Avez-vous les derniers succès de ____?** *ah-vay-voo lay dehr-nyay sewk-sseh duh*
Where is the ____ section?	**Où est le rayon de ____?** *oo eh luh reh-yohn duh*

■ blues   **blues** *blewz*

■ classical music   **musique classique** *mew-zeek klah-sseek*

■ jazz   **jazz** *zhahz*

■ French music   **musique française** *mew-zeek frahn-ssehz*

■ opera   **opéra (m.)** *oh-pay-rah*

■ pop music   **musique pop** *mew-zeek pohp*

■ rock music   **musique rock** *mew-zeek ruhk*

I'm looking for iPod (iPad) accessories.	**Je cherche les accessoires pour les iPod (iPad).** *zhuh shersh lay-zahk-seh-swahr poor lay zee-pohd (zee-pahd)*
I would like ____.	**Je voudrais ____.** *zhuh voo-dreh*

■ an armband   **un brassard** *zuhn brah-ssahr*

▥ a base	**une station d'accueil**	*zewn stah-ssyohn dah-kuhy*
▥ cables	**des cables**	*day kah-bluh*
▥ earpieces	**des écouteurs**	*day zay-koo-tuhr*
▥ a keyboard dock	**un clavier physique**	*zuhn klah-vyay fee-zeek*
▥ a jack	**une prise**	*zewn preez*
▥ a case	**une housse**	*zewn ooss*
▥ a memory card	**une carte mémoire**	*zewn kahrt may-mwahr*

NEWSSTAND

Do you carry newspapers (magazines) in English?	**Avez-vous des journaux (magazines) en anglais?** *ah-vay voo day zhoor-noh (mah-gah-zeen) ahn nahn-gleh*
How much is it?	**C'est combien?** *seh kohn-byan*
I'd like to buy some postcards.	**Je voudrais acheter des cartes postales.** *zhuh voo-dreh zahsh-tay day kahrt pohss-tahl*
Do you have stamps?	**Avez-vous des timbres?** *ah-vay voo day tan-bruh*

PHOTOGRAPHIC SUPPLIES

Where is there a camera shop?	**Où y a-t-il un magasin de photos?** *oo ee ah-teel uhn mah-gah-zan duh foh-toh*
Do you sell cameras?	**Vendez-vous des appareils?** *vahn-day voo day zah-pah-rehy*

How much does it cost?	**Ça coûte combien?** *sah koot kohn-byan*

I would like a(n) _____ camera.	**Je voudrais un appareil photo _____.** *zhuh voo-dreh zuhn nah-pah-rehy foh-toh*
disposable	**jetable** *zheh-tah-bluh*
inexpensive	**pas très cher** *pah treh shehr*
14-megapixel	**à quatorze megapixels** *ah kah-tohrz meh-gah-peek-sehl*
3-inch screen	**avec un écran de trois pouces** *ah-vehk uhn nay-krahn duh trwah poos*
5X-zoom	**à zoom cinq fois** *ah zoom sank fwah*
point-and-shoot	**point and shoot (compact)** *point ahnd shoot (kohn-pahkt)*
reflex	**reflex** *ruh-flehks*
waterproof	**étanche** *ay-tahnsh*
I need a camera with _____.	**J'ai besoin d'un appareil photo avec _____.** *zhay buh-zwan duhn ah-pah-rehy foh-toh ah-vehk*
movie mode	**mode film** *mohd feelm*
manual controls	**réglages manuels** *ray-glahzh mah-new-ehl*
interchangeable lenses	**des objectifs interchangeables** *day zohb-zhehk-teef an-tehr-shanzh-ah-bluh*

an adjustable screen	**écran orientable** *ay-krahn oh-ree-ahn-tah-bluh*

I need _____.	**J'ai besoin _____.** *zhay buh-zwan*
a memory card	**d'une carte-mémoire** *dewn kahrt-may-mwahr*
a case	**d'une housse** *dewn ooss*
a tripod	**d'un trépied (d'un pied)** *duhn tray-pyay (duhn pyay)*

Here's the card.	**Voici la carte.** *vwah-ssee lah kahrt*

Please make three prints from each frame.	**Faites trois épreuves de chaque cadre, s'il vous plait.** *feht trwah zay-pruhv duh shahk kah-druh seel voo pleh*

When can I pick up the pictures?	**Quand puis-je venir chercher les photos?** *kahn pweezh vuh-neer shehr-shay lay foh-toh*

SOUVENIRS

You may want to purchase specialties of certain cities or regions as gifts or as souvenirs.

Alençon	lace products
Aubusson, Beauvais	rugs
Baccarat	crystal
Besançon	watches and clocks
Grasse	perfume (Coty, Fragonard, Lanvin)
Grenoble	gloves
Limoges, Sèvres	fine porcelain
Nancy	crystal

Paris haute couture, high-style fashions at stores like Rive Gauche, Galeries Lafayette, Au Printemps, La Samaritaine

If you are in Paris, you may be able to pick up real bargains at the Flea Market (Marché aux Puces) and, at the small book shops along the Seine, old books, magazines, or comic strips.

Don't forget the famous wines and cheeses, of course!

GIFT SHOP

I'd like _____.	**Je voudrais _____.**	*zhuh voo-dreh*
▪ a pretty gift	**un joli cadeau**	*zuhn zhoh-lee kah-doh*
▪ a small gift	**un petit cadeau**	*zuhn puh-tee kah-doh*
▪ a souvenir	**un souvenir**	*zuhn soov-neer*
It's for _____.	**C'est pour _____.**	*seh poor*
Could you suggest something?	**Pourriez-vous me suggérer quelque chose?**	*poo-ree-yay voo muh sewg-zhay-ray kehl-kuh shohz*
I don't want to spend more than _____ euros.	**Je ne voudrais pas dépenser plus de _____ euros.**	*zhuh nuh voo-dreh pah day-pahn-ssay plew duh _____ ew-roh*

Travel Tips A wonderful gift that is very reasonably priced is a hand-painted watercolor scene, sold and packaged in heavy-duty cardboard tubes by artists from their stalls along the Seine in Paris.

ANTIQUE SHOPPING

French-speaking Europe boasts a large number of antique shops where you can find old books, watches, toys, and antiquities.

Haggle as much as you can!

Principal Shopping Areas for Antiques in Paris

Rue du Bac and Rue des Saints Pères	7ème arrondissement
Marché aux Puces	18ème arrondissement
Quai Voltaire	7ème arrondissement
Rue Jacob and Rue Bonaparte	6ème arrondissement

STATIONERY

I want to buy _____.	**Je voudrais acheter _____.**	*zhuh voo-dreh zahsh-tay*
a ball-point pen	**un stylo à bille**	*uhn stee-loh ah beey*
envelopes	**des enveloppes**	*day zahn-vlohp*
an eraser	**une gomme**	*ewn gohm*
glue	**de la colle**	*duh lah kohl*
a notebook	**un cahier**	*uhn kah-yay*
paper	**du papier**	*dew pah-pyay*
pencils	**des crayons**	*day kreh-yohn*
a pencil sharpener	**un taille-crayon**	*uhn tahy kreh-yohn*
a ruler	**une règle**	*ewn reh-gluh*
Scotch tape	**du scotch**	*dew skohtsh*

■ stationery **du papier à lettres** *dew pah-pyay ah leh-truh*

■ wrapping paper **du papier d'emballage** *dew pah-pyay dahn-bah-lahzh*

■ a writing pad **un bloc** *uhn blohk*

TOBACCO SHOP

Tobacco, cigarettes, and cigars may be purchased from a state-licensed tobacconist. Look for the signs with the red cones outside cafés and bars.

Newly promulgated laws have outlawed smoking in many public places and fines are imposed. Be careful to heed the no smoking signs: DÉFENSE DE FUMER.

A pack (carton) of cigarettes, please. **Un paquet (une cartouche) de cigarettes, s'il vous plaît.** *uhn pah-keh (ewn kahr-toosh) duh see-gah-reht seel voo pleh*

■ filtered **avec filtre** *ah-vehk feel-truh*

■ unfiltered **sans filtre** *sahn feel-truh*

■ menthol **mentholées** *mahn-toh-lay*

■ king-size **long format** *lohn fohr-mah*

Are these cigarettes (very) strong (mild)? **Ces cigarettes sont elles (très) fortes (douces)?** *say see-gah-reht sohn tehl (treh) fohrt (dooss)*

Do you have American cigarettes? **Avez-vous des cigarettes américaines?** *ah-vay voo day see-gah-reht ah-may-ree-kehn*

What brands? **Quelles marques?** *kehl mahrk*

Please give me a pack of matches also. **Donnez-moi aussi une boîte d'allumettes, s'il vous plaît.** *doh-nay mwah oh-ssee ewn bwaht dah-lew-meht seel voo pleh*

Do you sell ____?	**Vendez-vous ____?** *vahn-day voo*
▓ cigars	**des cigares** *day see-gahr*
▓ lighter fluid	**de l'essence à briquet** *duh leh-ssahnss ah bree-keh*
▓ lighters	**des briquets** *day bree-keh*
▓ pipes	**des pipes** *day peep*
▓ pipe tobacco	**du tabac pour pipe** *dew tah-bah poor peep*

TOILETRIES

There are pharmacies, **drogueries**, and *drugstores* in France.

A green cross identifies a pharmacy, which sells over-the-counter and prescription drugs, personal hygiene items, and some cosmetics.

A **droguerie** sells chemical products, paints, household cleaners, detergents, and accessories such as mops, brooms, buckets, and some personal hygiene items and cosmetics.

The *drugstores* in France resemble small department stores. They sell newspapers, international magazines, books, maps, guides, small gifts, records, and have fast-food restaurants for items such as ice cream, sandwiches, or drinks. Many of these drugstores even have a counter where prescriptions can be filled. Perfumes and cosmetics may also be purchased at a *parfumerie*.

Do you have ____?	**Avez-vous ____?** *ah-vay voo*
▓ a brush	**une brosse** *ewn brohss*
▓ cleansing cream	**une crème démaquillante** *ewn krehm day-mah-kee-yahnt*
▓ a comb	**un peigne** *uhn peh-nyuh*
▓ condoms	**des préservatifs** *day pray-zehr-vah-teef*

▥ (disposable) diapers	**des couches (jetables)**	*day koosh (zheh-tah-bluh)*
▥ emery boards	**des limes à ongles**	*day leem ah ohn-gluh*
▥ eyeliner	**du traceur à paupières**	*dew trah-ssuhr ah poh-pyehr*
▥ eyebrow pencil	**un crayon pour les yeux**	*uhn kreh-yohn poor lay zyuh*
▥ eye shadow	**du fard à paupières**	*dew fahr ah poh-pyehr*
▥ gel	**du gel coiffant**	*dew zhehl kwah-fahn*
▥ hairspray	**de la laque**	*duh lah lahk*
▥ lipstick	**du rouge à lèvres**	*dew roozh ah leh-vruh*
▥ makeup	**du maquillage**	*dew mah-kee-yahzh*
▥ mascara	**du mascara**	*dew mahss-kah-rah*
▥ a mirror	**un miroir**	*uhn meer-wahr*
▥ mousse	**de la mousse coiffante**	*duh lah mooss kwah-fahnt*
▥ mouthwash	**de l'eau dentifrice**	*deh-loh dahn-tee-freess*
▥ nail clippers	**un coupe-ongles**	*uhn koop ohn-gluh*
▥ a nail file	**une lime à ongles**	*ewn leem ah ohn-gluh*
▥ nail polish	**du vernis à ongles**	*dew vehr-nee ah ohn-gluh*
▥ nail polish remover	**du dissolvant**	*dew dee-ssohl-vahn*
▥ a razor	**un rasoir**	*uhn rah-zwahr*

▓ razor blades	**une lame de rasoir**	*ewn lahm duh rah-zwahr*
▓ rouge	**du fard**	*dew fahr*
▓ sanitary napkins	**des serviettes hygiéniques**	*day sehr-vyeht ee-zhyay-neek*
▓ scissors	**des ciseaux**	*day see-zoh*
▓ shampoo	**du shampooing**	*dew shahn-pwan*
▓ shaving lotion	**la lotion à raser**	*lah loh-ssyohn ah rah-zay*
▓ soap	**du savon**	*dew sah-vohn*
▓ a sponge	**une éponge**	*ewn ay-pohnzh*
▓ talcum powder	**du talc**	*dew tahlk*
▓ tampons	**des tampons périodiques**	*day tahn-pohn pay-ree-oh-deek*
▓ tissues	**des mouchoirs en papier**	*day moo-shwahr ahn pah-pyay*
▓ toilet paper	**du papier hygiénique**	*dew pah-pyay ee-zhyay-neek*
▓ a toothbrush	**une brosse à dents**	*ewn brohss ah dahnt*
▓ toothpaste	**de la pâte dentifrice**	*duh lah paht dahn-tee-freess*
▓ tweezers	**une pince à épiler**	*ewn panss ah ay-pee-lay*

PERSONAL CARE AND SERVICES

If your hotel doesn't offer these amenities, ask the desk clerk to recommend someone nearby.

AT THE BARBER/BEAUTY SALON

Where is there a good _____?	**Où y a-t-il un bon _____?** *oo ee ah teel uhn bohn*
barber shop	**coiffeur** *kwah-fuhr*
beauty salon	**salon de beauté** *sah-lohn duh boh-tay*
I'd like an appointment for (day) at (hour).	**Je voudrais prendre rendez-vous pour _____ à _____.** *zhuh voo-dreh prahndr rahn-day-voo poor _____ ah*
Do I have to wait long?	**Faut-il attendre long temps?** *foh teel ah-tahn-druh lohn-tahn*
I would like _____.	**Je voudrais _____.** *zhuh voo-dreh*
a color rinse	**un shampooing colorant** *uhn shahn-pwan koh-loh-rahn*
a facial massage	**un massage facial** *uhn mah-ssahzh fah-ssyahl*
a haircut	**une coupe de cheveux** *ewn koop duh shuh-vuh*
blunt	**en carré** *ahn kah-ray*
layered	**dégradée** *day-grah-day*
highlights	**des reflets** *day ruh-fleh*
a manicure	**une manucure** *ewn mah-new-kewr*
a pedicure	**une pédicurie** *ewn pay-dee-kew-ree*

▥ a permanent	**une permanente**	*ewn pehr-mah-nahnt*
▥ a shampoo	**un shampooing**	*uhn shahn-pwan*
▥ a shave	**me faire raser**	*muh fehr rah-zay*
▥ a tint	**des reflets**	*day ruh-fleh*
▥ a touch-up	**une retouche**	*ewn ruh-toosh*
▥ a wash and set	**un shampooing et une mise en plis**	*uhn shahn-pwan ay ewn meez ahn plee*
▥ a waxing	**une épilation**	*ewn ay-pee-lah-syohn*

I'd like to see a color chart.	**Je voudrais voir une échelle de teintes.**	*zhuh voo-dreh vwahr ewn ay-shehl duh tant*
I want _____.	**Je voudrais _____.**	*zhuh voo-dreh*
▥ auburn	**auburn**	*oh-buhrn*
▥ black	**noir**	*nwahr*
▥ (light)blond	**blond (clair)**	*blohn (klehr)*
▥ brunette	**brun**	*bruhn*
▥ a darker color	**une teinte plus foncée**	*ewn tant plew fohn-ssay*
▥ a lighter color	**une teinte plus claire**	*ewn tant plew klehr*
▥ the same color	**la même couleur**	*lah mehm koo-luhr*

You can cut a little _____.	**Vous pouvez dégager un peu _____.**	*voo poo-vay day-gah-zhay uhn puh*
▥ in back	**derrière**	*deh-ryehr*
▥ in front	**devant**	*duh-vahn*
▥ off the top	**dessus**	*duh-ssew*
▥ on the sides	**aux côtés**	*oh koh-tay*

I part my hair _____. **Je fais la raie _____.** *zhuh feh lah ray*

- on the left   **à gauche** *ah gohsh*
- on the right   **à droite** *ah drwaht*
- in the middle   **au milieu** *oh meel-yuh*

I comb my hair straight back.   **Je me peigne en arrière.** *zhuh muh peh-nyuh ah<u>n</u> nah-ryehr*

Cut a little bit more here.   **Coupez un peu plus ici.** *koo-pay uh<u>n</u> puh plew ee-ssee*

That's enough.   **Ça suffit.** *sah sew-fee*

It's fine that way.   **C'est parfait comme ça.** *seh pahr-feh kohm sah*

I (don't) want _____.   **Je (ne) veux (pas de) _____.** *zhuh (nuh) vuh (pah duh)*

- hairspray   **la laque** *lah lahk*
- shampoo   **un shampooing** *uh<u>n</u> sha<u>n</u>-pwa<u>n</u>*
- lotion   **une lotion** *ewn loh-ssyoh<u>n</u>*

I would like my _____ trimmed.	**Je voudrais me faire rafraîchir** _____. *zhuh voo-dreh muh fehr rah-freh-sheer*
■ beard	**la barbe** *lah bahrb*
■ moustache	**la moustache** *lah mooss-tahsh*
■ sideburns	**les favoris** *lay fah-voh-ree*
I'd like to look at myself in the mirror.	**Je voudrais me regarder dans le miroir.** *zhuh voo-dreh muh ruh-gahr-day dahn luh meer-wahr*
How much do I owe you?	**Je vous dois combien?** *zhuh voo dwah kohn-byan*

LAUNDRY AND DRY CLEANING

Where is the nearest _____?	**Où est la _____ la plus proche?** *oo eh lah _____ lah plew prohsh*
■ laundry	**blanchisserie** *blahn-sheess-ree*
■ laundromat	**laverie automatique** *lah-vree oh-toh-mah-teek*
■ dry cleaner's	**teinturerie** *tan-tew-ruh-ree*
I have clothes to be _____.	**J'ai des vêtements à faire _____.** *zhay day veht-mahn ah fehr*
■ dry-cleaned	**nettoyer à sec** *neh-twah-yay ah sehk*
■ washed	**laver** *lah-vay*
■ mended	**réparer** *ray-pah-ray*
■ ironed	**repasser** *ruh-pah-ssay*
This isn't my laundry.	**Ce n'est pas ma lessive.** *suh neh pah mah lay-sseev*

Travel Tips Every traveler needs to carry a few small items for emergencies. Sealed, pre-wet washcloths, Band-Aids, a fold-up toothbrush, a small tube of toothpaste, a tiny sewing kit, notebook and pen, and aspirin are musts for the handbag or backpack. Skip Swiss army knives or any object that could be considered a weapon by airport security guards.

SHOE REPAIRS

Put on (half) soles and rubber heels.	**Mettez les (demi-) semelles et les talons en caoutchouc.** *meh-tay lay (duh-mee) suh-mehl ay lay tah-lohn ahn kah-oo-tshoo*
I'd like to have my shoes shined (too).	**Je voudrais un cirage (aussi).** *zhuh voo-dreh zuhn see-rahzh (oh-ssee)*

AT THE OPTICIAN

I've broken a lens (the frame).	**J'ai cassé un verre (la monture).** *zhay kah-ssay uhn vehr (lah mohn-tewr)*
It's a progressive lens.	**C'est un verre progressif.** *seh tuhn vehr proh-greh-seef*
Can you fix (replace) it?	**Pouvez-vous le (la) réparer (remplacer)?** *poo-vay voo luh (lah) ray-pah-ray (rahn-plah-ssay)*
Can you tighten the screw?	**Pouvez-vous reserrer la vis?** *poo-vay voo ruh-sseh-ray lah vees*

I don't have another pair.	**Je n'ai pas d'autre paire.** *zhuh nay pah doh-truh pehr*
I've lost a contact lens.	**J'ai perdu un verre de contact.** *zhay pehr-dew uhn vehr duh kohn-tahkt*
Can you replace it right away?	**Pouvez-vous le remplacer tout de suite?** *poo-vay voo luh rahn-plah-ssay toot sweet*
Do you sell sunglasses?	**Vendez-vous des lunettes de soleil?** *vahn-day voo day lew-neht duh soh-lehy*

PHOTOCOPIES

Some drugstores and stationery stores will have photocopy machines.

Do you have a photocopier?	**Avez-vous un photo-copieur?** *ah-vay-voo uhn fot-toh-koh-pyuhr*

I would like to make a photocopy of this paper (this document).	**Je voudrais faire une photocopie de ce papier (ce document).** *zhuh voo-dreh fehr ewn foh-toh-koh-pee duh suh pah-pyay (suh doh-kew-mahn)*
What is the cost per page?	**Quel est le prix par page?** *kehl eh luh pree pahr pahzh*
Can you enlarge it (by 25 percent)?	**Pouvez-vous l'élargir (de vingt-cinq pour cent)?** *poo-vay voo lay-lahr-zheer (duh van-sank poor sahn)*
Can you reduce it (by 50 percent)?	**Pouvez-vous le réduire (de cinquante pour cent)?** *poo-vay voo luh ray-dweer (duh san-kahnt poor sahn)*
Can you make a color copy?	**Pouvez-vous en faire une copie en couleurs?** *poo-vay voo ahn fehr ewn koh-pee ahn koo-luhr*

MEDICAL CARE

AT THE PHARMACY

A green cross indicates a pharmacy, where you buy over-the-counter or prescription drugs. If the pharmacy is closed there will be a sign on the door to indicate which pharmacies are open in the neighborhood.

Where is the nearest (all-night) pharmacy?	**Où se trouve la pharmacie de garde (de nuit) la plus proche?** *oo suh troov lah fahr-mah-ssee duh gahrd (duh nwee) lah plew prohsh*
At what time does the pharmacy open (close)?	**À quelle heure ouvre (ferme) la pharmacie?** *ah kehl uhr oo-vruh (fehrm) lah fahr-mah-ssee*
I need medicine for___.	**J'ai besoin d'un médicament pour ___.** *zhay buh-zwan duhn may-dee-kah-mahn poor*

- a cold **un rhume** *uhn rewm*
- constipation **la constipation** *lah kohn-sstee-pah-ssyohn*
- a cough **une toux** *ewn too*
- diarrhea **la diarrhée** *lah dee-ah-ray*
- a fever **une fièvre** *ewn fyeh-vruh*
- hay fever **le rhume des foins** *luh rewm day fwan*
- a headache **un mal de tête** *uhn mahl duh teht*
- insomnia **l'insomnie** *lan-sohm-nee*
- the flu **la grippe** *lah greep*
- nausea **la nausée** *lah noh-zay*
- sunburn **les coups de soleil** *lay koo duh soh-lehy*

■ a toothache	**un mal de dents**	*uhn mahl duh dahn*
■ an upset stomach	**les indigestions**	*lay zan-dee-zhehss-tyohn*
Is a prescription needed?	**Faut-il avoir une ordonnance?**	*foh-teel ah-vwahr ewn nohr-doh-nahnss*
Can you fill this prescription for me now?	**Pourriez-vous me préparer cette ordonnance maintenant?**	*poo-ree-yay voo muh pray-pah-ray seht ohr-doh-nahnss mant-nahn*
It's an emergency.	**C'est urgent.**	*seh tewr-zhahn*
Can I wait for it?	**Puis-je l'attendre?**	*pweezh lah-tahn-druh*
How long will it take?	**Ça prendra combien de temps?**	*sah prahn-drah kohn-byan duh tahn*
When can I come for it?	**Quand puis-je venir la chercher?**	*kahn pweezh vuh-neer lah shehr-shay*
How many times a day should I take it?	**Je le prends combien de fois par jour?**	*zhuh luh prahn koh-byan duh fwah pahr zhoor*
Will this medicine make me drowsy?	**Ce médicament me donnera-t-il envie de dormir?**	*suh may-dee-kah-mahn muh dohn-rah-teel ahn-vee duh dohr-meer*
Do I take it with food?	**Je le prends avec de la nourriture?**	*zhuh luh prahn ah-vehk duh lah noo-ree-tewr*
Are there any contraindications?	**Y a-t-il des contra-indications?**	*ee ah-teel day kohn-trah-an-dee-kah-ssyohn*

Do you have the morning-after pill?	**Avez-vous la pilule du lendemain?** *ah-vay voo lah pee-lewl dew lahn-duh-man*	
I would like _____.	**Je voudrais _____.** *zhuh voo-dreh*	
▥ alcohol	**de l'alcool** *duh lahl-kohl*	
▥ an antacid	**un anti-acide** *zuhn nahn-tee ah-sseed*	
▥ an antiseptic	**un antiseptique** *zuhn nahn-tee-ssehp-teek*	
▥ aspirins	**des aspirines** *day zahss-pee-reen*	
▥ bandages	**des pansements** *day pahnss-mahn*	
▥ Band-Aids	**des pansements adhésifs** *day pahnss-mahn ahd-ay-zeef*	
▥ (absorbent) cotton	**du coton** *dew koh-tohn*	
▥ cough drops	**des pastilles contre la toux** *day pahss-tee kohn-truh lah too*	
▥ cough syrup	**du sirop contre la toux** *dew see-roh kohn-truh lah too*	
▥ eardrops	**des gouttes pour les oreilles** *day goot poor lay zoh-rehy*	
▥ eyedrops	**des gouttes pour les yeux** *day goot poor lay zyuh*	
▥ iodine	**de la teinture d'iode** *duh lah tan-tewr dyohd*	
▥ a (mild) laxative	**un laxatif (léger)** *zuhn lahk-ssah-teef (lay-zhay)*	
▥ milk of magnesia	**le lait de magnésie** *luh leh duh mah-nyay-zee*	
▥ sleeping pills	**des somnifères** *day sohm-nee-fehr*	
▥ syringes	**des seringues** *day suh-rang*	
▥ a thermometer	**un thermomètre** *uhn tehr-moh-meh-truh*	
▥ vitamins	**des vitamines** *day vee-tah-meen*	

DOCTORS

You never know when you may need a doctor while on vacation. In Paris the U.S. Embassy (tel: (01) 43 12 22 22) has a list of English-speaking doctors. There is also an American Hospital where most of the doctors speak English (tel: (01) 46 41 25 25) and the Hertford British Hospital (tel: (01) 46 39 22 22). In other areas and situations, the following phrases will help you:

I don't feel well.	**Je ne me sens pas bien.**	*zhuh nuh muh sahn pah byan*
I need a (woman) doctor (who speaks English).	**J'ai besoin d'un médecin (d'une femme médecin) (qui parle anglais).**	*zhay buh-zwan duhn mayd-ssan (dewn fahm mayd-ssan) (kee pahrl ahn-gleh)*
Where is his (her) office?	**Où se trouve son cabinet?**	*oo suh troov sohn kah-bee-neh*

TELLING THE DOCTOR

I've run out of medicine.	**Je n'ai plus de médicaments.**	*zhuh nay plew duh may-dee-kah-mahn*
I've been vaccinated for ____.	**Je me suis fait(e) vacciné(e) contre ____.**	*zhuh muh swee feh(t) vahk-ssee-nay kohn-truh*
▧ chicken pox	**la varicelle**	*lah vah-ree-sehl*
▧ influenza	**la grippe**	*lah greep*
▧ measles	**la rougeole**	*lah roo-zhohl*
▧ mumps	**les oreillons**	*lay zoh-reh-yohn*

▨ pneumonia	**la pneumonie**	*lah puh-nuh-moh-nee*
▨ polio	**la poliomyélite**	*lah poh-lee-oh-mee-ay-leet*
▨ tuberculosis	**la tuberculose**	*lah tew-behr-kew-lohz*
▨ whooping cough	**la coqueluche**	*lah kohk-lewsh*
I have _____.	**J'ai _____.**	*zhay*
▨ an abscess	**un abcès**	*uhn nahb-sseh*
▨ a broken bone	**une fracture**	*ewn frahk-tewr*
▨ a bruise	**une contusion**	*ewn kohn-tew-zyohn*
▨ a burn	**une brûlure**	*ewn brew-lewr*
▨ the chills	**des frissons**	*day free-ssohn*
▨ a cold	**un rhume**	*uhn rewm*
▨ cramps	**des crampes**	*day krahnp*
▨ a cut	**une coupure**	*ewn koo-pewr*
▨ diarrhea	**la diarrhée**	*lah dee-ah-ray*
▨ a fever	**de la fièvre**	*duh lah fyeh-vruh*
▨ a fracture	**une fracture**	*ewn frahk-tewr*
▨ a headache	**mal à la tête**	*mahl ah lah teht*
▨ an infection	**une infection**	*ewn an-fehk-ssyohn*
▨ a lump	**une grosseur**	*ewn groh-ssuhr*
▨ something in my eye	**quelque chose dans l'oeil**	*kehl-kuh shohz dahn luhy*
▨ a sore throat	**mal à la gorge**	*mahl ah lah gohrzh*
▨ a stomachache	**mal à l'estomac**	*mahl ah lehss-toh-mah*
▨ swelling	**une enflure**	*ewn ahn-flewr*
▨ a wound	**une blessure**	*ewn bleh-ssewr*
I am constipated.	**Je suis constipé(e).**	*zhuh swee kohn-sstee-pay*

I have a pain here.	**J'ai une douleur ici.** *zhay ewn doo-luhr ee-ssee*
My ___ hurts since (yesterday, two days ago, last week).	**J'ai mal ___ depuis (hier, deux jours, la semaine passée).** *zhay mahl duh-pwee (yehr, duh zhoor, lah suh-mehn pah-ssay)*
I have a pain in my ___.	**J'ai une douleur ___** *zhay ewn doo-luhr*

- ankle   **à la cheville** *ah lah shuh-vee*
- arm   **au bras** *oh brah*
- back   **au dos** *oh doh*
- chest   **à la poitrine** *ah lah pwah-treen*
- ear   **à l'oreille** *ah loh-rehy*
- elbow   **au coude** *oh kood*
- eyes   **aux yeux** *oh zyuh*
- face   **à la figure** *ah lah fee-gewr*
- finger   **au doigt** *oh dwah*
- foot   **au pied** *oh pyay*
- glands   **aux ganglions** *oh gahn-glee-yohn*
- hand   **à la main** *ah lah man*
- head   **à la tête** *ah lah teht*
- heart   **au cœur** *oh kuhr*
- hip   **à la hanche** *ah lah ahnsh*
- knee   **au genou** *oh zhuh-noo*
- leg   **à la jambe** *ah lah zhahnb*
- lip   **à la lèvre** *ah lah leh-vruh*
- mouth   **à la bouche** *ah lah boosh*
- neck   **au cou** *oh koo*
- nose   **au nez** *oh nay*
- shoulder   **à l'épaule** *ah lay-pohl*
- throat   **à la gorge** *ah lah gohrzh*

▥ thumb	**au pouce**	*oh pooss*
▥ toe	**à l'orteil**	*ah lohr-tehy*
▥ tooth	**aux dents**	*oh dahn*
▥ wrist	**au poignet**	*oh pwah-nyeh*

There is (no) _____ in my family. — **Il y a (Il n'y a pas) _____ dans ma famille.** *eel yah (eel nyah pah) _____ dahn mah fah-mee*

▥ asthma	**l'asthme (m.)**	*lahs-muh*
▥ diabetes	**la diabète**	*lah dee-yah-beht*
▥ heart disease	**la maladie cardiaque**	*lah mah-lah-dee kahr-dyahk*

I'm allergic ____. — **Je suis allergique ____.** *zhuh swee zah-lehr-zheek*

▥ to antibiotics	**aux antibiotiques**	*oh zahn-tee-bee-oh-teek*
▥ to anti-inflammatories	**aux anti-inflammatoires**	*oh zahn-tee-an-flah-mah-twahr*
▥ to bees	**aux abeilles**	*oh zah-behy*
▥ to codeine	**à la codéine**	*ah lah koh-day-een*
▥ to penicillin	**à la pénicilline**	*ah lah pay-nay-see-leen*

I had ____ ____ years ago. — **J'ai eu ____ il y a ____ ans.** *zhay ew ___ eel yah ____ ahn*

▥ a heart attack	**une crise cardiaque**	*ewn kreez kahr-dee-ahk*
▥ cancer	**le cancer**	*luh kahn-sehr*
▥ chemotherapy	**la chimiothérapie**	*lah kee-mee-oh-tay-rah-pee*
▥ radiation	**la radiothérapie**	*lah rah-dee-oh-tay-rah-pee*
▥ a stroke	**une attaque d'apoplexie**	*ewn nah-tahk dah-poh-plehk-ssee*

I have ____.	**J'ai____.** *zhay*
■ high blood pressure	**la hypertension** *lah ee-pehr-tahn-ssyohn*
■ high cholesterol	**un taux élevé de cholestérol** *uhn toh ay-luh-vay duh koh-lehss-tay-rohl*
■ diabetes	**le diabète** *luh dee-ah-beht*
■ AIDS	**le sida** *luh see-dah*

I'm taking this medicine.

Je prends ce médicaments. *zhuh prahn ssuh may-dee-kah-mahn*

I'm pregnant.

Je suis enceinte. *zhuh swee zahn-sant*

I'm on the pill.

Je prends la pilule. *zhuh prahn lah pee-lewl*

I'm dizzy.

J'ai des vertiges. *zhay day vehr-teezh*

I have the chills.

J'ai des frissons. *zhay day free-ssohn*

I'm nauseous.

J'ai des nausées. *zhay day noh-zay*

I vomited.

J'ai vomi. *zhay voh-mee*

I fainted.

Je me suis évanoui(e) *zhuh muh swee zay-vah-nwee*

I can't sleep.

Je n'arrive pas à dormir. *zhuh nah-reev pah zah dohr-meer*

I have diarrhea.

J'ai la diarrhée. *zhay lah dee-ah-ray*

I've been injured.	**J'ai été blessé.** *zhay ay-tay bleh-ssay*
I've run out of medicine.	**Je n'ai plus de médicaments.** *zhuh nay plew duh may-dee-kah mahn*
I feel weak.	**Je me sens faible.** *zhuh muh sahn feh-bluh*
I feel better.	**Je vais mieux.** *zhuh veh myuh*
I feel worse.	**Je me sens moins bien.** *zhuh muh sahn mwan byan*
Is my illness serious (contagious)?	**Ma maladie est-elle grave (contagieuse)?** *mah mah-lah-dee eh-tehl grahv (kohn-tah-zhyuhz)*

Do I have to go to the hospital?	**Dois-je aller à l'hôpital?** *dwahzh ah-lay ah loh-pee-tahl*
When can I continue my trip?	**Quand pourrai-je pour-suivre mon voyage?** *kahn poo-rayzh poor-swee-vruh mohn vwah-yahzh*

DOCTOR'S INSTRUCTIONS

Open your mouth. **Ouvrez la bouche.** *oo-vray lah boosh*

Stick out your tongue. **Tirez la langue.** *tee-ray lah lahng*

Cough. **Toussez.** *too-ssay*

Breathe deeply. **Respirez profondément.** *rehss-pee-ray proh-fohn-day-mahn*

Take off your clothing (to the waist). **Déshabillez-vous (jusqu'à la ceinture).** *day-zah-bee-yay voo (zhewss-kah lah san-tewr)*

Lie down. **Étendez-vous.** *ay-tahn-day voo*

Stand up. **Levez-vous.** *luh-vay voo*

It is necessary to do a blood test. **Il faut faire une analyse de sang.** *eel foh fehr ewn ah-nah-leez duh sahn*

Are you taking any medication? **Vous prenez des médicaments?** *voo pruh-nay day may-dee-kah-mahn?*

Are you under treatment for a medical condition? **Recevez-vous des soins médicaux?** *ruh-suh-vay voo day swan may-dee-koh*

Get dressed. **Habillez-vous.** *ah-bee-yay voo*

Here is a prescription. **Voici une ordonnance.** *vwah-ssee ewn nohr-doh-nahnss*

Take this medicine two times a day (with food, with water). **Prenez ce médicament deux fois par jour (avec de la nourriture, avec de l'eau).** *pruh-nay suh may-dee-kah-mahn duh fwah pahr zhoor (ah-vehk duh lah new-ree-tewr, ah-vehk duh loh)*

Have this checked when you get home.	**Consultez votre docteur en rentrant.** *kohn-sool-tay voh-truh dohk-tuhr ahn rahn-trahn*
You have to be admitted to the hospital.	**Il faut vous faire hospitaliser.** *eel foh voo fehr oh-sspee-tah-lee-zay*

PATIENT

(How long) do I have to stay in bed?	**(Combien de temps) dois-je garder le lit?** *(kohn-byan duh tahn) dwahzh gahr-day luh lee*
Thank you (for everything), doctor.	**Merci bien (pour tout), docteur.** *mehr-ssee byan (poor too) dohk-tuhr*
What is your fee?	**Quels sont vos honoraires?** *kehl sohn voh zoh-noh-rehr*
I have medical insurance.	**J'ai une assurance médicale.** *zhay ewn ah-ssew-rahnss may-dee-kahl*
Please fill out this medical form.	**Remplissez cette feuille de maladie, s'il vous plaît.** *rahn-plee-ssay seht fuhy duh mah-lah dee seel voo pleh*
May I please have a receipt for my medical insurance?	**Puis-je avoir une quittance pour mon assurance médicale, s'il vous plaît?** *Pweezh ah-vwahr ewn kee-tahnss poor mohn nah-sew-rahnss may-dee-kahl seel voo pleh*

SPECIAL NEEDS

Where can I get _____?	**Où puis-je obtenir _____?** *oo pweezh ohb-tuh-neer*
■ a cane	**une canne** *ewn kahn*
■ crutches	**des béquilles (f.)** *day bay-kee*

■ a hearing aid **un audiophone** *uhn noh-dyoh-fohn*

■ a walker **un déambulateur** *uhn day-ahn-bew-lah-tuhr*

■ a wheelchair **un fauteuil roulant** *uhn foh-tuhy roo-lahn*

What services do you have for the handicapped. **Quels services avez-vous pour les handicapés?** *kehl sehr-veess ah-vay voo poor lay zahn-dee-kah-pay*

I need assistance. **J'ai besoin d'aide.** *zhay buh-zwan dehd*

Is there wheelchair access for the handicapped? **Il y a accès aux handicapés?** *eel yah ahk-sseh oh zahn-dee-kah-pay*

Are there toilet facilities for the handicapped? **Il y a des toilettes avec accès aux handicapés?** *eel yah day twah-leht ah-vehk ahk-seh oh zahn-dee-kah-pay*

Are there stairs? **Il y a des marches?** *eel yah day mahrsh*

Are there bars in the bathrooms? **Il y a des barres dans les salles de bain?** *eel yah day bahr dahn lay sahl duh ban?*

Is there an elevator? **Il y a un ascenseur?** *eel yah uhn nah-sahn-suhr*

Is there a ramp? **Il y a une rampe d'accès pour les handicapés?** *eel yah ewn rahnp dahk-sseh poor lay zahn-dee-kah-pay*

Is there a refrigerator in the room? **Il y a un réfrigérateur dans la chambre?** *eel yah uhn ray-free-zhay-rah-tuhr dahn lah shahn-bruh*

Are there parking spaces for the disabled?	**Il y a des emplacements de stationnement pour les handicapés?** *eel yah day zahn-plahss-mahn duh stah-ssyohn-mahn poor lay zahn-dee-kah-pay*
Are guide dogs allowed?	**Les chiens d'aveugle sont permis?** *lay shyan dah-vuh-gluh sohn pehr-mee*
Do you have accessories for the hearing impaired?	**Avez-vous des accessoires pour les malentendants?** *ah-vay voo day zahk-sseh-sswahr poor lay mahl-ahn-tahn-dahn*
Do you have closed-captioned TVs?	**Avez-vous des télévisions avec sous-titres?** *ah-vay voo day tay-lay-vee-zyohn ah-vehk soo-tee-truh*

IN THE HOSPITAL (ACCIDENTS)

Help!	**Au secours!** *oh suh-koor*
Help me, please.	**Aidez-moi, s'il vous plaît.** *eh-day mwah seel voo pleh*
Get a doctor, quick!	**Vite, appelez un médecin!** *veet ah-play uhn mayd-ssan*
Call an ambulance!	**Faites venir une ambulance!** *feht vuh-neer ewn nahn-bew-lahnss*
Take me (him, her) to the hospital.	**Emmenez-moi (le, la) à l'hôpital.** *ahn-muh-nay mwah (luh, lah) ah loh-pee-tahl*
I need first aid.	**J'ai besoin de premiers soins.** *zhay buh-zwan duh pruh-myay swan*

I fell.	**Je suis tombé(e).** *zhuh swee tohn-bay*
I burned myself.	**Je me suis brûlé(e).** *zhuh muh swee brew-lay*
I cut myself.	**Je me suis coupé(e).** *zhuh muh swee koo-pay*
He's lost a lot of blood.	**Il a perdu beaucoup de sang.** *eel ah pehr-dew boh-koo duh sahn*
My leg is swollen.	**Ma jambe est enflée.** *mah zhahnb eh tahn-flay*
Is there outpatient surgery?	**Il y a un centre de traitement ambulatoire?** *eel yah uhn sahn-truh duh treht-mahn ahn-bew-lah-twahr*

AT THE DENTIST

I have to go to the dentist.	**Je dois aller chez le dentiste.** *zhuh dwah zah-lay shay luh dahn-teesst*
Can you recommend a dentist?	**Pouvez-vous me recommander un dentiste?** *poo-vay voo muh ruh-koh-mahn-day uhn dahn-teesst*
Where is his/her office?	**Où se trouve son cabinet?** *oo suh troov sohn kah-bee-neh*
I have a bad toothache.	**J'ai un mal de dents à tout casser. (J'ai une rage de dents.)** *zhay uhn mahl duh dahn ah too kah-ssay (zhay ewn rahzh duh dahn)*
What is your fee?	**Combien je vous dois?** *kohn-byan zhuh voo dwah*

I've lost a filling.	**J'ai perdu un plombage.**	*zhay pehr-dew uhn plohn-bahzh*

I've broken a tooth.	**Je me suis cassé une dent.**	*zhuh muh swee kah-ssay ewn dahn*
My gums hurt me.	**Les gencives me font mal.**	*lay zhahn-sseev muh fohn mahl*
Is there an infection?	**Il y a une infection?**	*eel yah ewn an-fehk-ssyohn*
Will you have to pull the tooth?	**Faut-il arracher la dent?**	*foh teel ah-rah-shay lah dahn*
Can you fill it temporarily?	**Pouvez-vous l'obturer provisoirement?**	*poo-vay voo lohp-tew-ray proh-vee-zwahr-mahn*
Can you fix _____?	**Pouvez-vous réparer _____?**	*poo-vay voo ray-pah-ray*
■ this bridge	**ce bridge**	*suh breedzh*
■ this crown	**cette couronne**	*seht koo-rohn*
■ this denture	**ce dentier**	*suh dahn-tyay*
When should I come back?	**Quand faut-il revenir?**	*kahn foh-teel ruh-vuh-neer*
How much is it?	**C'est combien?**	*seh kohn-byan*

COMMUNICATIONS

POST OFFICE

Bright yellow signs that say **La Poste** or **Bureau de Poste** indicate French post offices. Mailboxes are hard to miss because they are painted the same bright yellow. Post offices are generally open Monday through Friday from 8:00 A.M. to 5:00 P.M. and Saturdays from 8:00 A.M. until noon. During the week, some post offices may be closed for lunch.

Most post offices have automated stamp machines marked **Affranchissement** (*ah-frah<u>n</u>-sheess-mah<u>n</u>*), from which you may buy postage without having to stand in line. You may choose the language in which you want to transact business and you must enter the weight of your letter or package. These machines accept only coins. You may also buy pre-stamped envelopes.

Many post offices have an inside sign indicating their busiest times. If you're in a hurry, you may purchase stamps at tobacco shops, newspaper kiosks, and souvenir shops.

I want to mail a letter (a package).	**Je voudrais envoyer une lettre (un colis).** *zhuh voo-dreh ahn-vwah-yay ewn leh-truh (uhn koh-lee)*

Where's the post office?	**Où se trouve le bureau de poste?** *oo suh troov luh bew-roh duh pohsst*
Where's a mailbox?	**Où se trouve une boîte aux lettres?** *oo suh troov ewn bwaht oh leh-truh*

What is the postage on _____ to the United States?	**Quel est l'affranchissement _____ pour les États-Unis?** *kehl eh lah-frahn-sheess-mahn _____ poor lay zay-tah zew-nee*
■ a letter	**d'une lettre** *dewn leh-truh*
■ an air mail letter	**pour une lettre envoyée par avion** *poor ewn leh-truh ahn-vwah-yay pahr ah-vyohn*
■ an insured letter	**pour une lettre recommandée** *poor ewn leh-truh ruh-koh-mahn-day*
■ a registered letter	**pour une lettre recommandée** *poor ewn leh-truh ruh-koh-mahn-day*
■ a special delivery letter	**pour une lettre par exprès** *poor ewn leh-truh pahr ehkss-preh*
■ a postcard	**d'une carte postale** *dewn kahrt pohss-tahl*
When will it arrive?	**Quand arrivera-t-il (t-elle)?** *kahn tah-ree-vrah teel (tehl)*
Where is the _____ window?	**Où est le guichet _____?** *oo eh luh gee-sheh*
■ general delivery	**pour la poste restante** *poor lah pohsst rehss-tahnt*
■ stamp	**pour les timbres** *poor lay tan-bruh*
I'd like _____.	**Je voudrais _____.** *zhuh voo-dreh*
■ 10 postcards	**dix cartes postales** *dee kahrt pohss-tahl*
■ 5 (air mail) stamps	**cinq timbres (courrier aérien)** *sank tahn-bruh (koo-ryay ah-ay-ryan)*
■ one prepaid envelope	**une enveloppe prêt à poster** *ewn nahn-vuh-lohp preh tah pohss-tay*

■ a phone card	**une carte téléphonique** *ewn kahrt tay-lay-foh-neek*

You may come across the following postal terms:

accusé de réception *ah-kew-zay duh ray-ssehp-ssyohn*	acknowledgement of receipt
adresse de réexpédition *ah-drehss duh ray-ehkss-pay-dee-ssyohn*	forwarding address
destinataire inconnu *dehss-tee-nah-tuhr an-koh-new*	address unknown
expéditeur *ehkss-pay-dee-tuhr*	sender
la levée *lah luh-vay*	mail collection
port payé *pohr pay-yay*	postage paid
retour à l'envoyeur *ruh-toor ah lahn-vway-yuhr*	return to sender

TELEPHONES

All telephone numbers in France have 10 digits and are given in pairs. The first two digits represent an area code:

Paris and surrounding regions	01
Northwest France	02
Northeast France	03
Southeast France and Corsica	04
Southwest France	05
Mobile phone services	06–07
Skype	08

You may not drop these codes even if you are calling someone in the same zone. Directory assistance is free, but the operators don't always speak English. Dial 0899 15 6000 to find out who owns a specific French landline or mobile phone.

Some public pay phones are still available in post offices, cafés, tobacconists, convenience stores, supermarket checkouts, train, metro, and bus stops, and on the streets of larger cities. To call the United States or Canada, dial **00 + 1 + area code + number**. Although a few public phones still accept coins, the overwhelming majority will only accept a phone card. These phone cards allow for differing numbers of units (shown on the left of the card), so be sure to give some thought to how much time you'll need. When you insert the card into a phone, the display indicates how many minutes you have left. As you speak, you can watch the countdown of the remaining minutes.

Hotels tend to charge exorbitant rates for international as well as domestic calls. It's an excellent idea, therefore, to purchase a **Télécarte**, available at the places previously listed and in any location with a sign that reads "**Télécartes en vente ici**," which enables you to buy 50 or 120 message units of calls. The number of message units required for the call depends on the total speaking time and the area phoned: One unit entitles you to one three-minute call during the normal rate period, and up to nine minutes of calls after 10:50 P.M. It also allows you to make 10 minutes worth of calls within France, or a four-minute call to the United States. It can also connect you with an operator to call home. The pictures on these cards vary and change over time, so some of the **Télécartes** are already collectors' items that are on display at the market at Rond Point des Champs-Elysées.

CALLING

You have to _____.	**Vous devez _____.**	*voo duh-vay*
■ call back	**rappeler**	*rah-play*
■ dial	**composer le numéro**	*kohn-poh-zay luh new-may-roh*
■ hang up (the receiver)	**raccrocher**	*rah-kroh-shay*

■ insert the card	**introduire la carte**	*an-troh-dweer lah kahrt*
■ know the area code (of the country) (of the city)	**savoir l'indicatif (du pays) (de la ville)**	*sah-vvwahr lan-dee-kah-teef (dew pay-ee)(duh lah veel)*
■ leave a message	**laisser un message**	*leh-say uhn meh-sahzh*
■ listen for the dial tone	**attendre la tonalité**	*ah-tahndr lah toh-nah-lee-tay*
■ pick up (the receiver)	**décrocher**	*day-kroh-shay*
■ telephone	**téléphoner**	*tay-lay-foh-nay*
Where is _____?	**Où y a-t-il _____?**	*oo ee ah-teel*
■ a public telephone	**un téléphone public**	*uhn tay-lay-fohn pew-bleek*
■ a telephone booth	**une cabine téléphonique**	*ewn kah-been tay-lay-foh-neek*

■ a telephone directory	**un annuaire téléphonique**	*uhn nah-new-ehr tay-lay-foh-neek*
May I use your phone?	**Puis-je me servir de votre téléphone?**	*pweezh muh sehr-veer duh voh-truh tay-lay-fohn*

I would like to make a _____.	**Je voudrais téléphoner _____.** *zhuh voo-dreh tay-lay-foh-nay*
■ collect call	**en P.C.V.** *ahn pay-say-vay*
■ local call	**en ville** *ahn veel*
■ long-distance call	**à l'extérieur** *ah lehkss-tay-ryuhr*
■ person-to-person call	**avec préavis** *ah-vehk pray-ah-vee*
How do I get an operator?	**Que fait-on pour parler à la téléphoniste?** *kuh feh-tohn poor pahr-lay ah lah tay-lay-foh-neesst*
I'd like to buy a prepaid phone card.	**Je voudrais acheter une carte téléphonique pré-payée.** *zhuh voo-dreh zahsh-tay ewn kahrt tay-lay-foh-neek pray-pay-ay*
I'd like to buy a prepaid cell phone.	**Je voudrais acheter un portable pré-payé.** *zhuh voo-dreh zahsh-tay uhn pohr-tah-bluh pray-pay-ay*
How much does a three-minute call cost?	**Combien coûte une communication de trois minutes?** *kohn-byan koot ewn koh-mew-nee-kah-ssyohn duh trwah mee-newt*
How much does each additional minute cost?	**Combien coûte chaque minute supplémentaire?** *kohn-byan koot shahk mee-newt sew-plee-mahn-tehr*
My number is _____.	**Mon numéro est _____.** *mohn new-may-roh eh*
I'd like to speak to _____.	**Je voudrais parler à _____.** *zhuh voo-dreh pahr-lay ah*
Is Mr. _____ in?	**Monsieur _____, est là?** *muh-ssyuh _____ eh lah*

What's your phone number?	**Quel est votre (ton) numéro de téléphone?** *kehl eh voh-truh (toh<u>n</u>) new-may-roh duh tay-lay-fohn*
What's your cell phone number?	**Quel est le numéro de votre (ton) portable?** *kehl eh luh new-may-roh duh voh-truh (toh<u>n</u>) pohr-tah-bluh*

Why don't you answer your cell phone?	**Pourquoi ne répondez-vous (réponds-tu) pas à votre (ton) portable?** *poor-kwah nuh ray-poh<u>n</u>-day-voo (nuh ray-poh<u>n</u>-tew) pah zah voh-truh (toh<u>n</u>) pohr-tah-bluh*
I have to recharge my phone.	**Je dois recharger mon portable.** *zhuh dwah ruh-shahr-zhay moh<u>n</u> pohr-tah-bluh*
I can't find my cell phone. Have you seen it?	**Je ne trouve pas mon portable. Vous l'avez vu? (Tu l'as vu?)** *zhuh nuh troov pah moh<u>n</u> pohr-tah-bluh voo lah-vay vew (tew lah vew)*
Do you text?	**Vous textez? (Tu textes?)** *voo tehkss-tay (tew-tehksst)*
Can I text you?	**Je peux vous (te) texter?** *zhuh puh voo (tuh) tehkss-tay*
Do you have Bluetooth?	**Avez-vous (As-tu) Bluetooth?** *ah-vay voo (ah-tew) bloo-toot*

Hello.	**Allô.** *ah-loh*
This is _____.	**Ici _____.** *ee-ssee*
Who is calling?	**Qui est à l'appareil?** *kee eh tah lah-pah-rehy*
I can't hear.	**Je ne peux pas vous entendre.** *zhuh nuh puh pah voo zahn-tahn-druh*
Speak louder.	**Parlez plus fort.** *pahr-lay plew fohr*
Don't hang up.	**Ne quittez pas.** *nuh kee-tay pah*
Do you have an answering machine?	**Avez-vous (As-tu) un répondeur?** *ah-vay-voo (ah-tew) uhn ray-pohn-duhr*
I want to leave a message.	**Je voudrais laisser un message.** *zhuh voo-dreh leh-ssay uhn meh-ssahzh*

PROBLEMS

What number are you calling?	**Vous demandez quel numéro?** *voo duh-mahn-day kehl new-may-roh*
It's an error.	**C'est une erreur.** *seh tewn eh-ruhr*
You have the wrong number.	**Vous avez le mauvais numéro.** *voo zah-vay luh moh-veh new-may-roh*
We got disconnected.	**On nous a coupés.** *ohn noo zah koo-pay*
The phone isn't working.	**Le téléphone est en panne.** *luh tay-lay-fohn eh tahn pahn*
There's a lot of static.	**Il y a beaucoup de parasites.** *eel yah boh-koo duh pah-rah-seet*

Travel Tips   Hotels often levy a service charge for calls made from a guest room. To avoid paying too much, make all calls from a cell phone compatible with the French system or use a French telephone company calling card, especially for long distance.

FAXES

Although the correct way to say "to fax" is **envoyer une télécopie** *(ahn-vwah-yay ewn tay-lay-koh-pee)*, informal French allows the use of the verb **faxer** *(fahk-ssay)* and the noun **un fax** *(uhn fahkss)*.

Do you have a fax machine?	**Avez-vous un fax?** *ah-vay voo uhn fahkss*
What is your fax number?	**Quel est le numéro de votre fax?** *kehl eh luh new-may-roh duh vohtr fahkss*
I'd like to send a fax.	**Je voudrais envoyer un fax.** *zhuh voo-dreh zahn-vwah-yay uhn fahkss*

May I fax this, please?	**Puis-je faxer ceci, s'il vous plaît?** *pweezh fahk-ssay suh-see seel voo pleh*

May I fax this letter (document) to you?	**Puis-je vous faxer cette lettre (ce document)?** *pweezh voo fahk-ssay seht lehtr (suh doh-kew-mah<u>n</u>)*
Fax it to me.	**Faxez-le (-la) –moi.** *fahk-ssay-luh (lah) mwah.*
I didn't get your fax.	**Je n'ai pas reçu votre fax.** *zhuh nay pah ruh-sew vohtr fahkss.*
Did you receive my fax?	**Avez-vous reçu mon fax?** *ah-vay voo ruh-sew moh<u>n</u> fahkss*
Your fax is illegible.	**Votre fax n'est pas lisible.** *vohtr fahkss neh pah lee-zee-bluh*
Please send it again.	**Veuillez le (la) faxer de nouveau.** *vuh-yay luh (lah) fahk-ssay duh noo-voh*

COMPUTERS

To get information on the Internet you may use one of the sites given on pages 218–219.

What kind of computer do you have?	**Quel type d'ordinateur utilizez-vous?** *kehl teep dohr-dee-nah-tuhr oo-tee-lee-zay voo*
Do you use___?	**Utilisez-vous___?** *oo-tee-lee-zay-voo*
What is your e-mail address	**Quelle est votre (ton) adresse e-mail?** *kehl eh voh-truh (toh<u>n</u>) ah-drehss ee-mehl*
Are you on Facebook?	**Êtes-vous (Es-tu) sur Facebook?** *eht-voo (eh-tew) sewr fayss-book*

Do you have a blog?	**Avez-vous (As-tu) un blogue?** *ah-vay-voo (ah-tew) uhn blohg*
I'm looking for an Internet café.	**Je cherche un cybercafé.** *zhuh shehrsh uhn see-behr-kah-fay*
Is there one nearby? Where?	**Il y en a un par ici? Où?** *eel yahn nah uhn pahr ee-ssee oo*
How do you get there?	**Comment y va-ton?** *koh-mahn ee vah-tohn*
Can you show me how to burn a CD?	**Pouvez-vous (Peux-tu) me montrer comment brûler un CD?** *poo-vay voo (puh-tew) muh mohn-tray koh-mahn brew-lay uhn say-day*
My computer has broken down.	**Mon ordinateur est en panne.** *mohn nohr-dee-nah-tuhr eh tahn pahn*
My computer has crashed.	**Mon ordinateur s'est planté.** *mohn nohr-dee-nah-tuhr say plahn-tay*

MINI-DICTIONARY OF COMPUTER TERMS AND PHRASES

access	**l'accès (m.)**	*lahk-sseh*
accessory	**l'accessoire (m.)**	*lahk-sseh-sswahr*

app(lication)	**l'app(lication) (f.)**	*lah-p(lee-kah-ssyohn)*
back-up drive	**le disque de sauvegarde**	*luh deessk duh sohv-gahrd*
Blackberry	**le Blackberry**	*luh blahk-beh-ree*
blog	**le blog(ue)**	*luh blohg*
bookmark	**le signet**	*luh see-nyeh*
(to) boot	**démarrer**	*day-mah-ray*
brand name	**la marque**	*lah mahrk*
(to) break down	**être en panne**	*eh-truh ahn pahn*
browser	**le logiciel de navigation**	*luh loh-zhee-ssyehl duh nah-vee-gah-ssyohn*
(to) burn (a CD)	**brûler (un CD)**	*brew-lay (uhn say-day)*
cable	**le câble**	*luh kah-bluh*
(to) chat	**causer**	*koh-zay*
(to) click	**cliquer**	*klee-kay*
CPU	**l'unité centrale (f.)**	*lew-nee-tay sahn-trahl*
computer science	**l'informatique (f.)**	*lan-fohr-mah-teek*
computer scientist	**l'informaticien (ne)**	*lan-fohr-mah-tee-syan (syehn)*

(to) crash	**se planter**	*suh plahn-tay*
cursor	**le curseur**	*luh kuhr-suhr*
database	**la base de données**	*lah bahz duh doh-nay*
disk drive	**le lecteur de disques**	*luh lehk-tuhr duh deessk*
(to) download	**télécharger**	*tay-lay-shahr-zhay*
e-mail	**le e-mail**	*luh ee-mehl*
Facebook	**le Facebook**	*luh fayss-book*
file	**le fichier**	*luh feesh-yay*
firewall	**la barrière de sécurité**	*lah bah-ree-yehr duh say-kew-ree-tay*
flash (thumb) drive	**la clé USB**	*lah klay ew-ehss-bay*
graphics	**la grafique**	*lah grah-feek*
home page	**la page d'accueil**	*lah pahzh dah-kuhy*
Internet	**l'Internet**	*lan-tehr-neht*
Internet café	**le cybercafé**	*luh see-behr kah-fay*
joystick	**la manette de jeux**	*lah mah-neht duh zhuh*
key	**la touché**	*lah toosh*
keyboard	**le clavier**	*luh klah-vyay*

| laptop computer | **l'ordinateur portable (m.)** | *lohr-dee-nah-tuhr pohr-tah-bluh* |

memory	**la mémoire**	*lah may-mwahr*
monitor	**le moniteur**	*luh moh-nee-tuhr*
mouse	**la souris**	*lah soo-ree*
network	**le réseau**	*luh ray-zoh*
newsgroup	**le forum**	*luh foh-ruhm*
printer	**l'imprimante**	*lan-pree-mahnt*
■ laser	**laser**	*lah-zehr*
■ ink jet	**jet d'encre**	*zheh dahn-kruh*
scanner	**le scanneur**	*luh skah-nuhr*
screen	**l'écran (m.)**	*lay-krahn*
search engine	**le moteur de recherche**	*luh moh-tuhr duh ruh-shehrsh*
site	**le site**	*luh seet*
software	**le logiciel**	*luh loh-zhee-ssyehl*
speed	**la vitesse**	*lah vee-tehss*

spell-checker	**le correcteur orthographique**	*luh koh-rehk-tuhr ohr-toh-grah-feek*
thesaurus	**le thesaurus**	*luh tuh-soh-rewss*
thread	**le fil (de la discussion)**	*luh feel (duh lah deess-kew-ssyoh<u>n</u>)*
touch screen	**l'écran tactile**	*lay-krah<u>n</u> tahk-teel*
tweet	**le tweet**	*luh tweet*
Twitter	**twitter**	*twee-tay*
webmaster	**l'administrateur de site**	*lah-mee-nee-strah-tuhr duh seet*
WiFi	**le WiFi**	*luh wee-fee*
You Tube	**You Tube**	*yoo tewb*
zip drive	**le lecteur zip**	*luh lehk-tuhr zeep*

WEB SITES AND SEARCH ENGINES

These web sites and search engines can give you the most up-to-date information on France and French-speaking countries:

www.yahoo.fr —France and French-speaking countries

www.pratique.fr —France and French-speaking countries

www.admin.ch —Switzerland

www.gouv.qc.ca —Quebec

www.primature.sn —Senegal

www.travelang.com —for worldwide travelers; you can reserve hotel accommodations, rent a car, book your flight, and figure currency conversions. There's also a travel calendar listing holidays and festivals

http://www.info-france-usa.org—the French embassy in Washington, D.C.; information in English on economic, political, scientific, and linguistic topics

http://www.francophonie.org—news and announcements in French pertaining to international relations, conferences, and English publications covering French government, the arts and sciences, and traveling

http://www.paris.org—information in English on Paris: maps, museums, monuments, travel

http://www.utm.edu/departments/french/french.html— 5,000 links to French-related sites

http://pariscope.fr—the French weekly *Pariscope* magazine, which gives current information about Paris: plays, festivals, flea markets, concerts

http://www.babelfish.altavista.com—an Internet language translator (works better for one word than a full sentence)

http://www.africaonline.co.ci—information about Africa

http://www.afp.com/—site of L'Agence France-Presse; allows links with principal newspapers and magazines from France and French-speaking countries

http://www.admifrance.gouv.fr—directory of Internet services for French and French-speaking countries

GENERAL INFORMATION

TELLING TIME

What time is it?	**Quelle heure est-il?**	*kehl uhr eh teel*
It is _____.	**Il est _____.**	*eel eh*
■ noon	**midi**	*mee-dee*
■ 8:00	**huit heures**	*weet uhr*
■ 1:05	**une heure cinq**	*ewn uhr sank*
■ 2:10	**deux heures dix**	*duh zuhr deess*
■ 3:15	**trois heures et quart**	*trwah zuhr ay kahr*
■ 4:20	**quatre heures vingt**	*kah-truh uhr van*
■ 5:25	**cinq heures vingt-cinq**	*sank uhr van-sank*
■ 6:30	**six heures et demie**	*seez uhr ay duh-mee*
■ 7:35	**sept heures trente-cinq**	*seht uhr trahnt-sank*
■ 8:40	**neuf heures moins vingt**	*nuhv uhr mwan van*
■ 9:45	**dix heures moins le quart**	*deez uhr mwan luh kahr*
■ 10:50	**onze heures moins dix**	*ohnz uhr mwan deess*
■ 11:55	**midi moins cinq**	*mee-dee mwan sank*

EXPRESSIONS OF TIME

At what time?	**À quelle heure ____?**	*ah kehl uhr*
When?	**Quand?**	*kah<u>n</u>*
at ____ o'clock	**à ____ heures**	*ah ____ uhr*
at exactly noon	**à midi précis**	*ah mee-dee pray-ssee*
at exactly 5 o'clock	**à cinq heures précises**	*ah sa<u>n</u>k uhr pray-sseez*
in an hour	**dans une heure**	*dah<u>n</u> zewn-uhr*
in 2 hours	**dans deux heures**	*dah<u>n</u> duhz-uhr*
not before 2:00 A.M.	**pas avant deux heures du matin**	*pah zah-vah<u>n</u> duhz-uhr dew mah-ta<u>n</u>*
after 3:00 P.M.	**après trois heures de l'après-midi**	*ah-preh trwah-zuhr duh lah-preh mee-dee*
at about 9:00 P.M.	**vers neuf heures du soir**	*vehr nuhv-uhr dew swahr*
between 8 and 9 o'clock	**entre huit et neuf heures**	*ah<u>n</u>-truh weet ay nuhv uhr*
until 5 o'clock	**jusqu'à cinq heures**	*zhewss-kah sa<u>n</u>k uhr*
since what time ____?	**depuis quelle heure ____?**	*duh-pwee kehl uhr*

since 7 o'clock	**depuis sept heures**	*duh-pwee seht uhr*
per hour	**par heure**	*pahr uhr*
three hours ago	**il y a trois heures**	*eel yah trwah zuhr*
early	**tôt**	*toh*
	de bonne heure	*duh bohn uhr*
late	**tard**	*tahr*
late (in arriving)	**en retard**	*ah<u>n</u> ruh-tahr*
on, in time	**à l'heure**	*ah luhr*
noon	**midi**	*mee-dee*
midnight	**minuit**	*mee-nwee*
in the morning	**le matin**	*luh mah-ta<u>n</u>*
in the afternoon	**l'après-midi**	*lah-preh-mee-dee*
in the evening	**le soir**	*luh swahr*

at night	**la nuit** *lah nwee*
second	**une seconde** *ewn suh-goh<u>n</u>d*
minute	**une minute** *ewn mee-newt*
hour	**une heure** *ewn uhr*
a quarter of an hour	**un quart d'heure** *uh<u>n</u> kahr duhr*
a half hour	**une demi-heure** *ewn duh-mee uhr*

Official time is based on the 24-hour clock. You will find schedules for planes, trains, radio and television programs, movies, sports events, and the like expressed in terms of a point within the 24-hour sequence. The time may be written as follows:

Noon	12 h 00	12.00
1:15 A.M.	01 h 15	1.15
1:15 P.M.	13 h 15	13.15
Midnight	00 h 00	00.00

To calculate the conventional time, subtract 12 from the official time for the hours between noon and midnight:

16 h 30   4:30 P.M.

The train leaves at 15:30.	**Le train part à 15:30.** *luh tra<u>n</u> pahr ah ka<u>n</u>z-uhr trah<u>n</u>t*
The time is now 21:15.	**Il est maintenant 21 heures 15.** *eel eh ma<u>n</u>t-nah<u>n</u> va<u>n</u>-tay-ewn uhr ka<u>n</u>z*

To calculate official time, add 12 to the conventional time for the hours between noon and midnight:

| 9:45 A.M. | 09 h 45 | 9.45 |
| 9:45 P.M. | 21 h 45 | 21.45 |

DAYS OF THE WEEK

What day is today?	**Quel jour est-ce aujourd' hui?** *kehl zhoor ehss oh-zhoor-dwee* **Quel jour sommes-nous aujourd'hui?** *kehl zhoor sohm noo oh-zhoor-dwee*
Today is _____.	**C'est aujourd'hui _____.** *seh toh-zhoor-dwee* **Nous sommes _____.** *noo sohm*
■ Monday	**lundi** *luhn-dee*
■ Tuesday	**mardi** *mahr-dee*
■ Wednesday	**mercredi** *mehr-kruh-dee*
■ Thursday	**jeudi** *zhuh-dee*
■ Friday	**vendredi** *vahn-druh-dee*
■ Saturday	**samedi** *sahm-dee*
■ Sunday	**dimanche** *dee-mahnsh*

NOTE: In French, the names of the days and the months and seasons are written in small letters.

last Monday	**lundi dernier** *luhn-dee dehr-nyay*
the eve	**la veille** *lah vehy*
the day before yesterday	**avant-hier** *ah-vahn-tyehr*
yesterday	**hier** *yehr*

today	**aujourd'hui**	*oh-zhoor-dwee*
tomorrow	**demain**	*duh-ma<u>n</u>*
the day after tomorrow	**après-demain**	*ah-preh-duh-ma<u>n</u>*
the next day	**le lendemain**	*luh lah<u>n</u>-duh-ma<u>n</u>*
next Monday	**lundi prochain**	*lu<u>n</u>-dee proh-sha<u>n</u>*
the day	**le jour**	*luh zhoor*
2 days ago	**il y a deux jours**	*eel yah duh zhoor*
in 2 days	**dans deux jours**	*dah<u>n</u> duh zhoor*
every day	**tous les jours**	*too lay zhoor*
day off	**(le) jour de congé**	*(luh) zhoor duh koh<u>n</u>-zhay*
holiday	**(le) jour de fête**	*(luh) zhoor duh feht*
birthday	**l'anniversaire**	*lah-nee-vehr-ssehr*
per day	**par jour**	*pahr zhoor*
during the day	**pendant la journée**	*pah<u>n</u>-dah<u>n</u> lah zhoor-nay*
from this day on	**dès aujourd'hui**	*deh zoh-zhoor-dwee*
the week	**la semaine**	*lah suh-mehn*
a weekday	**un jour de semaine**	*uh<u>n</u> zhoor duh suh-mehn*
the weekend	**le week-end**	*luh week-ehnd*
last week	**la semaine passée**	*lah suh-mehn pah-ssay*
this week	**cette semaine**	*seht suh-mehn*

next week	**la semaine prochaine** *lah suh-mehn proh-shehn*
a week from today	**dans une semaine** *dahn zewn suh-mehn*
2 weeks from tomorrow	**de demain en quinze** *duh duh-man ahn kanz*
during the week	**pendant la semaine** *pahn-dahn lah suh-mehn*

MONTHS OF THE YEAR

January	**janvier** *zhan-vee-yay*
February	**février** *fay-vree-yay*
March	**mars** *mahrss*
April	**avril** *ah-vreel*
May	**mai** *meh*
June	**juin** *zhwan*
July	**juillet** *zhwee-yeh*
August	**août** *oo or oot*
September	**septembre** *sehp-tahn-bruh*
October	**octobre** *ohk-toh-bruh*
November	**novembre** *noh-vahn-bruh*
December	**décembre** *day-ssahn-bruh*
the month	**le mois** *luh mwah*
2 months ago	**il y a deux mois** *eel yah duh mwah*
last month	**le mois dernier** *luh mwah dehr-nyay*

this month	**ce mois** *suh mwah*
next month	**le mois prochain** *luh mwah proh-shan*
during the month of	**pendant le mois de** *pahn-dahn luh mwah duh*
since the month of	**depuis le mois de** *duh-pwee luh mwah duh*
for the month of	**pour le mois de** *poor luh mwah duh*
every month	**tous les mois** *too lay mwah*
per month	**par mois** *pahr mwah*
What is today's date?	**Quelle est la date d'aujourd'hui?** *kehl ay lah daht doh-zhoor-dwee*
Today is _____.	**C'est aujourd'hui _____.** *seht oh-zhoor-dwee*
■ Monday, May 1	**lundi, le premier mai** *luhn-dee luh pruh-myay meh*
■ Tuesday, June 2	**mardi, le deux juin** *mahr-dee luh duh zhwan*

NOTE: Use the ordinal number only for the first of the month.

the year	**l'an/l'année** *lahn/lah-nay*
per year	**par an** *pahr ahn*
all year	**toute l'année** *toot lah-nay*
every year	**chaque année** *shahk ah-nay*
during the year	**pendant l'année** *pahn-dahn lah-nay*

THE FOUR SEASONS

spring	**le printemps**	*luh pran-tahn*
summer	**l'été**	*lay-tay*
autumn	**l'automne**	*loh-tohn*
winter	**l'hiver**	*lee-vehr*
in the spring	**au printemps**	*oh pran-tahn*
in the summer	**en été**	*ahn nay-tay*
in the autumn	**en automne**	*ahn noh-tohn*
in the winter	**en hiver**	*ahn nee-vehr*

WEATHER

What is the weather like?	**Quel temps fait-il?**	*kehl tahn feh-teel*
It is beautiful.	**Il fait beau.**	*eel feh boh*
It is hot.	**Il fait chaud.**	*eel feh shoh*
It is sunny.	**Il fait du soleil.**	*eel feh dew soh-lehy*
It is bad.	**Il fait mauvais.**	*eel feh moh-veh*
It is cold.	**Il fait froid.**	*eel feh frwah*
It is cool.	**Il fait frais.**	*eel feh freh*
It is windy.	**Il fait du vent.**	*eel feh dew vahn*
It is foggy.	**Il fait du brouillard.**	*eel feh dew broo-yahr*
It is humid.	**Il fait lourd.**	*eel feh loor*
It is snowing.	**Il neige.**	*eel nehzh*
It is raining.	**Il pleut.**	*eel pluh*

TEMPERATURE

The average annual daily temperatures in Paris in Fahrenheit and Centigrade are:

MONTH	°F	°C	MONTH	°F	°C
January	42°	5°	July	77°	25°
February	45°	7°	August	75°	24°
March	54°	12°	September	70°	21°
April	61°	16°	October	61°	16°
May	68°	20°	November	50°	10°
June	73°	23°	December	44°	7°

What heat!	**Quelle chaleur!**	*kehl shah-luhr*
What cold!	**Quel froid!**	*kehl frwah*

RELIGIOUS SERVICES

France has many cathedrals and churches that you may wish to visit. There are churches and synagogues in major cities that do conduct some services in English. For more information, speak to the concierge at your hotel.

Is there a _____ near here?	**Y a-t-il _____ près d'ici?** *ee ah teel _____ preh dee-ssee*
■ Catholic church	**une église catholique** *ewn nay-gleez kah-toh-leek*
■ Protestant church	**un temple** *uhn tah<u>n</u>-pluh*
■ synagogue	**une synagogue** *ewn see-nah-gohg*
■ mosque	**une mosquée** *ewn mohss-kay*

At what time is the service (mass)?	**À quelle heure commence l'office (la messe)?** *ah kehl uhr koh-mah<u>n</u>ss l'oh-feess (lah mehss)*

I would like to speak to a _____.	**Je voudrais parler à un _____.** *zhuh voo-dreh pahr-lay ah uh<u>n</u>*
■ priest	**prêtre** *preh-truh*
■ minister	**pasteur** *pahss-tuhr*
■ rabbi	**rabbin** *rah-ba<u>n</u>*

PUBLIC HOLIDAYS AND CELEBRATIONS

Jan. 1	Le Jour de l'An Le Nouvel An	New Year's Day
May 1	La Fête du Travail	Labor Day
July 14	La Fête Nationale	Bastille Day
Aug. 15	L'Assomption	Assumption Day
Nov. 1	La Toussaint	All Saints' Day
Nov. 2	Le Jour des Morts	All Souls' Day
Nov. 11	L'Armistice	Armistice Day
Dec. 25	Noël	Christmas
February	Le Carnaval	Carnival
Last day of carnival	Le Mardi gras	Mardi-Gras
Mar./Apr.	Les Rameaux	Palm Sunday
Mar./Apr.	Le Vendredi-Saint	Good Friday

Mar./Apr.	Pâques	Easter
Mar./Apr.	Le Dimanche de Quasimodo	1st Sunday after Easter
40 days after Easter	L'Ascension	Ascension Thursday
7 Mondays after Easter	Lundi de la Pentecôte	Whit Monday
May	La Fête de Jeanne d'Arc	Feast of Joan of Arc

COUNTRIES AND NATIONALITIES

| Where are you from? | **D'où êtes-vous?** | *doo eht voo* |
| I am (from) _____. | **Je suis de _____.** | *zhuh swee duh* |

| I am _____. | **Je suis _____.** | *zhuh swee* |

NOTE: The feminine form of the adjective is indicated after the masculine form. For this form remember to pronounce the last consonant.

	COUNTRY	NATIONALITY
Australia	**d'Australie** *doh-strah-lee*	**australien/ne** *oh-strah-lya<u>n</u>/lyehn*
Austria	**d'Autriche** *doh-treesh*	**autrichien/ne** *oh-tree-shya<u>n</u>/shyehn*
Belgium	**de Belgique** *duh behl-zheek*	**belge** *behlzh*
Canada	**(du) Canada** *(dew) kah-nah-dah*	**canadien/ne** *kah-nah-dya<u>n</u>/dyehn*
China	**(de) Chine** *(duh) sheen*	**chinois/e** *shee-nwah/nwahz*
Denmark	**(du) Danemark** *(dew) dahn-mahrk*	**danois/e** *dah-nwah/nwahz*
England	**d'Angleterre** *dah<u>n</u>-gluh-tehr*	**anglais/e** *ah<u>n</u>-gleh/glehz*
Finland	**(de) Finlande** *(duh) feen-lah<u>n</u>d*	**finlandais/e** *feen-lah<u>n</u>-deh/dehz*
France	**de France** *duh frah<u>n</u>ss*	**français/e** *frah<u>n</u>-sseh/sehz*
Germany	**d'Allemagne** *dahl-mah-nyuh*	**allemand/e** *ahl-mah<u>n</u>/mah<u>n</u>d*
Greece	**de Grèce** *duh grehss*	**grec/que** *grehk*
Haiti	**d'Haïti (m.)** *dahy-ee-tee*	**haïtien/ne** *ahy-ee-ssya<u>n</u>/ssyehn*
India	**d'Inde (f.)** *da<u>n</u>d*	**indien/ne** *a<u>n</u>-dya<u>n</u>/dyehn*

NOTE: When nationality refers to a person (noun) it is capitalized, i.e., **Un(e) Francais(e) parle français.** When the nationality is used as an adjective it begins with a lower case letter, i.e., **C'est un plat chinois.**

	COUNTRY	NATIONALITY
Ireland	**d'Irlande (f.)** *deer-lah<u>nd</u>*	**irlandais/e** *eer-lah<u>n</u>-deh/dehz*
Israel	**d'Israël (m.)** *deez-rah-ehl*	**israélite** *eez-rah-ay-leet*
Italy	**d'Italie (f.)** *dee-tah-lee*	**italien/ne** *ee-tah-lya<u>n</u>/lyehn*
Japan	**du Japon** *dew zhah-poh<u>n</u>*	**japonais/e** *zhah-poh-neh/nehz*
Luxembourg	**du Luxembourg** *dew lewkss-ah<u>n</u>-boor*	**luxembourgeois/e** *lewkss-ah<u>n</u>-boor- zhwah/zhwahz*
Morocco	**du Maroc** *dew mah-rohk*	**marocain/e** *mah-roh-ka<u>n</u>/kehn*
Norway	**de Norvège** *duh norh-vehzh*	**norvégien/ne** *nohr-vay-zhya<u>n</u>/ zhyehn*
Portugal	**du Portugal** *dew pohr-tew-gahl*	**portugais/e** *pohr-tew-geh/gehz*
Russia	**de Russie** *duh roo-se<u>e</u>*	**russe** *rooss*
Scotland	**d'Ecosse** *day-kohss*	**écossais/e** *ay-koh-sseh/ssehz*
Senegal	**du Sénégal** *dew say-nay-gahl*	**sénégalais/e** *say-nay-gah-leh/lehz*
Spain	**d'Espagne** *dehss-pah-nyuh*	**espagnol/e** *ehss-pah-nyohl*
Sweden	**de Suède** *duh swehd*	**suédois/e** *sway-dwah/dwahz*
Switzerland	**de Suisse** *duh sweess*	**suisse** *sweess*

	COUNTRY	NATIONALITY
Tunisia	**de Tunisie** *duh tew-nee-zee*	**tunisien/ne** *tew-nee-zyan/zyehn*
U.S.	**des États-Unis** *day-zay-tah-zew-nee*	**américain/e** *ah-may-ree-kan/ kehn*
Wales	**du pays de Galles** *dew pay-ee duh gahl*	**gallois/e** *gahl-wah/wahz*

DIRECTIONS

le nord	*luh nohr*	the north
le sud	*luh sewd*	the south
l'est	*lehsst*	the east
l'ouest	*lwehsst*	the west

IMPORTANT SIGNS

À louer	*ah loo-ay*	For rent, hire
Ascenseur	*ah-sahn-ssuhr*	Elevator
Attention	*ah-tahn-ssyohn*	Careful
À vendre	*ah vahn-druh*	For sale
Dames	*dahm*	Ladies
Danger	*dahn-zhay*	Danger
Danger de mort	*dahn-zhay duh mohr*	Danger of death
Défense de ____	*day-fahnss duh*	Do not ____

Défense d'entrer	*day-fahnss dahn-tray*	Do not enter
Défense de cracher	*day-fahnss duh krah-shay*	No spitting
Défense de fumer	*day-fahnss duh few-may*	No smoking
Défense de marcher sur l'herbe	*day-fahnss duh mahr-shay sewr lehrb*	Keep off the grass
Eau non potable	*oh nohn poh-tah-bluh*	Don't drink the water
École	*ay-kohl*	School
Entrée	*ahn-tray*	Entrance
Entrée interdite	*ahn-tray an-tehr-deet*	No Entrance
Entrée libre	*ahn-tray lee-bruh*	Free Admission
Fermé	*fehr-may*	Closed
Fumeurs	*few-muhr*	Smokers
Hommes	*ohm*	Men
Hôpital	*oh-pee-tahl*	Hospital
Horaire	*oh-rehr*	Schedule
Libre	*lee-bruh*	Free/Unoccupied
Messieurs	*meh-ssyuh*	Gentlemen
Ne pas toucher	*nuh pah too-shay*	Don't touch
Non-fumeurs	*nohn few-muhr*	Nonsmokers
Occupé	*oh-kew-pay*	Occupied

Ouvert	*oo-vehr*	Open
Passage souterrain	*pah-ssahzh soo-teh-ran*	Underground Passage
Poussez	*poo-ssay*	Push
Privé	*pree-vay*	Private
Quai/Voie	*kay/vwah*	Track, Platform
Renseignements	*rahn-sseh-nyuh-mahn*	Information
Réservé	*ray-zehr-vay*	Reserved
Salle d'attente	*sahl dah-tahnt*	Waiting room
Soldes	*sohld*	Sales
Sonnez	*soh-nay*	Ring
Sortie	*sohr-tee*	Exit
Sortie de secours	*sohr-tee duh-suh-koor*	Emergency exit
Stationnement inderdit	*stah-ssyohn-mahn an-tehr-dee*	No parking
Tirez	*tee-ray*	Pull
Toilettes	*twah-leht*	Toilets

COMMON ABBREVIATIONS

ACF	Automobile Club de France	Automobile Club of France
apr. J.-C.	après Jésus-Christ	A.D.
av. J.-C.	avant Jésus-Christ	B.C.
bd.	boulevard	boulevard
c.-à-d.	c'est-à-dire	that is to say, i.e.
CGT	Compagnie générale transatlantique	French Line
Cie.	compagnie	Company
EU	États-Unis	United States (U.S.)
h.	heure(s)	hour, o'clock
M.	Monsieur	Mr.
Mlle	Mademoiselle	Miss
MM	Messieurs	Gentlemen
Mme	Madame	Mrs.
ONU	Organisation des Nations Unies	United Nations (U.N.)
p.	page	page
p. ex.	par example	for example
RATP	Régie Autonome des Transports Parisiens	Paris Transport Authority
RD	Route Départementale	local road
RN	Route Nationale	national road
SA	Société anonyme	Ltd., Inc.
SI	Syndicat d'initiative	Tourist Information Office
SNCF	Société Nationale des Chemins de fer Français	French National Railways
s.v.p.	s'il vous plaît	please

CENTIMETERS/INCHES

It is usually unnecessary to make exact conversions from your customary inches to the metric system used in France, but to give you an approximate idea of how they compare, we give you the following guide.

Centimètres

Pouces

To convert centimeters into inches, multiply by .39.
To convert inches into centimeters, multiply by 2.54.

METERS/FEET

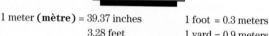

1 meter (**mètre**) = 39.37 inches   1 foot = 0.3 meters
3.28 feet   1 yard = 0.9 meters
1.09 yards

How tall are you in meters? See for yourself.

FEET	METERS	FEET	METERS
5'	1.52	5'7"	1.70
5'1"	1.54	5'8"	1.73
5'2"	1.57	5'9"	1.75
5'3"	1.59	5'10"	1.78
5'4"	1.62	5'11"	1.80
5'5"	1.64	6'	1.83
5'6"	1.68	6'1"	1.85

WHEN YOU WEIGH YOURSELF

1 kilogram (kilo) = 2.2 pounds
1 pound = 0.45 kilograms

KILOS	POUNDS	KILOS	POUNDS
40	88	75	165
45	99	80	176
50	110	85	187
55	121	90	198
60	132	95	209
65	143	100	220
70	154	105	231

LIQUID MEASUREMENTS

1 liter = 1.06 quarts
4 liters = 1.06 gallons
For quick, approximate conversions multiply the number of gallons by 4 to get liters (**litres**). Divide the number of liters by 4 to get gallons.

MINI-DICTIONARY FOR BUSINESS TRAVELERS

amount	le montant	*luh mohn-tahn*
appraise	évaluer	*ay-vah-lew-ay*
authorize	autoriser	*oh-toh-ree-zay*
authorized edition	l'édition autorisée (f.)	*lay-dee-ssyohn oh-toh-ree-zay*
bill (noun)	la facture	*lah fahk-tewr*

bill of exchange	la lettre de change	*lah leh-truh duh shah<u>n</u>zh*
bill of lading	le connaissement	*luh koh-nehss-mah<u>n</u>*
bill of sale	la lettre de vente	*lah leh-truh duh vah<u>n</u>t*
business operation	■ l'affaire (f.) ■ le commerce	*lah-fehr* *luh koh-mehrss*
cash (noun)	l'argent (m.)	*lahr-zhah<u>n</u>*
to buy for cash	payer comptant	*peh-yay koh<u>n</u>-tah<u>n</u>*
to sell for cash	vendre au comptant	*vah<u>n</u>-druh oh koh<u>n</u>-tah<u>n</u>*
to cash a check	toucher un chèque	*too-shay uh<u>n</u> shehk*
certified check	le chèque assuré	*luh shehk ah-ssew-ray*
chamber of commerce	la chambre de commerce	*lah shah<u>n</u>-bruh duh koh-mehrss*
compensation for damage	le dédommagement	*luh day-doh-mahzh-mah<u>n</u>*
competition	la concurrence	*lah koh<u>n</u>-kew-rah<u>n</u>ss*
competitive price	le prix de concurrence	*luh pree duh koh<u>n</u>-kew-rah<u>n</u>ss*
contract	le contrat	*luk koh<u>n</u>-trah*
contractual obligations	les obligations du contrat	*lay-zoh-blee-gah-ssyoh<u>n</u> dew koh<u>n</u>-trah*
controlling interest	le droit d'autorité	*luh drwah doh-toh-ree-tay*

co-owner	le co-propriétaire	*luh koh-proh-pree-ay-tehr*
copartner	le co-associé	*luh koh-ah-ssoh-ssyay*
down payment	■ l'acompte (m.) ■ payer en compte	*lah kohnt* *peh-yay ahn-kohnt*
due	■ échu ■ arrivé à l'échéance	*ay-shew* *ah-ree-vay ah lay-shay-ahnss*
enterprise	l'entreprise (f.)	*lahn-truh-preez*
expedite delivery (of letters)	expédier la livraison	*ehkss-pay-dee-ay lah lee-vreh-zohn*
expedite delivery (of goods)	expédier la distribution	*ehkss-pay-dee-ay lah deess-tree-bew-ssyohn*
expenses	les frais (m. pl.)	*lay freh*
goods	■ les produits ■ les biens (m. pl.)	*lay proh-dwee* *lay byan*
infringement of patent rights	l'infraction de bre-vet d'invention	*lan-frahk-ssyohn duh bruh-veh dan-vahn-ssyohn*
insurance against all risks	l'assurance contre tous risques	*lah-ssew-rahnss kohn-truh too reessk*
international law	le droit international	*luh drwah an-tehr-nah-ssyoh-nahl*
lawful possession	la possession légitime	*lah poh-sseh-ssyohn lay-zhee-teem*

lawsuit	le procès	*luh proh-sseh*
lawyer	l'avocat(e)	*lah-voh-kah(t)*
letter of credit	la lettre de crédit	*lah leh-truh duh kray-dee*
mail-order business	l'établissement de vente par correspondance (m.)	*lay-tah-bleess-mah<u>n</u> duh vah<u>n</u>t pahr koh-rehss-poh<u>n</u>-dah<u>n</u>ss*
market value	le cours du marché	*luh koor dew mahr-shay*
manager	le gérant	*luh zhay-rah<u>n</u>*
payment	le versement	*luh vehrss-mah<u>n</u>*
partial payment	l'acompte (m.)	*lah-koh<u>n</u>t*
past due	■ arriéré ■ en retard	*ah-ree-yay-ray* *ah<u>n</u> ruh-tahr*
post office box	la boîte postale	*lah bwaht pohss-tahl*
property	■ la propriété ■ les biens	*lah proh-pree-ay-tay* *lay bya<u>n</u>*
purchasing agent	l'acquéreur	*lah-kay-ruhr*
to put on the American market	mettre au marché américain	*meh-truh oh mahr-shay ah-may-ree-ka<u>n</u>*
sale	la vente	*lah vah<u>n</u>t*
to sell	vendre	*vah<u>n</u>-druh*
to send	envoyer	*ah<u>n</u>-vwah-yay*
to send back	renvoyer	*rah<u>n</u>-vwah-yay*

to send C.O.D.	envoyer payable à l'arrivée	*ahn-vwah-yay peh-yah-bluh ah lah-ree-vay*
shipment	l'expédition (f.)	*lehkss-pay-dee-ssyohn*
tax	l'impôt (m.)	*lan-poh*
tax-exempt	exempt d'impôts	*ehg-zahn dan-poh*
sales tax	la taxe de luxe	*lah tahkss duh lewkss*
value-added tax	la taxe sur la valeur ajoutée	*lah tahkss sewr lah vah-luhr ah-zhoo-tay*
trade	le commerce	*luh koh-mehrss*
transact business	faire des affaires	*fehr day-zah-fehr*
to transfer	transférer	*trahnss-fay-ray*
transportation charges	les frais de transport	*lay freh duh trahnss-pohr*
via	par	*pahr*
yield a profit	rendre un bénéfice	*rahn-druh uhn bay-nay-feess*

QUICK GRAMMAR GUIDE

NOUNS

1. All nouns in French have a gender (masculine or feminine) and a number (singular or plural).

2. There is no easy way to determine gender, so a noun must be learned with its identifying article and its gender memorized.

3. To change a singular noun to the plural, an unpronounced **S** is usually added. Add nothing if the noun ends in **S**, **X**, or **Z**.

ARTICLES

Articles agree in gender and number with the nouns they modify.

DEFINITE ARTICLES (THE)			
	MASC. (THE)		FEM. (THE)
SING.	LE	**le livre** the book	LA	**la carte** the map
PLUR.	LES	**les livres** the books	LES	**les cartes** the maps

NOTE: LE and LA become L' before a noun beginning with a vowel or an H: **l'avion**, **l'homme**.

INDEFINITE ARTICLES (A, AN, SOME)			
	MASC. (A, AN, SOME)		FEM. (A, AN, SOME)
SING.	UN	**un restaurant** a restaurant	UNE	**une voiture** a car
PLUR.	DES	**des restaurants** some restaurants	DES	**des voitures** some cars

THE PARTITIVE (SOME, ANY)		
SINGULAR		
DU (de + le) + masc. sing. noun with consonant	**du pain**	some bread
DE LA + fem. sing. noun with consonant	**de la glace**	some ice cream
DE L' + masc. or fem. sing. noun with vowel or "H"	**de l'eau**	some water
PLURAL		
DES (de + les) + all plural nouns	**des glaces**	some ice creams
NEGATIVE		
DE is used in negative sentences	**Je n'ai pas d'argent.**	I don't have any money.
	Elle n'a pas de cartes.	She doesn't have any maps.

NOTE: DE becomes D' before a vowel or a vowel sound (H, Y).

ADJECTIVES

1. Adjectives agree in number and gender with the nouns they modify.
2. To form the feminine of most adjectives, add **E** to the masculine form. If the masculine form ends in **E**, add nothing to get the feminine form.
3. To form the plural of most adjectives, add **S** to the singular form. If the singular form ends in **S**, add nothing to get the plural form.

un livre intéressant   une femme intéressant<u>e</u>
des livres intéressant<u>s</u> des femmes intéressant<u>es</u>

4. Adjectives usually follow the nouns they modify. A few common exceptions that precede the noun are: **bon/bonne** good; **grand/grande** big; **jeune** young; **joli/jolie** pretty; **petit/petite** small.

un grand appartement

POSSESSIVE ADJECTIVES

Possessive adjectives agree in number and gender with the object possessed, not with the possessor. They precede the noun.

ENGLISH	MASC. SING. OR FEM. SING. WITH VOWEL	FEM. SING. WITH CONS.	ALL PLURALS
my	mon	ma	mes
your	ton	ta	tes
his/her/its	son	sa	ses
our	notre	notre	nos
your	votre	votre	vos
their	leur	leur	leurs

EXAMPLES:

mon ami(e)	my friend	*ami(e) starts with vowel
ma chemise	my shirt	*chemise is fem. sing. with cons.
mes chemises	my shirts	
ton gant	your glove	*gant is masc. sing.
tes gants	your gloves	

NOTE: **sa valise** can mean his or her valise
son argent can mean his or her money
ses parents can mean his or her parents.

Another way to show possession is by using the preposition DE (OF) or any of its forms:

SINGULAR	PLURAL
DU masculine noun with consonant	DES all nouns
DE LA feminine noun with consonant	
DE L' masculine or feminine noun with vowel	
DE proper noun (name)	

EXAMPLES:

la valise de Paul	Paul's valise
l'argent de la femme	the woman's money
la soupe du garçon	the boy's soup
la chemise de l'homme	the man's shirt
les cartes des touristes	the tourists' maps

DEMONSTRATIVE ADJECTIVES (THIS/THAT; THESE/THOSE)

SINGULAR	
CE masc. noun with consonant	THIS/THAT
CET masc. noun with vowel or H	THIS/THAT
CETTE fem. noun	THIS/THAT
PLURAL	
CES all nouns	THESE/THOSE

EXAMPLES:

ce livre	this/that book
cet hôtel	this/that hotel
cette fille	this/that girl
cette eau	this/that water (**eau** is fem.)
ces arbres	these/those trees

PRONOUNS

Subject pronouns come at the beginning of the sentence before the verb.

Je parle	I speak
Nous sommes	We are

Direct object pronouns come before the verb except in an affirmative command when they come after the verb.

Il la voit.	He sees **it**.
Prenez-les!	Take **them**!

Indirect object pronouns come before the verb except in an affirmative command when they come after the verb.

Elle lui parle.	She speaks **to him** (**to her**).
Écrivez-leur!	Write **to them**!

Object of a preposition is a pronoun that comes after a preposition.

Après vous.	After you.
Avec eux.	With them.

SUBJECT	DIRECT OBJECT	INDIRECT OBJECT	OBJECT OF A PREPOSITION
Je I	**me** me	**me** to me	**moi** me
Tu You*	**te** you	**te** to you	**toi** you
Il He	**le** him	**lui** to him	**lui** him
Elle She	**la** her	**lui** to her	**elle** her
Nous We	**nous** us	**nous** to us	**nous** us
Vous You*	**vous** you	**vous** to you	**vous** you
Ils They m.	**les** them	**leur** to them	**eux** them
Elles They f.	**les** them	**leur** to them	**elles** them
On One			

*NOTE: Use **tu** for familiar conversation with a relative, a young child or a friend; **tu** is a singular subject pronoun only.

Use **vous** to be polite and to show respect when speaking to people with whom you are not intimate. **Vous** is a singular or plural subject or object pronoun and is used when addressing a group of people.

Use **ils** to refer to a group of males or to a mixed group consisting of males and females.

REGULAR VERBS

Regular verbs follow a specific pattern of conjugation (changing the verb to agree with the subject pronoun) depending upon the infinitive ending.

PRESENT TENSE			
	-ER ENDING	-IR ENDING	-RE ENDING
SUBJECT	PARLER	FINIR	VENDRE
	to speak	to finish	to sell
Je	parle	finis	vends
Tu	parles	finis	vends
Il/Elle	parle	finit	vend
Nous	parlons	finissons	vendons
Vous	parlez	finissez	vendez
Ils/Elles	parlent	finissent	vendent
COMMANDS	Parlez!	Finissez!	Vendez!

In order to conjugate a verb, the infinitive ending (-ER, -IR, -RE) must be removed and replaced by the appropriate ending found in the above table.

EXAMPLES:

désirer to desire, want	I desire	**Je désire**
choisir to choose	We choose	**Nous choisissons**
attendre to wait for	You wait for	**Vous attendez**

COMMON VERBS IN THE –ER FAMILY

admirer to admire	**donner** to give
aider to help	**écouter** to listen to
aimer to like, to love	**entrer** to enter
chercher to look for	**fermer** to close
coûter to cost	**fumer** to smoke
déjeuner to eat lunch	**marcher** to walk
demander to ask	**montrer** to show
dépenser to spend money	**penser** to think
désirer to wish, to desire	**regarder** to look at
dîner to eat dinner	**tourner** to turn
	trouver to find

COMMON VERBS IN THE -IR FAMILY

agir to act	**grossir** to become fat
avertir to warn	**maigrir** to become thin
choisir to choose	**nourrir** to feed
finir to finish	**obéir** to obey
grandir to grow	**remplir** to fill

COMMON VERBS IN THE -RE FAMILY

attendre to wait for	**pendre** to hang
correspondre to correspond	**perdre** to lose
défendre to defend	**rendre** to give back
descendre to descend	**répondre (à)** to answer
entendre to hear	**vendre** to sell

NOTE: Je + verb beginning with a vowel = J'

Je + écoute = J'écoute

Tu + vowel never drops the **u** from **tu**

Tu aimes le français

HELPING VERBS

The auxiliary verbs **avoir** (to have) and **être** (to be) must be memorized. They are used by themselves in the present or with other verbs to form compound tenses.

AVOIR—to have	
J'ai I have	**Nous avons** We have
Tu as you have	**Vous avez** You have
Il a he has	**Ils ont** They have
Elle a she has	**Elles ont** They have

ETRE—to be	
Je suis I am	**Nous sommes** We are
Tu es You are	**Vous êtes** You are
Il est He is	**Ils sont** They are
Elle est She is	**Elles sont** They are

IRREGULAR VERBS

Irregular verbs must be memorized. Here are some common irregular verbs that you will find helpful.

PRESENT TENSE			
SUBJECT	ALLER to go	FAIRE to make, do	POUVOIR can, be able to
Je	vais	fais	peux
Tu	vas	fais	peux
Il/Elle	va	fait	peut
Nous	allons	faisons	pouvons
Vous	allez	faites	pouvez
Ils/Elles	vont	font	peuvent
COMMAND	Allez!	Faites!	

PRESENT TENSE	
VOIR to see	VOULOIR to wish, want
vois	veux
vois	veux
voit	veut
voyons	voulons
voyez	voulez
voient	veulent
Voyez!	

The following verbs will also be helpful to you in a more limited sense.

SUBJECT	BOIRE to drink	DIRE to say	ÉCRIRE to write
Je	bois	dis	écris
Vous	buvez	dites	écrivez
COMMAND	Buvez!	Dites!	Écrivez!

SUBJECT	METTRE to put (on)	OUVRIR to open	RECEVOIR to receive
Je	mets	ouvre	reçois
Vous	mettez	ouvrez	recevez
COMMAND	Mettez!	Ouvrez!	Recevez!

REFLEXIVE VERBS

Reflexive verbs show that the subject is acting upon itself. Reflexive verbs consist of a reflexive pronoun and a conjugated verb. Reflexive pronouns agree with their subjects.

JE	ME		NOUS	NOUS
TU	TE		VOUS	VOUS

IL SE	ILS SE
ELLE SE	ELLES SE

NOTE: ME, TE, and SE become M', T', and S' before a vowel or an H.

Verbs that are reflexive in French are not necessarily reflexive in English. Common reflexive verbs are:

s'appeler   to call oneself, to be called

s'asseoir   to sit down

se coucher   to go to bed

se dépêcher   to hurry up

s'habiller   to get dressed

se laver   to wash oneself

se lever   to get up

se peigner   to comb one's hair

se promener   to go for a walk

se raser   to shave oneself

se réveiller   to wake up

Follow this formula:

SUBJECT	REFLEXIVE PRONOUN	VERB
Je	**m'**	**appelle** My name is (I call myself)
Nous	**nous**	**réveillons** We wake up
Tu NE	**te**	**rases PAS** You don't shave

NOTE: A verb is reflexive only if the subject is acting upon itself. If the subject is acting upon another person or thing, the verb is NOT reflexive.

EXAMPLE:

Je me lave.	I wash myself.
Je lave l'enfant.	I wash the child.
Je lave la voiture.	I wash the car.

The infinitive of a reflexive verb is always preceded by the pronoun SE.

NEGATIVES

Form the negative by putting NE before the conjugated verb, and PAS (not) after the verb.

OTHER NEGATIVE CONSTRUCTIONS

NE . . . **RIEN** nothing

NE . . . **JAMAIS** never

NE . . . **PERSONNE** nobody

NE . . . **PLUS** no longer

NOTE: NE becomes N' before a vowel or H.

Il parle anglais.	**Il ne parle pas anglais.**
He speaks English.	He doesn't speak English.
Je veux manger.	**Je ne veux plus manger.**
I want to eat.	I don't want to eat any more.
Elle écoute.	**Elle n'écoute rien.**
She listens.	She doesn't listen to anything.

QUESTIONS

The four most common ways to ask a yes/no question are:

1. Raise your voice at the end of a phrase.
   Vous parlez francais?

2. Add the tag n'est-ce pas (isn't that so?) at the end of a phrase:
   Vous parlez français, n'est-ce pas?

3. Put EST-CE QUE *(ehss-kuh)* in front of a phrase.
   Vous parlez anglais.   **Est-ce que vous parlez anglais?**

4. Invert the order of the subject pronoun (ONLY) and the verb.
   Vous parlez anglais.   **Parlez-vous anglais?**

NOTE: a) Do NOT invert with the pronoun JE. Use EST-CE QUE.
   b) If the verb ends in a vowel and the pronoun begins with a vowel
   (IL or ELLE) then –t– must separate the two vowels.

   Il parle anglais.   **Parle-t-il anglais?**

   Elle a une voiture.   **A-t-elle une voiture?**

To ask for information:

1. Put the information word at the end of the phrase:
   Vous arrivez quand?

2. Use the information word + EST-CE QUE at the beginning of the sentence:
   Quand est-ce que vous arrivez?

3. Use the information word followed by inversion:
   Quand arrivez-vous?

PREPOSITIONS

Study the list of the following prepositions. The prepositions **à** (to, at) and **de** (of, from) have contracted forms.

a + le = au	**de + le = du**
à + les = aux	**de + les = des**
à la (no change)	**de la** (no change)
à l' (no change)	**de l'** (no change)

EXAMPLES:

to the movies	**au cinéma**
to the museums	**aux musées**
to the kitchen	**à la cuisine**
of the boy	**du garçon**
of the children	**des enfants**
of the year	**de l'année**

COMMON PREPOSITIONS

about	**de**	*duh*
according to	**selon**	*suh-lohn*
across	**à travers**	*ah trah-vehr*
after	**après**	*ah-preh*
among	**parmi**	*pahr-mee*
around	**autour de**	*oh-toor duh*
at	**à**	*ah*
at the house of	**chez**	*shay*
before	**avant**	*ah-vahn*
behind	**derrière**	*deh-ryehr*

between	**entre**	*ah<u>n</u>-truh*
by	**par**	*pahr*
down/downstairs	**en bas**	*ah<u>n</u> bah*
during	**pendant**	*pah<u>n</u>-dah<u>n</u>*
except	**sauf**	*sohf*
for	**pour**	*poor*
from	**de**	*duh*
in	**dans, en**	*dah<u>n</u>, ah<u>n</u>*
in front of	**devant**	*duh-vah<u>n</u>*
in order to	**pour**	*poor*
inside	**dedans**	*duh-dah<u>n</u>*
on	**sur**	*sewr*
opposite	**en face de**	*ah<u>n</u> fahss duh*
outside	**dehors**	*duh-ohr*
through	**à travers**	*ah trah-vehr*
to	**à**	*ah*
toward	**vers**	*vehr*
under	**sous**	*soo*
until	**jusqu'à**	*zhewss-kah*
up/upstairs	**en haut**	*ah<u>n</u> oh*
with	**avec**	*ah-vehk*
without	**sans**	*sah<u>n</u>*

ENGLISH-FRENCH DICTIONARY*

A

a, an un (m.) *uhn*, une (f.) *ewn*

able: to be able pouvoir *poo-vwahr*

about à peu près *ah-puh-preh*; environ *ahn-vee-rohn*

above dessus *duh-ssew*

abroad à l'étranger *ah lay-trahn-zhay*

according to selon *suh-lohn*

accountant comptable *kohn-tah-bluh*

ache (noun) le mal *luh mahl*; **(head)** mal de tête *mahl duh teht*; **(stomach)** mal d'estomac *mahl dehss-toh-mah*; **(tooth)** mal de dents *mahl duh dahn*

acquaintance: make the . . . of faire la connaissance de *fehr lah koh-neh-ssahnss duh*

across à travers *ah trah-vehr*

add ajouter *ah-zhoo-tay*

address une adresse *ewn ah-drehss*

adjust arranger *ah-rahn-zhay*

advertisement une réclame *ewn ray-klahm*; une annonce *ewn ah-nohnss*

advice l'avis (m.) *lah-vee*; le conseil *luh kohn-sschy*

advise conseiller *kohn-say-yay*

aerobics de l'aérobic (m.) *duh lahy-roh-beek*

afraid: to be afraid of avoir peur de *ah-vwahr puhr duh*

after après *ah-preh*

afternoon l'après-midi (m.) *lah-preh mee-dee*

again encore une fois *ahn-kohr ewn fwah*

against contre *kohn-truh*

agency une agence *ewn ah-zhahnss*; **(travel)** une agence de voyage *ewn ah-zhahnss duh vwah-yahzh*

ago il y a + time *eel yah*

agree être d'accord *eh-truh dah-kohr*

air conditioner le climatiseur *luh klee-mah-tee-zuhr*

air mail par avion *pahr ah-vyohn*

airplane un avion *uhn nah-vyohn*

airport un aéroport *uhn nahy-roh-pohr*

alcohol l'alcool (m.) *lahl-kol*

all tout (m.), toute (f.) *too, toot*

allergic allergique *ah-lehr-zheek*

alley la ruelle *lah rew-ehl*

almond une amande *ewn ah-mahnd*

almost presque *prehss-kuh*

alone seul(e) *suhl*

already déjà *day-zhah*

also aussi *oh-ssee*

always toujours *too-zhoor*

ambulance une ambulance *ewn ahn-bew-lahnss*

among parmi *pahr-mee*

and et *ay*

ankle la cheville *lah shuh-vee*

annoy gêner *zheh-nay*; ennuyer *ahn-nwee-yay*

answer (noun) la réponse *lah ray-pohnss*; **(verb)** répondre *ray-pohn-druh*

---

*Underscored letters indicate nasals.

answering machine le répondeur automatique *luh ray-pohn-duhr oh-toh-mah-teek*

antiseptic un antiseptique *uhn nahn-tee-ssehp-teek*

any ne . . . aucun(e) *nuh . . . oh-kuhn, oh-kewn*

appendicitis l'appendicite *lah-pahn-dee-sseet*

apple la pomme *lah pohm*

apricot un abricot *uhn nah-bree-koh*

argument la dispute *lah deess-pewt*

arm le bras *luh brah*

around autour de *oh-toor duh*

arrival l'arrivée (f.) *lah-ree-vay*

artichoke l'artichaut *lahr-tee-shoh*

artificial sweetener le sucre artificiel *luh sew-kruh ahr-tee-fee-syehl*

artist (m. and f.) artiste *ahr-teesst*

ashtray le cendrier *luh ssahn-dree-yay*

ask demander *duh-mahn-day*

asparagus l'asperge (f.) *lahss-pehrzh*

asthma l'asthme (m.) *lahs-muh*

at à *ah*

ATM le guichet automatique *luh gee-sheh oh-toh-mah-teek*

August août *oo*

author l'auteur (m.) *loh-tuhr*

avoid éviter *ay-vee-tay*

awaken réveiller *ray-veh-yay*

B

back (noun) le dos *luh doh;* **in back of** derrière *deh-ryehr*

backup disk la copie de sauvegarde *lah koh-pee duh sohv-gahrd*

backward en arrière *ahn nah-ryehr*

bacon le lard *luh lahr*

bad mauvais(e) *moh-veh(z)*

badly mal *mahl*

bag le sac *luh sahk*

baggage room la consigne *lah kohn-ssee-nyuh*

baked au four *oh foor*

baked Alaska (f.) l'omelette norvégienne *lohm-leht nohr-vay-zhyehn*

bakery la boulangerie *lah boo-lahn-zhree*

balcony le balcon *luh bahl-kohn*

ballet le ballet *luh bah-leh*

banana la banane *lah bah-nahn*

bandage (noun) la bande *lah bahnd*

bank la banque *lah bahnk*

bank [branch] la succursale *lah sew-kewr-ssahl*

banking window le guichet *luh gee-sheh*

bar le bistro *luh beess-troh*

barber le coiffeur *luh kwah-fuhr*

bargain (noun) l'occasion *loh-kah-zyohn*

basket le panier *luh pah-nyay*

bath le bain *luh ban*

bathe se baigner *suh beh-nyay*

bathing suit le maillot de bain *luh mah-yoh duh ban*

bathrobe la robe de chambre *lah rohb duh shahn-bruh*

bathroom la salle de bains *lah sahl duh ban*

battery la batterie *lah bah-tree;* la pile *lah peel*

be être *eh-truh*

beach la plage *lah plahzh*

bean le haricot *luh ah-ree-koh*

beard la barbe *lah bahrb*

beautiful beau (m.) *boh,* belle (f.) *behl*

beauty salon   le salon de beauté *luh sah-lohn duh boh-tay*

because   parce que *pahrss kuh*

become   devenir *duh-vuh-neer*

bed   le lit *luh lee*

bedroom   la chambre à coucher *lah shahn-bruh ah koo-shay*

beef (noun)   le bœuf *luh buhf*

beer   la bière *lah byehr*

beet   la betterave *lah beht-rahv*

before   avant *ah-vahn*

begin   commencer (à) *koh-mahn-ssay (ah)*

behind   en arrière *ahn nah-ryehr*; derrière *deh-ryehr*

beige   beige *behzh*

believe   croire *krwahr*

bell   la cloche *lah klohsh*

bellboy   le chasseur *luh shah-ssuhr*

belong   appartenir *ah-pahr-tuh-neer*

belt   la ceinture *lah-san-tewr*; **seat belt**   la ceinture de sécurité *lah san-tewr duh say-kew-ree-tay*

bench   le banc *luh bahn*

beneath   dessous *duh-ssoo*

berth   la couchette *lah koo-sheht*

beside   à côté de *ah koh-tay duh*

better (adj.)   meilleur(e) *meh-yuhr*

better (adv.)   mieux *myuh*

between   entre *ahn-truh*

big   grand(e) *grahn(d)*

bill   la facture *lah fahk-tewr*; la note *lah noht*

birthday   l'anniversaire (m.) *lah-nee-vehr-ssehr*

bitter   amer(ère) *ah-mehr*

black   noir(e) *nwahr*

blanket   la couverture *lah koo-vehr-tewr*

blood   le sang *luh sahn*

blood test   analyse (f.) de sang *ah-nah-leez duh sahn*

blouse   la chemisier *luh shuh-mee-zyay*

blue   bleu *bluh*; **navy blue**   bleu marine *bluh mah-reen*

boat   le bateau *luh bah-toh*; **boating**   le canotage *luh kah-noh-tahzh*

body   le corps *luh kohr*

bodybuilding   la musculation *lah mew-skew-lah ssyohn*

boiled   bouilli(e) *boo-yee*

bone   l'os (m.) *lohss*

book   le livre *luh lee-vruh*

bookstore   la librairie *lah lee-breh-ree*

boots   les bottes (f.) *lay boht*

boot (v.)   démarrer *day-mah-ray*

border   la frontière *lah frohn-tyehr*

borrow   emprunter *ahn-pruhn-tay*

boss   le patron *luh pah-trohn*; le propriétaire *luh proh-pree-ay-tehr*

bother   gêner *geh-nay*; ennuyer *ahn-nwee-yay*

bottle   la bouteille *lah boo-tehy*

bowl   un bol *uhn bohl*

box   la boîte *lah bwaht*

box office   le bureau de location *luh bew-roh duh loh-kah-ssyohn*

boy   le garçon *luh gahr-ssohn*

bra   le soutien-gorge *luh soo-tyan gohrzh*

braised   braisé *breh-zay*

brakes   les freins (m. pl.) *lay fran*

brand   la marque *lah mahrk*

bread   le pain *luh pan*; **French**   la baguette *lah bah-geht*; **pumpernickel**   le pain bis *luh pan bee*; **rye**   le pain de seigle *luh pan duh seh-gluh*;

white le pain blanc *luh pan blahn*; **whole wheat** le pain de froment *luh pan duh froh-mahn*

break briser *bree-zay*; casser *kah-ssay*

breakdown (auto) la panne *lah pahn*; **broken down** en panne *ahn pahn*

breakfast le petit déjeuner *luh puh-tee day-zhuh-nay*

bridge le pont *luh pohn*

bring apporter *ah-pohr-tay*

broiled grillé *gree-yay*

brother le frère *luh frehr*

brown brun(e) *bruhn (brewn)*; marron *mah-rohn*; **browned** gratiné *grah-tee-nay*

bruise (noun) la contusion *lah kohn-tew-zyohn*

brush (noun) la brosse *lah brohss*; **(verb)** brosser *broh-ssay*; **toothbrush** la brosse à dents *lah brohss ah dahn*

Brussels sprouts les choux (m. pl.) de Bruxelles *lay shoo duh brewk-ssehl*

building le bâtiment *luh bah-tee-mahn*

bulb (electric) l'ampoule (f.) *lahn-pool*

bumper le pare-choc *luh pahr-shohk*

bun (roll) la brioche *lah bree-ohsh*

burn (noun) la brûlure *lah brew-lewr*; **(verb)** brûler *brew-lay*

bus l'autobus *loh-toh-bewss*; **bus station** la gare routière *lah gahr roo-tyehr*; **bus stop** l'arrêt de bus (m.) *lah-reh duh bewss*

businessperson homme (femme) d'affaires *ohm (fehm) dah-fehr*

busy occupé(e) *oh-kew-pay*

but mais *meh*

butcher shop la boucherie *lah boosh-ree*

butter le beurre *luh buhr*

button le bouton *luh boo-tohn*

buy acheter *ahsh-tay*

by par *pahr*; en *ahn*

C

cabbage le chou *luh shoo*

cake le gâteau *luh gah-toh*

call (verb) appeler *ah-play*

camera l'appareil (m.) photographique *lah-pah-rehy foh-toh-grah-feek*

can (verb) pouvoir *poo-vwahr*

candle la bougie *lah boo-zhee*

candy store la confiserie *lah kohn-feess-ree*

cane une canne *ewh kahn*

car la voiture *lah vwah-tewr*

carburetor le carburateur *luh kahr-bew-rah-tuhr*

card la carte *lah kahrt*; **credit card** la carte de crédit *lah kahrt duh kray-dee*; **debit card** la carte de débit *la kahrt duh day-bee*; **identification card** la carte d'identité *lah kahrt dee-dahn-tee-tay*

care le soin *luh swan*

carefully avec soin *ah-vehk swan*

carefulness la prudence *lah prew-dahnss*

carrot la carotte *lah kah-roht*

carry porter *pohr-tay*; **carry away** emporter *ahn-pohr-tay*

cashier le caissier *luh kehss-yay*

cash register la caisse *lah kehss*

castle le château *luh shah-toh*

cat le chat *luh shah*

catch attraper *ah-trah-pay*

caution attention *ah-tahn-ssyohn*

CD player le lecteur de CD *luh lehk-tuhr duh say-day*

ceiling le plafond *luh plah-fohn*

cell phone le portable *luh pohr-tah-bluh*

cellar la cave *lah kahv*

cemetery le cimetière *luh seem-tyehr*

chain (jewelry) la chaînette *lah sheh-neht*

chair la chaise *lah shehz*

change (noun) le changement *luh shahnzh-mahn*; **money** la monnaie *lah moh-nay*

change (verb) changer *shahn-zhay*; **change plane or train** faire la correspondance *fehr lah koh-rehss-pohn-dahnss*

charge (noun) les frais (m. pl.) *lay freh*

charge (verb) charger *shahr-zhay*

charm (noun) le porte-bonheur *luh pohrt boh-nuhr*

cheap bon marché *bohn mahr-shay*; **cheaper** meilleur marché *meh-yuhr mahr-shay*

check (noun) (restaurant) l'addition (f.) *lah-dee-ssyohn*; **(money)** le chèque *luh shehk*; **traveler's check** le chèque de voyage *luh shehk duh vwah-yahzh*; **cash a check** toucher un chèque *too-shay uhn shehk*; encaisser un chèque *ahn-keh-ssay uhn shehk*

check (verb) vérifier *vay-ree-fyay*; **check bags** enregistrer *ahn-ruh-zheess-tray*

checked (material) à carreaux *ah kah-roh*

cheek la joue *lah zhoo*

cheese le fromage *luh froh-mahzh*

cherry la cerise *lah suh-reez*

chest la poitrine *lah pwah-treen*

chicken le poulet *luh poo-leh*

chick-peas les pois (m. pl.) chiches *lay pwah sheesh*

chiffon la mousseline de soie *lah mooss-leen duh swah*

child l'enfant (m./f.) *lahn-fahn*

chin le menton *luh mahn-tohn*

chip la puce *lah pews*

choose choisir *shwah-zeer*

chop (noun) la côtelette *lah koht-leht*

church l'église (f.) *lay-gleez*; le temple (Prot.) *luh tahn-pluh*

cigar le cigare *luh see-gahr*

cigarette la cigarette *lah see-gah-reht*

cigarette lighter le briquet *luh bree-keh*

city la ville *la veel*

clam la palourde *lah pah-loord*

clean (verb) nettoyer *neh-twah-yay*

clean (adj.) propre *proh-pruh*; **dry cleaner's** la teinturerie *lah tan-tew-ruh-ree*; **dry-clean** nettoyer à sec *neh-twah-yay ah-sehk*

click (verb) cliquer *klee-kay*

clipboard le presse-papiers *luh prehss-pah-pyay*

clock la pendule *lah pahn-dewl*; l'horloge (f.) *lohr-lohzh*; **alarm clock** le réveil *luh ray-vehy*

close (verb) fermer *fehr-may*

closet l'armoire (f.) *lahr-mwahr*

clothes les habits (m. pl.) *lay zah-bee*; les vêtements (m. pl.) *lay veht-mahn*

coast la côte *lah koht*

coat le manteau *luh mahn-toh*;
    coat check le vestiaire *luh
    vehss-tyehr*

coconut la noix de coco *lah
    nwah duh koh-koh*

coffee le café *luh kah-fay*;
    black le café noir *luh kah-
    fay nwahr*; **with cream** le
    café crème *luh kah-fay krehm*;
    decaffeinated décaféiné
    day-kah-fay-ee-nay; **iced** le
    café glacé *luh kah-fay glah-
    ssay*; **with milk** le café au
    lait *luh kah-fay oh leh*;
    espresso le café express
    luh kah-fay ehkss-prehss

cold (noun) (weather) le
    froid *luh frwah*; **(verb) to be
    cold (weather)** faire froid
    fehr frwah; **to be cold
    (person)** avoir froid *ah-
    vwahr frwah*

cold (noun) (respiratory) le
    rhume *luh rewm*

cold cuts la charcuterie *lah
    shahr-kew-tree*

collar le col *luh kohl*

color la couleur *lah koo-luhr*

comb le peigne *luh peh-nyuh*

come venir *vuh-neer*; **come
    back** revenir *ruh-vuh-neer*

company la compagnie *lah
    kohn-pah-nyee*

complaint la plainte *lah plant*

computer l'ordinateur (m.)
    lohr-dee-nah-tuhr

computerize (verb)
    informatiser *an-fohr-mah-
    tee-zay*

computer science
    l'informatique (f.) *lan-fohr-
    mah-teek*

concert le concert *luh kohn-
    ssehr*; **concert hall** la salle
    de concert *lah sahl duh
    kohn-ssehr*

condom le préservatif *luh
    pray-zehr-vah-teef*

conductor le contrôleur *luh
    kohn-troh-luhr*

congratulations félicitations
    fay-lee-ssee-tah-ssoyhn

connect relier *ruh-lee-yay*

contact lens le verre de
    contact *luh vehr duh kohn-
    tahkt*

contagious contagieux(ieuse)
    kohn-tah-zhuh(z)

contain contenir *kohn-tuh-
    neer*

contents le contenu *luh
    kohnt-new*

cook (noun) le cuisinier *luh
    kwee-zee-nyay*

cooked cuit(e) *kwee(t)*

cookie le biscuit *luh beess-kwee*

cooking la cuisine *lah kwee-
    zeen*

corduroy le velours côtelé *luh
    vuh-loor koht-lay*

corkscrew le tire-bouchon *luh
    teer boo-shohn*

corn le maïs *luh mah-eess*

corner le coin *luh kwan*

cost coûter *koo-tay*

costly coûteux(euse) *koo-tuh(z)*

cotton le coton *luh koh-tohn*;
    absorbent cotton l'ouate
    (f.) *lwaht*

cough (noun) la toux *lah too*;
    cough drops les pastilles
    contre la toux *lay pahss-teey
    kohn-truh lah too*; **cough
    syrup** le sirop contre la
    toux *luh see-roh kohn-truh
    lah too*

cough (verb) tousser *too-ssay*

count (verb) compter *kohn-
    tay*

country (nation) le pays *luh
    pay-ee*; la campagne *lah
    kahn-pah-nyuh*

countryside le paysage *luh pay-ee-zahzh*

courtyard la cour *lah koor*

cover (verb) couvrir *koo-vreer*

cover charge le couvert *luh koo-vehr*

crab le crabe *luh krahb*

cramp la crampe *lah krahnp*

cream la crème *lah krehm*; **whipped cream** la crème fouettée *lah krehm foo-eh-tay*

CPU l'unité centrale (f.) *lew-nee-tay sahn-trahl*

crib le berceau *luh behr-soh*

cross (verb) traverser *trah-vehr-ssay*

crust la croûte *lah kroot*

crutches les béquilles (f.) *lay bay-kee*

cry pleurer *pluh-ray*

cucumber le concombre *luh kohn-kohn-bruh*

cup la tasse *lah tahss*

cursor le curseur *luh kuhr-suhr*

custard le flan *luh flahn*

customer le client *luh klee-ahn*

customs la douane *lah dwahn*

customs official le douanier *luh dwah-nyay*

cut couper *koo-pay*

D

daily quotidien(ne) *koh-tee-dyan (yehn)*

dance (noun) la danse *lah dahnss*

dance (verb) danser *dahn-ssay*

dangerous dangereux(-euse) *dahn-zhuh-ruh(z)*

dark (color) foncé(e) *fohn-ssay*

database la base de données *lah bahz duh doh-nay*

date la date *lah daht*

date (fruit) la datte *lah daht*

daughter la fille *lah feey*

day le jour *luh zhoor*; **day before yesterday** avant-hier *ah-vahn-tyehr*; **day after tomorrow** après-demain *ah-preh-duh-man*

dear cher, chère *shehr*

deceive tromper *trohn-pay*

decide décider *day-ssee-day*

declare déclarer *day-klah-ray*

delay le retard *luh ruh-tahr*

delicatessen la charcuterie *lah shahr-kew-tree*

deliver livrer *lee-vray*

denim jean *zheen*

dentist dentiste (m. f.) *dahn-teesst*

deodorant le déodorant *luh day-oh-doh-rahn*

department (in store) le rayon *luh reh-yohn*

deserve mériter *may-ree-tay*

desire désirer *day-zee-ray*

desk le bureau *luh bew-roh*

detective story le roman policier *luh roh-mahn poh-lee-ssyay*

diabetes la diabète *lah dee-yah-beht*

diaper la couche *lah koosh*

dictionary le dictionnaire *luh deek-ssyoh-nehr*

different différent(e) *dee-fay-rahn(t)*

difficult difficile *dee-fee-sseel*

diminish diminuer *dee-mee-new-ay*

dine dîner *dee-nay*

dining car le wagon-restaurant *luh vah-gohn rehss-toh-rahn*

dining room la salle à manger *lah sahl ah mahn-zhay*

dirty sale *sahl*

disappointed déçu(e) *day-ssew*

disco(theque) la disco(thèque) *lah deess-koh(tehk)*

discount la reduction *lah ray-dewk-ssyohn*

dish (of food) le plat *luh plah*; **plate** l'assiette *lah-ssyeht*; **disposable** jetable *zheh-tah-bluh*

distance le trajet *luh trah-zheh*

district le quartier *luh kahr-tyay*

diving le plongeon *luh plohn-zhohn*; **diving suit** le scaphandre *luh skah-fahn-druh*

do faire *fehr*

doctor le docteur *luh dohk-tuhr*; le médecin *luh mayd-ssan*

dog le chien *luh shyan*

door la porte *lah pohrt*

down: to go down descendre *day-ssahn-druh*

download télécharger *tay-lay-shahr-zhay*

downstairs en bas *ahn bah*

dozen la douzaine *lah doo-zehn*

dress (noun) la robe *lah rohb*

dress (verb) s'habiller *sah-bee-yay*

dressing room le vestiaire *luh vehss-tyehr*

drink (noun) la boisson *lah bwah-ssohn*; la consommation *lah kohn-ssoh-mah-ssyohn*; **soft drink** la boisson non-alcoolisée *lah bwah-ssohn nohn nahl-koh-lee-zay*

drink (verb) boire *bwahr*

drinkable potable *poh-tah-bluh*; **undrinkable** non potable *nohn poh-tah-bluh*

drive conduire *kohn-dweer*

driver's license le permis de conduire *luh pehr-mee duh kohn-dweer*

drunk ivre *ee-vruh*; soûl(e) *soo*

dry (adj.) sec (sèche) *sehk (sehsh)*

dry (verb) sécher *say-shay*

duck le canard *luh kah-nahr*

during pendant *pahn-dahn*

E

each chaque *shahk*

each one chacun(e) *shah-kuhn (kewn)*

ear l'oreille (f.) *loh-rehy*

early tôt *toh*; de bonne heure *duh bohn-uhr*

earn gagner *gah-nyay*

earring la boucle d'oreille *lah boo-kluh doh-rehy*

east l'est *lehsst*

easy facile *fah-sseel*

eat manger *mahn-zhay*

egg l'oeuf *luhf*; **eggs** les oeufs *lay zuh*; **fried** au plat *oh plah*; **hard-boiled** durs *dewr*; **medium-boiled** mollets *moh-leh*; **poached** pochés *poh-shay*; **soft-boiled** à la coque *ah lah kohk*; **sunny-side up** poêlés *pwah-lay*; **scrambled** brouillés *broo-yay*

eggplant l'aubergine (f.) *loh-behr-zheen*

eight huit *weet*

eighteen dix-huit *deez weet*

eighty quatre-vingts *kah-truh van*

elbow le coude *luh kood*

elevator l'ascenseur (m.) *lah-ssahn-ssuhr*

eleven onze *ohnz*

elsewhere ailleurs *ah-yuhr*

e-mail le e-mail *luh ee-mehl*

emergency le cas urgent *luh kah zewr-zhahn*; **in case of emergency** en cas d'urgence *ahn kah dewr-zhahnss*

empty vide *veed*

end (noun) la fin *lah fan*

end (verb) finir *fee-neer*

endorse endosser *ahn-doh-ssay*

English anglais (m.) *ahn-gleh*

enlarge élargir *ay-lahr-zheer*

enough assez (de) *ah-ssay (duh)*
enter entrer *ahn-tray*
entire entier(ière) *ahn-tyay (yehr)*
entrance l'entrée (f.) *lahn-tray*
envelope l'enveloppe (f.) *lahn-vlohp*
eraser la gomme *lah gohm*
especially surtout *sewr-too*
evening la soirée *lah swah-ray*
evening gown la robe de soir *lah rohb duh swahr*
every tout(e) *too(t)*; **chaque** *shahk*; **everybody** tout le monde *too luh mohnd*; **every day** tous les jours *too lay zhoor*; **everywhere** partout *pahr-too*
example l'exemple (m.) *lehg-zahn-pluh*; **for example** par exemple *pahr ehg-zahn-pluh*
excellent excellent(e) *ehkss-eh-lahn(t)*
exchange échanger *ay-shahn-zhay*; **exchange office** le bureau de change *luh bew-roh duh shahnzh*; **exchange rate** le cours du change *luh koor dew shahnzh*
excursion l'excursion (f.) *lehkss-kewr-zyohn*
excuse (verb) pardonner *pahr-doh-nay*; **excuse me** pardon *pahr-dohn*; excusez-moi *ehkss-kew-zay mwah*
exhaust l'echappement (m.) *lay-shahp-mahn*
exhausted épuisé(e) *ay-pwee-zay*
exit la sortie *lah sohr-tee*
expense les frais (m. pl.) *lay freh*
expensive cher, chère *shehr*
express express *ehkss-prehss*
eye l'oeil (m.) *luhy*; **eyes** les yeux (m. pl.) *lay zyuh*

eyebrow le sourcil *luh soor-ssee*
eyeglasses les lunettes (f. pl.) *lay lew-neht*
eyelash le cil *luh seel*
eyelid la paupière *lah poh-pyehr*
eyeliner le traceur à paupières *luh trah-ssuhr ah poh-pyehr*
eye shadow le fard à paupières *luh fahr ah poh-pyehr*

F

face (noun) la figure *lah fee-gewr*; le visage *luh vee-zahzh*
facing en face de *ahn fahss duh*
factory l'usine (f.) *lew-zeen*
fall tomber *tohn-bay*; **fall sick** tomber malade *tohn-bay mah-lahd*
fair (market) la foire *lah fwahr*
false faux (fausse) *foh (fohss)*
family la famille *lah fah-meey*
fan le ventilateur *luh vahn-tee-lah-tuhr*
fan belt la courroie de ventilateur *lah koor-wah duh vahn-tee-lah-tuhr*
far (from) loin de *lwan duh*
farm la ferme *lah fehrm*
fast rapide *rah-peed*; vite *veet*
fat gros(se) *groh(ss)*
father le père *luh pere*
faucet le robinet *luh roh-bee-neh*
fax le fax *luh fahkss*
fear la peur *lah puhr*; **to be afraid** avoir peur *ah-vwahr puhr*
February février *fay-vree-yay*
feel (se) sentir *(suh) sahn-teer*
felt le feutre *luh fuh-truh*
fender l'aile (f.) *lehl*
festival la fête *lah feht*
fever la fièvre *lah fyeh-vruh*; **hay fever** le rhume des foins *luh rewm day fwan*

few peu de *puh duh*; **a few** quelques *kehl-kuh*

field le champ *luh shahn*

fifteen quinze *kanz*

fifty cinquante *san-kahnt*

fig la figue *lah feeg*

figure (body) la taille *lah tahy*

file (noun) le fichier *luh feesh-yay*

fill (out) remplir *rahn-pleer*

film le film *luh feelm*; la pellicule *lah peh-lee-kewl*

finger le doigt *luh dwah*

finish finir *fee-neer*; terminer *tehr-mee-nay*

fire le feu *luh fuh*; l'incendie (m.) *lan-sahn-dee*

first premier(ière) *pruh-myay (yehr)*; **at first** d'abord *dah-bohr*; **first aid** le premier secours *luh pruh-myay suh-koor*

fish (noun) le poisson *luh pwah-ssohn*

fish (verb) pêcher *peh-shay*

fishing la pêche *lah pehsh*; **deep-sea fishing** la pêche sous-marine *lah pehsh soo-mah-reen*; **fishing rod** la canne à pêche *lah kahn ah pehsh*

five cinq *sank*

flannel la flanelle *lah flah-nehl*

flashlight la lampe de poche *lah lahnp duh pohsh*

flat plat(te) *plah(t)*

flavor le parfum *luh pahr-fuhn*

flight le vol *luh vohl*

floor le plancher *luh plahn-shay*; **(story)** l'étage (m.) *lay-tahzh*

florist le fleuriste *luh fluh-reesst*

flounder la sole *lah sohl*

flower la fleur *lah fluhr*

flu la grippe *lah greep*

fly (verb) voler *voh-lay*

follow suivre *swee-vruh*; **following** suivant(e) *swee-vahn(t)*

food les aliments (m. pl.) *lay zah-lee-mahn*; la nourriture *lah noo-ree-tewr*

food processor le robot ménager *luh roh-boh may-nah-zhay*

foot le pied *luh pyay*

for pour *poor*

forbid interdire *an-tehr-deer*; défendre *day-fahn-druh*; **forbidden** interdit(e) *an-tehr-dee(t)*; défendu(e) *day-fahn-dew*; **it is forbidden to** défense de *day-fahnss duh*

forehead le front *luh frohn*

foreign étranger(ère) *ay-trahn-zhay (zhehr)*

forest la forêt *lah foh-reh*

forget oublier *oo-blee-yay*

fork la fourchette *lah foor-sheht*

form (noun) la fiche *lah feesh*; la formule *lah fohr-mewl*

former ancien(ne) *ahn-ssyan (ssyehn)*

forty quarante *kah-rahnt*

forward (adv.) en avant *ahn nah-vahn*

fountain la fontaine *lah fohn-tehn*

four quatre *kah-truh*

fourteen quatorze *kah-tohrz*

free libre *lee-bruh*; **for free** gratuit(e) *grah-twee(t)*; **free of charge (adv.)** gratuitement *grah-tweet-mahn*

French le français *luh frahn-sseh*

fresh frais, fraîche *freh, frehsh*

Friday vendredi *vahn-druh-dee*

fried frit(e) *free(t)*

friend ami(e) *ah-mee*

frog's legs les cuisses (f. pl.) de grenouille *lay kweess duh gruh-nuhy*

front: in front of devant *duh-vahn*

fruit le fruit *luh frwee*

fruit salad la macédoine de fruits *lah mah-ssay-dwahn duh frwee*

fuel pump la pompe à essence *lah pohmp ah eh-ssahnss*

function (verb) fonctionner *fohnk-ssyoh-nay*

furnished meublé(e) *muh-blay*

G

gabardine la gabardine *lah gah-bahr-deen*

game le jeu *luh zhuh*; la partie *lah pahr-tee*

game (meat) le gibier *luh zhee-byay*

garden le jardin *luh zhahr-dan*

garlic l'ail (m.) *lahy*

gas l'essence (f.) *leh-ssahnss*

gas station le poste d'essence *luh pohsst deh-ssahnss*; la station-service *lah stah-ssyohn sehr-veess*

gas tank le réservoir à essence *luh ray-zehr-vwahr ah eh-ssahnss*

gears l'engrenage (m.) *lahn-gruh-nahzh*

gear shift le changement de vitesse *luh shahnzh-mahn duh vee-tehss*

get up se lever *suh luh-vay*

gift le cadeau *luh kah-doh*

girl la fille *lah feey*

give donner *doh-nay*

gladly volontiers *voh-lohn-tyay*

glass le verre *luh vehr*

glove le gant *luh gahn*

glue la colle *lah kohl*

go aller *ah-lay*; **go down** descendre *day-ssahn-druh*; **go home** rentrer *rahn-tray*; **go in** entrer *ahn-tray*; **go out** sortir *sohr-teer*; **go shopping** faire des emplettes *fehr day zahn-pleht*; **go to bed** se coucher *suh koo-shay*; **go up** monter *mohn-tay*

gold l'or (m.) *lohr*

golf course le terrain de golf *luh teh-rah duh gohlf*

good bon(ne) *bohn, bohn*

goose l'oie (f.) *lwah*

GPS le système de navigation GPS *luh seess-tehm duh nah-vee-gah-ssyohn zhay-pay-ehss*

grape le raisin *luh reh-zan*

grapefruit le pamplemousse *luh pahn-pluh-mooss*

graphics la graphique *lah grah-feek*

grass l'herbe (f.) *lehrb*

grave (adj.) sérieux(ieuse) *say-ree-uh(z)*; grave *grahv*

gray gris(e) *gree(z)*

green vert(e) *vehr(t)*

greet saluer *sah-lew-ay*

grilled grillé(e) *gree-yay*

grocery store l'épicerie (f.) *lay-peess-ree*

ground le terrain *luh teh-ran*; la terre *lah tehr*; **campground** le terrain de camping *luh teh-ran duh kahn-peeng*; **golf course** le terrain de golf *luh teh-ran duh golf*; **playing field** le terrain de sport *luh teh-ran duh spohr*; **on the ground** par terre *pahr tehr*

ground floor le rez-de-chaussée *luh ray-duh-shoh-ssay*

guava la goyave *lah goh-yahv*

guide le guide *luh geed*; **entertainment guide** le

programme des spectacles *luh pro-grahm day spehk-tah-kluh*; **guidebook** le guide touristique *luh geed too-reess-teek*

gums (mouth) les gencives (f.) *lay zhah<u>n</u>-sseev*

gym le gymnase *luh zheem-nahz*

H

hair les cheveux (m. pl.) *lay shuh-vuh*

haircut la coupe de cheveux *lah koop duh shuh-vuh*

hairdresser le (la) coiffeur (-euse) *luh (lah) kwah-fuhr (fuhz)*

hair dryer le sèche-cheveux *luh sehsh shuh-vuh*

hairspray la laque *lah lahk*

half (noun) la moitié *lah mwah-tyay*

half (adj.) demi(e) *duh-mee*

ham le jambon *luh zhah<u>n</u>-boh<u>n</u>*

hamburger le hamburger *luh ah<u>n</u>-boor-gehr*

hand la main *lah ma<u>n</u>*

handicapped handicapé *ah<u>n</u>-dee-kah-pay*

handkerchief le mouchoir *luh moo-shwahr*

handmade fait à la main *feh tah lah ma<u>n</u>*

handsome beau (m.), belle (f.) *boh, behl*

hanger le cintre *luh sa<u>n</u>-truh*

hang up accrocher *ah-kroh-sshay*

happy heureux(euse) *uh-ruh(z)*

hardware store la quincaillerie *lah kah<u>n</u>-kahy-ree*

have avoir *ah-vwahr*; **have just** venir de *vuh-neer duh*;

have to avoir à *ah-vwahr ah*; devoir *duh-vwahr*

he il *eel*

head la tête *lah teht*

headlight le phare *luh fahr*

health la santé *lah sah<u>n</u>-tay*

hear entendre *ah<u>n</u>-tah<u>n</u>-druh*

hearing aid l'audiophone (m.) *loh-dyoh-fohn*

heart le coeur *luh kuhr*

heat (noun) la chaleur *lah shah-luhr*

heat (verb) chauffer *shoh-fay*

heating le chauffage *luh shoh-fahzh*

heel le talon *luh tah-loh<u>n</u>*

height la hauteur (f.) *lah oh-tuhr*

hello bonjour *boh<u>n</u>-zhoor*

help (noun) le secours *luh suh-koor*; **help!** au secours! *oh suh-koor*

help (verb) aider *eh-day*

here ici *ee-ssee*

here is, are voici *vwah-ssee*

herring les harengs (m. pl.) *lay ah-rah<u>n</u>*; **smoked herring** les harengs fumés *lay ah-rah<u>n</u> few-may*

high haut(e) *oh(t)*

high school le lycée *luh lee-ssay*

highway l'autoroute (f.) *loh-toh-root*

hip la hanche *lah ah<u>n</u>sh*

hire louer *loo-ay*

hit frapper *frah-pay*

hockey le hockey *luh oh-kee*

hold tenir *tuh-neer*

hole le trou *luh troo*

holiday la fête *lah feht*

hood (car) le capot *luh kah-poh*

hope (verb) espérer *ehss-pay-ray*

horn le klaxon *luh klahk-ssoh<u>n</u>*

horse le cheval *luh shuh-vahl*; les chevaux (pl.) *lay shuh-voh*

horseback riding l'équitation (f.) *lay-kee-tah-ssyohn*

horseradish le raifort *luh reh-fohr*

hospital l'hôpital (m.) *loh-pee-tahl*

host l'hôte (m.) *loht*

hostel (youth) l'auberge (f.) de jeunesse *loh-behrzh duh zhuh-nehss*

hostess l'hôtesse (f.) *loh-tehss*

hot chaud *shoh*; **be hot (person)** avoir chaud *ah-vwahr shoh*; **be hot (weather)** faire chaud *fehr shoh*

hotel l'hôtel (m.) *loh-tehl*

hour l'heure (f.) *luhr*

house la maison *lah meh-zohn*; **at the house of** chez *shay*; **boardinghouse** la pension *lah pahn-ssyohn*

house porter le concierge *luh kohn-ssyehrzh*

how comment *koh-mahn*; **how far** à quelle distance *ah kehl deess-tahnss*; **how long** depuis quand *duh-pwee kahn*

how many, much combien *kohn-byan*

hundred cent *sahn*

hunger la faim *lah fan*; **to be hungry** avoir faim *ah-vwahr fan*

hunting la chasse *lah shahss*

hurry se dépêcher *suh day-peh-shay*; **be in a hurry** être pressé *eh-truh preh-ssay*

husband le mari *luh mah-ree*

I

I je *zhuh*

ice la glace *lah glahss*; **ice cream** la glace *lah glahss*; **ice cubes** les glaçons (m. pl.) *lay glah-ssohn*; **ice-skating** le patin à glace *luh pah-tan ah glahss*; **ice water** l'eau (f.) glacée *loh glah-ssay*

if si *see*

ignition l'allumage (m.) *lah lew-mahzh*

ill malade *mah-lahd*

illness la maladie *lah mah-lah-dee*

immediately immédiatement *ee-may-dyaht-mahn*

important important(e) *an-pohr-tahn(t)*

impossible impossible *an-poh-ssee-bluh*

improbable invraisemblable *an-vreh-sahn-blah-bluh*

in dans *dahn*; en *ahn*

incapable incapable *an-kah-pah-bluh*

included compris(e) *kohn-pree(z)*

indefinite imprécis(e) *an-pray-ssee(z)*

infection l'infection (f.) *lan-fehk-ssyohn*

information (m. pl.) les renseigne-ments *lay rahn-seh-nyuh-mahn*

inn l'auberge (f.) *loh-behrzh*

inside dedans *duh-dahn*

insomnia l'insomnie (f.) *lan-ssohm-nee*

in spite of malgré *mahl-gray*

instead of au lieu de *oh lyuh duh*

insufficient insuffisant(e) *an-ssew-fee-zahn(t)*

insurance l'assurance (f.) *lah-ssew-rahnss*

insure assurer *ah-ssew-ray*

intelligent intelligent(e) *an-teh-lee-zhahn(t)*

interesting intéressant(e) *an-tay-reh-ssahn(t)*

Internet l'Internet *lan-tehr-neht*

Internet café le cybercafé *luh see-behr-kah-fay*

interpret interpréter *an-tehr-pray-tay*

interpreter l'interprète (m.) *lan-tehr-preht*

intersection le croisement *luh krawhz-mahn*

introduce présenter *pray-zahn-tay*

invite inviter *an-vee-tay*

invoice la facture *lah fahk-tewr*

iron (noun) le fer *luh fehr*

iron (verb) repasser *ruh-pah-ssay*

island l'île (f.) *leel*

itinerary l'itinéraire *lee-tee-nay-rehr*

J

jack (auto) le cric *luh kreek*

jacket le veston *luh vehss-tohn*

jam (marmalade) la confiture *lah kohn-fee-tewr*

January janvier *zhahn-vyay*

jar la jarre *lah zhahr*

jaw la mâchoire *lah mah-shwahr*

jewel le bijou *luh bee-zhoo*

jeweler le bijoutier *luh bee-zhoo-tyay*

jewelry shop la bijouterie *lah bee-zhoo-tree*

jogging suit le survêt *luh sewr-veh*; le jogging *luh zhoh-geeng*

joystick la manette de jeux *lah mah-neht duh zhuh*

joke la plaisanterie *lah pleh-zahn-tree*

journey le voyage *luh vwah-yahzh*; le trajet *luh trah-zheh*

judge (noun) le juge *luh zhewzh*

judge (verb) juger *zhew-zhay*

juice le jus *luh zhew*

July juillet *zhwee-yeh*

jumper cables les câbles (m.) de démarrage *lay kah-bluh duh day-mah-rahzh*

June juin *zhwan*

just: have just venir de *vuh-neer duh*

K

keep garder *gahr-day*

ketchup le ketchup *luh keht-shuhp*

key la clef *lah klay*; (computer) la touche *lah toosh*

keyboard le clavier *luh klah-vyay*

kiss (verb) embrasser *ahn-brah-ssay*

kitchen la cuisine *lah kwee-zeen*

knee le genou *luh zhuh-noo*; **kneepads** les genouillères *lay zhuh-noo-yehr*

knife le couteau *luh koo-toh*

knock (verb) frapper *frah-pay*

know (facts) savoir *sah-vwahr*; **(people)** connaître *koh-neh-truh*

L

label l'étiquette (f.) *lay-tee-keht*

lace la dentelle *lah dahn-tehl*

lack (noun) le manque *luh mahnk*

lack (verb) manquer *mahn-kay*

lake le lac *luh lahk*

lamb l'agneau *lah-nyoh*

lamp la lampe *lah lahnp*

land (noun) la terre *lah tehr*

land (verb) (plane) atterrir *ah-teh-reer*; débarquer *day-bahr-kay*

landing l'atterrissage (m.) *lah-teh-ree-ssahzh*; le

débarquement *luh day-bahrk-mahn*

lane la ruelle *lah rew-ehl*

language la langue *lah lahng*

laptop computer l'ordinateur (m.) portable *lohr-dee-nah-tuhr pohr-tah-bluh*

last (adj.) dernier(ière) *dehr-nyay(nyehr)*

last (verb) durer *dew-ray*

late tard *tahr*; **(to be) late** (être) en retard *(eh-truh) ahn ruh-tahr*

laugh rire *reer*

launderette la laverie automatique *lah lah-vree oh-toh-mah-teek*

laundering le blanchissage *luh blahn-shee-ssahzh*

laundry la blanchisserie *lah blahn-sheess-ree*

lawyer l'avocat (m.), l'avocate (f.) *lah-voh-kah, lah-voh-kaht*

learn apprendre *ah-prahn-druh*

least: at least au moins *oh mwan*

leather le cuir *luh kweer*

leave (behind) laisser *leh-ssay*

leave (depart) partir *pahr-teer*; **to go out** sortir *sohr-teer*; **to leave + (place or person)** quitter *kee-tay*

left gauche *gohsh*; **to the left** à gauche *ah gohsh*

leg la jambe *lah zhahnb*

lemon le citron *luh see-trohn*

lemonade la citronnade *lah see-troh-nahd*

lend prêter *preh-tay*

less moins *mwan*

letter la lettre *lah leh-truh*

lettuce la laitue *lah leh-tew*

library la bibliothèque *lah bee-blee-oh-tehk*

life la vie *lah vee*

life preserver la ceinture de sauvetage *lah san-tewr duh sohv-tahzh*

light (noun) la lumière *lah lew-myehr*

light (color) clair(e) *klehr*

light (weight) léger(ère) *lay-zhay(zhehr)*

light (verb) allumer *ah-lew-may*

lighter le briquet *luh bree-keh*

like (prep.) comme *kohm*

like (verb) aimer *eh-may*

lime la limette *lah lee-meht*

line la ligne *lah lee-nyuh*; la voie *lah vwah*

line (of people) la queue *lah kuh*; **form a line** faire la queue *fehr lah kuh*

linen (cloth) le lin *luh lan*

lip la lèvre *lah leh-vruh*

lipstick le rouge à lèvres *luh roozh ah leh-vruh*

list la liste *lah leesst*

listen écouter *ay-koo-tay*

little (adj.) petit(e) *puh-tee(t)*; **(adv.)** peu (de) *puh (duh)*

live vivre *vee-vruh*

live in demeurer *duh-muh-ray*; habiter *ah-bee-tay*

liver le foie *luh fwah*

lobster le homard *luh oh-mahr*

lock (noun) la serrure *lah seh-rewr*

locker le casier *luh kah-zyay*

lodging le logis *luh loh-zhee*

long long (longue) *lohn (lohng)*

look at regarder *ruh-gahr-day*

look for chercher *shehr-shay*

lose perdre *pehr-druh*

loss la perte *lah pehrt*

lost: get lost s'égarer *say-gah-ray*

lot beaucoup de *boh-koo duh*

loudspeaker le haut-parleur *luh oh pahr-luhr*

love (noun) l'amour (m.) *lah-moor*

love (verb) aimer *eh-may*

low bas(se) *bah(ss)*

luck la chance *lah shah_n_ss;* **Good luck!** Bonne chance! *bohn shah_n_ss*

lunch (noun) le déjeuner *luh day-zhuh-nay*

lunch (verb) déjeuner *day-zhuh-nay*

lung le poumon *luh poo-moh_n_*

luxurious luxueux(euse) *lewk-ssew-uh(uhz)*

luxury le luxe *luh lewkss*

M

magazine le magazine *luh mah-gah-zeen*

mail le courrier *luh koo-ryay*

mailbox la boîte à lettres *lah bwaht ah leh-truh*

mailman le facteur *luh fahk-tuhr*

make faire *fehr*

man l'homme (m.) *lohm*

manager le gérant *luh zhay-rah_n_*

mango la mangue *lah mah_n_g*

many beaucoup de *boh-koo duh;* **too many** trop de *troh duh*

map la carte *lah kahrt;* **road map** la carte routière *lah kahrt roo-tyehr*

March mars *mahrss*

margarine la margarine *lah mahr-gah-reen*

market le marché *luh mahr-shay*

marvelous merveilleux(euse) *mehr-veh-yuh(z)*

mashed en purée *ah_n_ pew-ray*

match (noun) l'allumette (f.) *lah-lew-meht*

material le tissu *luh tee-ssew*

matter (noun) l'affaire (f.) *lah-fehr;* **it doesn't matter** n'importe na_n_-pohrt; **What's the matter?** Qu'est-ce qu'il y a? *kehss keel yah*

May mai *meh*

may (verb) pouvoir *poo-vwahr*

maybe peut-être *puh-teh-truh*

mayonnaise la mayonnaise *lah may-yoh-nehz*

meal le repas *luh ruh-pah*

mean (verb) vouloir dire *voo-lwahr deer;* signifier *see-nee-fyay*

mean (adj.) méchant(e) *may-shah_n_(t)*

meaning la signification *lah see-nee-fee-kah-ssyoh_n_*

measure (noun) la mesure *lah muh-zewr*

measure (verb) mesurer *muh-zew-ray*

meat la viande *lah vee-ah_n_d*

meatballs les boulettes *lay boo-leht*

mechanic le mécanicien *luh may-kah-nee-ssya_n_*

medicine le médicament *luh may-dee-kah-mah_n_*

medium (cooking) à point *ah pwa_n_*

meet rencontrer *rah_n_-koh_n_-tray*

meeting le rendez-vous *luh rah_n_-day-voo*

melon le melon *luh muh-loh_n_*

member le membre *luh mah_n_-bruh*

memory la mémoire *lah may-mwahr*

merchandise la marchandise *lah mahr-shah_n_-deez*

merchant le marchand *luh mahr-shah_n_*

mezzanine le parterre *luh pahr-tehr*

microwave oven le four à micro-ondes *luh foor ah mee-kroh ohnd*

middle le milieu *luh meel-yuh*; **in the middle of** au milieu de *oh meel-yuh duh*

midnight minuit *mee-nwee*

milk le lait *luh leh*

milk shake le frappé *luh frah-pay*

million le million *luh mee-lyohn*

minute la minute *lah mee-newt*

mirror le miroir *luh mee-rwahr*; la glace *lah glahss*

miss (verb) manquer *mahn-kay*

miss mademoiselle *mahd-mwah-zehl*

mistake la faute *lah foht*; l'erreur (f.) *leh-ruhr*; **make a mistake** se tromper *suh trohn-pay*

mister monsieur *muh-ssyuh*

misunderstanding le malentendu *luh mahl-ahn-tahn-dew*

modem le modem *luh moh-dehm*

modify modifier *moh-dee-fyay*

Monday lundi *luhn-dee*

money l'argent (m.) *lahr-zhahn*

money (coins) la monnaie *lah moh-nay*

money exchange le bureau de change *luh bew-roh duh shahnzh*

monitor le moniteur *luh moh-nee-tuhr*

month le mois *luh mwah*

monthly mensuel(le) *mahn-sswehl*

morning le matin *luh mah-tan*

mosque la mosquée *lah mohss-kay*

mother la mère *lah mehr*

motor le moteur *luh moh-tuhr*

mountain la montagne *lah mohn-tah-nyuh*

mouse (computer) la souris *lah soo-ree*

mouth la bouche (f.) *lah boosh*

mouthwash (f.) l'eau dentifrice *loh dahn-tee-freess*

movies le cinéma *luh see-nay-mah*

Mr. monsieur *muh-ssyuh*

Mrs. madame *mah-dahm*

museum le musée *luh mew-zay*

mushroom le champignon *luh shahn-pee-nyohn*

music la musique *lah mew-zeek*

mussels les moules (f. pl.) *lay mool*

mustard la moutarde *lah moo-tahrd*

mutton leg le gigot *luh zhee-goh*

N

nail l'ongle *lohn-gluh*

nail file la lime à ongles *lah leem ah ohn-gluh*

name le nom *luh nohn*; **family (last) name** le nom de famille *luh nohn duh fah-meey*; **first name** le prénom *luh pray-nohn*; **last name** le surnom *luh sewr-nohn*; **My name is** Je m'appelle *zhuh mah-pehl*

napkin la serviette *lah sehr-vyeht*; **sanitary napkin** la serviette hygiénique *lah sehr-vyeht ee-zhyay-neek*

nationality la nationalité *lah nah-ssyohn-nah-lee-tay*

nausea la nausée *lah noh-zay*

near (to) près de *preh duh*

nearby proche *prohsh*

nearly presque *prehss-kuh*

necessary nécessaire *nay-sseh-ssehr*; **it is necessary** il est nécessaire *eel eh nay-sseh-ssehr*; il faut *eel foh*

neck le cou *luh koo*

necklace le collier *luh koh-lyay*

need (verb) avoir besoin de *ah-vwahr buhz-wan duh*

needle l'aiguille (f.) *lay-gweey*

neighbor le voisin *luh vwah-san*; la voisine *lah vwah-zeen*

network le réseau *luh ray-zoh*

never jamais *zhah-meh*; ne ... jamais *nuh ... zhah-meh*

new nouveau (m.), nouvelle (f.) *noo-voh, noo-vehl*

newspaper le journal *luh zhoor-nahl*

next prochain(e) *proh-shan (shehn)*

night la nuit *lah nwee*

nightclub la boîte de nuit *lah bwaht duh nwee*

nine neuf *nuhf*

nineteen dix-neuf *deez-nuhf*

ninety quatre-vingt-dix *kah-truh-van-deess*

no non *nohn*

noise le bruit *luh brwee*

no longer ne ... plus *nuh ... plew*

none ne ... aucun(e) *nuh ... oh-kuhn(kewn)*

nonsmokers non-fumeurs *nohn few-muhr*

noon midi *mee-dee*

north le nord *luh nohr*

nose le nez *luh nay*

not ne ... pas *nuh ... pah*

not any ne ... aucun(e) *nuh ... oh-kuhn(kewn)*

notebook le cahier *luh kah-yay*

nothing ne ... rien *nuh ... ryan*

notice (noun) l'avis (m.) *lah-vee*

notice (verb) remarquer *ruh-mahr-kay*

novel le roman *luh roh-mahn*

novelty la nouveauté *lah noo-voh-tay*

now maintenant *mant-nahn*

number le numéro *luh new-may-roh*

number (quantity) le nombre *luh nohn-bruh*

nurse l'infirmière (f.) *lan-feer-myehr*

nut la noix *lah nwah*

nylon le nylon *luh nee-lohn*

O

observe observer *ohp-zehr-vay*

obtain obtenir *ohp-tuh-neer*

ocean l'océan (m.) *loh-ssay-ahn*

of de *duh*

of course bien entendu *byan nahn-tahn-dew*

offer offrir *oh-freer*

office le bureau *luh bew-roh*; **box office** le bureau de location *luh bew-roh duh loh-kah-ssyohn*; **exchange office** le bureau de change *luh bew-roh duh shahnzh*; **post office** le bureau de poste *luh bew-roh duh pohsst*

often souvent *soo-vahn*

oil l'huile (f.) *lweel*

O.K. d'accord *dah-kohr*

old vieux (m.), vieille (f.) *vyuh, vyay*; **How old are you?** Quel âge avez-vous? *kehl ahzh ah-vay voo?*

old-fashioned démodé(e) *day-moh-day*

olive l'olive (f.) *loh-leev*

olive oil l'huile d'olive *lweel doh-leev*

omelet l'omelette (f.) *lohm-leht*

on sur *sewr*

one un (m.), une (f.) *uhn, ewn*

onion l'oignon (m.) *loh-nyohn*

only ne . . . que *nuh . . . kuh*; seulement *suhl-mahn*

only (adj.) seul(e) *suhl*; unique *ew-neek*

open (verb) ouvrir *oo-vreer*

open (adj.) ouvert(e) *oo-vehr(t)*

opera l'opéra (m.) *loh-pay-rah*

operator la téléphoniste *lah tay-lay-foh-neesst*

opportunity l'occasion (f.) *loh-kah-zyohn*

opposite (noun) le contraire *luh kohn-trehr*

opposite (prep.) en face de *ahn fahss duh*

optician l'opticien (m.) *lohp-tee-ssyan*

or ou *oo*

orange l'orange (f.) *loh-rahnzh*

orangeade l'orangeade (f.) *loh-rahnzh-ahd*

orchestra l'orchestre (m.) *lohr-kehss-truh*

order (noun) la commande *lah koh-mahnd*

order (verb) commander *koh-mahn-day*

organic biologique *bee-oh-loh-zheek*

other autre *oh-truh*

outside dehors *duh-ohr*

over dessus *duh-ssew*

overcoat le manteau *luh mahn-toh*; le pardessus *luh pahr-duh-ssew*

overseas outre-mer *oo-truh-mehr*

owe devoir *duh-vwahr*

own posséder *poh-ssay-day*

owner le propriétaire *luh proh-pree-ay-tehr*

oyster l'huître (f.) *lwee-truh*

P

package le paquet *luh pah-keh*; le colis *luh koh-lee*

pad (writing) le bloc *luh blohk*

pain la douleur *lah doo-luhr*

painting le tableau *luh tah-bloh*

pair la paire *lah pehr*

pajamas le pyjama *luh pee-zhah-mah*

palace le palais *luh pah-leh*

panties la culotte *lah kew-loht*

pants le pantalon *luh pahn-tah-lohn*

panty hose les collants (m. pl.) *lay koh-lahn*

paper le papier *luh pah-pyay*; **toilet** le papier hygiénique *luh pah-pyay ee-zhyay-neek*; **wrapping** le papier d'emballage *luh pah-pyay dahn-bah-lahzh*; **writing** le papier à lettres *luh pah-pyay ah leh-truh*

park (noun) le parc *luh pahrk*

park (verb) garer *gah-ray*; stationner *stah-ssyoh-nay*

part la partie *lah pahr-tee*

pass (verb) passer *pah-ssay*

pastry la pâtisserie *lah pah-teess-ree*

path le sentier *luh sahn-tyay*

pay payer *peh-yay*

pear la poire *lah pwahr*

peas les pois (m. pl.) *lay pwah*

pedestrian le piéton *luh pyay-tohn*

pen la plume *lah plewm*; **ballpoint** le stylo à bille *luh stee-loh ah beey*

penalty l'amende (f.) *lah-mahnd*

pencil le crayon *luh kreh-yohn;* **pencil sharpener** le taille-crayon *luh tahy kreh-yohn*

people les gens *lay zhahn* [adj. before (f.); adj. after (m.)]

people (nation) le peuple *luh puh-pluh*

pepper le poivre *luh pwah-vruh*

perfect parfait(e) *pahr-feh(t)*

performance la représentation *lah ruh-pray-zahn-tah-ssyohn*

perfume le parfum *luh pahr-fuhn*

perhaps peut-être *puh-teh-truh*

permanent permanent(e) *pehr-mah-nahn(t)*

permanent press infroissable *an-frwah-ssah-bluh*

permit (noun) le permis *luh pehr-mee*

permit (verb) permettre *pehr-meh-truh;* **permitted** permis *pehr-mee*

person la personne *lah pehr-ssohn*

persuade persuader *pehr-sswah-day*

pharmacy la pharmacie *lah fahr-mah-ssee*

photocopy la photocopie *lah foh-toh-koh-pee*

photograph (noun) la photo *lah foh-toh*

photograph (verb) photographier *foh-toh-grah-fyay*

pickle le cornichon *luh kohr-nee-shohn*

picture (art) le tableau *luh tah-bloh*

pie la tarte *lah tahrt*

piece le morceau *luh mohr-ssoh*

pill la pilule *lah pee-lewl*

pillow l'oreiller (m.) *loh-reh-yay*

pin l'épingle (f.) *lay pan-gluh*

PIN le code confidentiel *luh kohd kohn-fee-dahn-ssyehl*

pineapple l'ananas (m.) *lah-nah-nah*

pink rose *rohz*

pipe (smoking) la pipe *lah peep;* **pipe tobacco** le tabac pour pipe *luh tah-bah poor peep*

pitcher la cruche *lah krewsh*

place (noun) l'endroit (m.) *lahn-drwah;* le lieu *luh lyuh*

place setting le couvert *luh koo-vehr*

plaid le tartan *luh tahr-tahn*

plan le plan *luh plahn;* **plan of the city** le plan de ville *luh plahn duh veel*

plate l'assiette (f.) *lah-ssyeht*

platform le quai *luh kay*

play (noun) la pièce *lah pyehss*

play (verb) jouer *zhoo-ay;* **play (a game)** jouer à *zhoo-ay ah;* **play (an instrument)** jouer de *zhoo-ay duh*

please s'il vous plaît *seel voo pleh;* (verb) plaire à *plehr ah*

pleasure le plaisir *luh pleh-zeer*

plum la prune *lah prewn*

pocket la poche *lah pohsh*

pocketbook le sac *luh sahk*

policeman l'agent (m.) de police *lah-zhahn duh poh-leess;* le gendarme *luh zhahn-dahrm*

police station le commissariat *luh koh-mee-ssah-ryah*

polka-dotted à pois *ah pwah*

polyester synthétique *san-tay-teek*

pool la piscine *lah pee-sseen*

poor pauvre *poh-vruh*

pork le porc *luh pohr*

portable portatif(tive) *pohr-tah-teef(teev)*

porter le porteur *luh pohr-tuhr*

possess posséder *poh-ssay-day*

postcard la carte postale *lah kahrt pohss-tahl*

poster l'affiche (f.) *lah-feesh*
postman le facteur *luh fahk-tuhr*
post office la poste *lah pohsst*;
le bureau de poste *luh bew-roh duh pohsst*
postpone remettre *ruh-meh-truh*
potato la pomme de terre *lah pohm duh tehr*
pottery la poterie *lah poh-tree*
pound (meas.) la livre *lah lee-vruh*
practice (noun) l'usage (m.) *lew-zahzh*
prefer préférer *pray-fay-ray*;
aimer mieux *eh-may myuh*
pregnant enceinte *ahn-sant*
prepare préparer *pray-pah-ray*
prescription l'ordonnance (f.) *lohr-doh-nahnss*
pretty joli(e) *zhoh-lee*
price le prix *luh pree*
printer l'imprimante (f.) *lan-pree-mahnt*
  laser laser *lah-zehr*
  ink jet jet d'encre *zheh dahn-kruh*
private privé(e) *pree-vay*
prize le prix *luh pree*
profession la profession *lah proh-feh-ssyohn*
prohibit interdire *an-tehr-deer*; **prohibited** interdit(e) *an-tehr-dee(t)*
promise (verb) promettre *proh-meh-truh*
promise (noun) la promesse *lah proh-mehss*
pronounce prononcer *proh-nohn-ssay*
property la propriété *lah proh-pree-ay-tay*
protect protéger *proh-tay-zhay*
protest (verb) protester *proh-tehss-tay*
prune le pruneau *luh prew-noh*

public (adj.) public(ique) *pew-bleek*
public (noun) le public *luh pew-bleek*
pull tirer *tee-ray*; arracher (tooth) *ah-rah-shay*
purchase (noun) l'achat (m.) *lah-shah*
purple violet *vee-oh-leh*; mauve *mohv*
purse le porte-monnaie *luh pohrt moh-nay*
push pousser *poo-ssay*
put mettre *meh-truh*; **to put on** mettre *meh-truh*; **to put back** remettre *ruh-meh-truh*

Q

quality la qualité *lah kah-lee-tay*
quantity la quantité *lah kahn-tee-tay*
quarter le quart *luh-kahr*
question la question *lah kehss-tyohn*
quickly vite *veet*; rapidement *rah-peed-mahn*
quickness la vitesse *lah vee-tehss*

R

rabbit le lapin *luh lah-pan*
radio la radio *lah rah-dyoh*
radish le radis *luh rah-dee*
railroad le chemin de fer *luh shuh-man duh fehr*
railroad station la gare *lah gahr*
rain la pluie *lah plwee*
raincoat l'imperméable (m.) *lan-pehr-may-ah-bluh*
raisin le raisin sec *luh reh-zan sehk*
rare rare *rahr*
rare (meat) saignant *seh-nyahn*

raspberry la framboise *lah frahn-bwahz*

rate le tarif *luh tah-reef*

rate of exchange le cours du change *luh koor dew shahnzh*

rather plutôt *plew-toh*

raw cru(e) *krew*

razor le rasoir *luh rah-zwahr*

read lire *leer*

ready prêt(e) *preh(t)*

really vraiment *vreh-mahn*

reason la raison *lah reh-zohn*

reasonable raisonnable *reh-zoh-nah-bluh*

receipt le reçu *luh ruh-ssew*

receive recevoir *ruh-ssuh-vwahr*

recently récemment *ray-sseh-mahn*

recommend recommander *ruh-koh-mahn-day*; conseiller *kohn-say-yay*

record le disque *luh deessk*

recover (health) se remettre *suh ruh-meh-truh*

recovery room la salle de repos *lah sahl duh ruh-poh*

recuperate récupérer *ray-kew-pay-ray*

red rouge *roozh*

reduction le rabais *luh rah-beh*

refreshments les rafraîchissements (m. pl.) *lay rah-freh-sheess-mahn*

refund rembourser *rahn-boor-ssay*

refuse (verb) refuser *ruh-few-zay*

regret regretter *ruh-greh-tay*

regular régulier(ière) *ray-gew-lyay(lyehr)*

regularly régulièrement *ray-gew-lyehr-mahn*

reimburse rembourser *rahn-boor-ssay*

remain rester *rehss-tay*

remedy le remède *luh ruh-mehd*

remember se rappeler *suh rah-play*; se souvenir de *suh soo-vuh-neer duh*

rent (noun) le loyer *luh lwah-yay*

rent (verb) louer *loo-ay*

repair (verb) réparer *ray-pah-ray*

repeat répéter *ray-pay-tay*

replace remplacer *rahn-plah-ssay*

resemble ressembler à *ruh-ssahn-blay ah*

reservation la réservation *lay ray-zehr-vah-ssyohn*

reserve réserver *ray-zehr-vay*

resolve résoudre *ray-zoo-druh*

responsible responsable *rehss-pohn-ssah-bluh*

rest (noun) le repos *luh ruh-poh*

rest (verb) se reposer *suh ruh-poh-zay*

restaurant le restaurant *luh rehss-toh-rahn*

result le résultat *luh ray-zewl-tah*

retain retenir *ruh-tuh-neer*

retired en retraite *ahn ruh-treht*

retrieve retrouver *ruh-troo-vay*

return retourner *ruh-toor-nay*; **return (give back)** rendre *rahn-druh*

reward (noun) la récompense *lah ray-kohn-pahnss*

reward (verb) récompenser *ray-kohn-pahn-ssay*

rice le riz *luh ree*

right: to be right avoir raison *ah-vwahr reh-zohn*

right (direction) droit *drwah*; **to the right** à droite *ah drwaht*

ring (noun) la bague *lah bahg*

ring (verb) sonner *soh-nay*

river le fleuve *luh fluhv*; la rivière *lah ree-vyehr*

road le chemin *luh shuh-man*

roasted (adj.) rôti(e) *roh-tee*

roll le petit pain *luh puh-tee pan*

roller skating le patin à roulettes *luh pah-tan ah roo-leht*

roof le toit *luh twah*

room la pièce *lah pyehss*; la salle *lah sahl*; la chambre *lah shahn-bruh*; **single room** une chambre à un lit *ewn shahn-bruh ah uhn lee*; **double room** une chambre à deux lits *ewn shahn-bruh ah duh lee*

round rond(e) *rohn(d)*

route la route *lah root*

row (noun) le rang *luh rahn*

rubber le caoutchouc *luh kah-oo-tshoo*; **rubbers** les caoutchoucs *lay kah-oo-tshoo*

rug le tapis *luh tah-pee*

rule la règle *lah reh-gluh*

ruler la règle *lah reh-gluh*

run courir *koo-reer*

runway la piste *lah peesst*

S

sad triste *treesst*

safe (strongbox) le coffre-fort *luh koh-fruh fohr*

sailboat le bateau à voiles *luh bah-toh ah vwahl*

sale la vente *lah vahnt*; **for sale** en vente *ahn vahnt*

sale (bargain) les soldes (m. pl.) *lay sohld*

salesman le vendeur *luh vahn-duhr*

saleswoman la vendeuse *lah vahn-duhz*

salmon le saumon *luh soh-mohn*

salt le sel *luh sehl*; **salted, salty** salé *sah-lay*

same même *mehm*

sample l'échantillon (m.) *lay-shahn-tee-yohn*

sand le sable *luh sah-bluh*

sandals les sandales (f.) *lay sahn-dahl*

sardine la sardine *lah sahr-deen*

satin le satin *luh sah-tan*

satisfied satisfait(e) *sah-teess-feh(t)*

Saturday samedi *sahm-dee*

sauerkraut la choucroute *lah shoo-kroot*

sausage la saucisse *lah soh-sseess*

say dire *deer*

scanner le scanneur *luh skah-nuhr*

scarf l'écharpe (f.) *lay-shahrp*

schedule l'horaire (m.) *loh-rehr*

school l'école (f.) *lay-kohl*

scissors les ciseaux (m. pl.) *lay see-zoh*

scrambled brouillé(e) *broo-yay*

screen l'écran (m.) *lay-krahn*

sea la mer *lah mehr*

seafood les fruits (m. pl.) de mer *lay frwee duh mehr*

search engine le moteur de recherche *luh moh-tuhr duh ruh-shehrsh*

season la saison *lah seh-zohn*

seasoned assaisonné *ah-sseh-zoh-nay*

seat la place *lah plahss*; le siège *luh syehzh*

secondhand usagé *ew-zah-zhay*

secondhand goods la marchandise d'occasion *lah mahr-shahn-deez doh-kah-zyohn*

secretary le (la) secrétaire *luh (lah) seh-kray-tehr*

security la sécurité *lah say-kew-ree-tay*

see voir *vwahr*

seem sembler *sahn-blay*; avoir l'air de *ah-vwahr lehr duh*

sell vendre *vahn-druh*

send envoyer *ahn-vwah-yay*; **send for** faire venir *fehr vuh-neer*, **send back** renvoyer *rahn-vwah-yay*

seniors les personnes du troisième âge *lay pehr-ssohn dew trwah-zyehm ahzh*

sentence la phrase *lah frahz*

serious sérieux(ieuse) *say-ryuh(z)*; grave *grahv*

serve servir *sehr-veer*

service le service *luh sehr-veess*

service station la station service *lah stah-ssyohn sehr-veess*

settle régler *ray-glay*; **settle an affair** régler une affaire *ray-glay ewn ah-fehr*

seven sept *seht*

seventeen dix-sept *dee seht*

seventy soixante-dix *swah-ssahnt-deess*

several plusieurs *plew-zyuhr*

sew coudre *koo-druh*

shade l'ombre (f.) *lohn-bruh*

shampoo le shampooing *luh shahn-pwan*

share partager *pahr-tah-zhay*

shark le requin *luh ruh-kan*

shave (verb) raser *rah-zay*

shawl le châle *luh shahl*

she elle *ehl*

sheet la feuille *lah fuhy*

shelf le rayon *luh reh-yohn*

shellfish le coquillage *luh koh-kee-yahzh*

sherbet le sorbet *luh sohr-beh*

shine (verb) cirer *see-ray*

shirt la chemise *lah shuh-meez*

shoe le soulier *luh soo-lyay*; la chaussure *lah shoh-ssewr*

shoelaces les lacets (m. pl.) *lay lah-sseh*

shoemaker le cordonnier *luh kohr-doh-nyay*

shop (noun) la boutique *lah boo-teek*

shop (verb) faire des achats *fehr day zah-shah*; faire des emplettes *fehr day zahn-pleht*

shop window la vitrine *lah vee-treen*

shore (bank) la rive *lah reev*

short court(e) *koor(t)*

shorts (briefs) le caleçon *luh kahl-ssohn*

short story le conte *luh kohnt*

shoulder l'épaule (f.) *lay-pohl*

show (verb) montrer *mohn-tray*

show (noun) le spectacle *luh spehk-tah-kluh*

shower la douche *lah doosh*

shrimp la crevette *lah kruh-veht*

sick malade *mah-lahd*

sickness la maladie *lah mah-lah-dee*

side le côté *luh koh-tay*

sidewalk le trottoir *luh troh-twahr*

significant other le/la partenaire *luh/lah pahr-tuh-nehr*

sightseeing le tourisme *luh too-reess-muh*

sign (noun) l'enseigne (f.) *lahn-sseh-nyuh*

sign (verb) signer *see-nyay*

signal (directional) le clignotant *luh klee-nyoh-tahn*

silk la soie *lah swah*

silver l'argent (m.) *lahr-zhahn*

since depuis *duh-pwee*

since when depuis quand *duh-pwee kahn*

sing chanter *shahn-tay*

single (unmarried) célibataire *say-lee-bah-tehr*

sir monsieur *muh-ssyuh*

sister la soeur *lah suhr*

sit s'asseoir *sah-sswahr*

site le site *luh seet*

six six *seess*

sixteen seize *sehz*

sixty soixante *swah-ssahnt*

size la taille *lah tahy*

skateboard la planche à roulettes *lah plahnssh ah roo-leht*

ski le ski *luh skee*; **water skis** les skis nautiques *lay skee-noh-teek*

ski lift le téléski *luh tay-lay-sskee*

ski slope la piste de ski *lah peesst duh skee*

skin la peau *lah poh*

skirt la jupe *lah zhewp*

sky le ciel *luh syehl*

skyscraper le gratte-ciel *luh graht-syehl*

sleep (verb) dormir *dohr-meer*

sleep, sleepiness le sommeil *luh soh-mehy*; **to be sleepy** avoir sommeil *ah-vwahr soh-mehy*; **sleeping pill** le somnifère *luh sohm-nee-fehr*

sleeve la manche *lah mahnsh*

slice la tranche *lah trahnsh*

slide (pictures) la diapositive *lah dee-ah-poh-zee-teev*

slip (clothing) la combinaison *lah kohn-bee-neh-zohn*; le jupon *luh zhew-pohn*

slippers les pantoufles (f. pl.) *lay pahn-too-fluh*

slope la piste *lah peesst*

slow (adj.) lent(e) *lahn(t)*

slowly (adv.) lentement *lahnt-mahn*

small petit(e) *puh-tee(t)*

smoke fumer *few-may*

smoker le fumeur *luh few-muhr*

snail l'escargot (m.) *lehss-kahr-goh*

snow (noun) la neige *lah nehzh*

snow (verb) neiger *neh-zhay*

so alors *ah-lohr*

soap le savon *luh sah-vohn*; **a bar of soap** une savonnette *ewn sah-voh-neht*

socket la prise de courant *lah preez duh koo-rahn*

socks les chaussettes (f. pl.) *lay shoh-sseht*

soda le soda *luh soh-dah*

soft doux, douce *doo(ss)*

softly doucement *dooss-mahn*

software le logiciel *luh loh-zhee-syehl*

sole (fish) la sole *lah sohl*

solid (colored) uni(e) *ew-nee*

some quelques *kehl-kuh*

some du *dew*; de la *duh lah*; de l' *duhl*; des *day*

someone quelqu'un *kehl-kuhn*

something quelque chose *kehl-kuh shohz*

sometimes quelquefois *kehl-kuh-fwah*

somewhere quelque part *kehl-kuh pahr*

son le fils *luh feess*

song la chanson *lah shahn-ssohn*

soon bientôt *byan-toh*; **see you soon** à bientôt *ah byan-toh*

sore throat le mal de gorge *luh mahl duh gohrzh*

sorry: to be sorry être désolé(e) *eh-truh day-zoh-lay*; regretter *ruh-greh-tay*

soup la soupe *lah soop*; le potage *luh poh-tahzh*

south le sud *luh sewd*

space l'espace (m.) *lehss-pahss*

spark plugs les bougies (f.) *lay boo-zhee*

speak parler *pahr-lay*

speed la vitesse *lah vee-tehss*

speed limit la vitesse maximum *lah vee-tehs mahk-ssee-muhm*

spell épeler *ay-play*

spell checker le correcteur orthographique *luh koh-rehk-tuhr ohr-toh-grah-feek*

spend (money) dépenser *day-pahn-ssay*

spend (time) passer *pah-ssay*

spicy épicé *ay-pee-say*

spinach les épinards (m. pl.) *lay zay-pee-nahr*

spoon la cuiller *lah kwee-yehr*; **teaspoon** la cuiller à café *lah kwee-yehr ah kah-fay*; **tablespoon** la cuiller à soupe *lah kwee-yehr ah soop*; **teaspoonful** la cuillerée à café *lah kwee-yuh-ray ah kah-fay*; **tablespoonful** la cuillerée à soupe *lah kwee-yuh-ray ah soop*

spouse l'époux (m.) (l'épouse (f.)) *lay-poo (lay-pooz)*

spring le printemps *luh pran-tahn*

square (adj.) carré(e) *kah-ray*

square (public) la place *lah plahss*

stadium le stade *luh stahd*

stain la tache *lah tahsh*

staircase l'escalier (m.) *lehss-kah-lyay*

stamp le timbre *luh tan-bruh*

stand (noun) le kiosque *luh kee-ohssk*; **newsstand** le kiosque à journaux *luh kee-ohssk ah zhoor-noh*

starter le démarreur *luh day-mah-ruhr*

state l'état (m.) *lay-tah*

station la gare *lah gahr*

stay, sojourn le séjour *luh say-zhoor*

stay (verb) rester *rehss-tay*

stay at loger *loh-zhay*

steak le bifteck *luh beef-tehk*

steal voler *voh-lay*

steamed à la vapeur *ah lah vah-puhr*

steering wheel le volant *luh voh-lahn*

stew le ragoût *luh rah-goo*

stewed en cocotte *ahn koh-koht*

stewardess l'hôtesse de l'air *loh-tehss duh lehr*

still encore *ahn-kohr*

stockings les bas (m. pl.) *lay bah*

stock market la bourse *lah boorss*

stomach l'estomac (m.) *lahss-toh-mah*; le ventre *luh van-truh*

stomachache mal à l'estomac *mahl ah lehss-toh-mah*

stone la pierre *lah pyehr*

stop (noun) l'arrêt (m.) *lah-reh*

stop (verb) arrêter *ah-reh-tay*

stop light le feu *luh fuh*

stopover une escale *ewn nehss-kahl*

store le magasin *luh mah-gah-zan*; **book** la librairie *lah lee-breh-ree*; **camera** le magasin de photographie *luh mah-gah-zan duh foh-toh-grah-fee*; **clothing** le magasin de vêtements *luh mah-gah-zan duh veht-mahn*; **department** le grand magasin *luh grahn mah-gah-zan*; **drug** la pharmacie *lah fahr-mah-ssee*; **grocery** l'épicerie (f.) *lay-peess-ree*; **hardware** la quincaillerie *lah kahn-kahy-ree*; **jewelry** la bijouterie *lah bee-zhoo-tree*; **liquor** le magasin de spiritueux *luh mah-gah-zan duh spee-ree-tew-uh*; **multimedia** le magasin multimédia *luh mah-*

gah-zan mool-tee-may-dee-ah; **shoe** le magasin de chaussures *luh mah-gah-zan duh shoh-ssewr*; **tobacco** le bureau de tabac *luh bew-roh duh tah-bah*; **toy** le magasin de jouets *luh mah-gah-zan duh zhoo-eh*

storm la tempête *lah tahn-peht*; l'orage (m.) *loh-rahzh*

story l'histoire (f.) *leess-twahr*

straw la paille *lah pahy*

strawberry la fraise *lah frehz*

stream la rivière *lah ree-vyehr*

street la rue *lah rew*

string la ficelle *lah fee-ssehl*

string beans les haricots (m. pl.) verts *lay ah-ree-koh vehr*

stripe la rayure *lah rah-yewr*; **striped** à rayures *ah rah-yewr*

strong fort(e) *fohr(t)*

stuffed farci(e) *fahr-ssee*

style la mode *lah mohd*; **in style** à la mode *ah lah mohd*

subtitles les sous-titres (m. pl.) *lay soo-tee-truh*

suburb la banlieue *lah bahn-lyuh*; le faubourg *luh foh-boor*

subway le métro *luh may-troh*

suede le daim *luh dan*

sugar le sucre *luh sew-kruh*

suit (man's) le complet *luh kohn-pleh*; **(woman's)** le tailleur *luh tah-yuhr*

suitcase la valise *lah vah-leez*

sum total le montant *luh mohn-tahn*

summer l'été (m.) *lay-tay*

sun le soleil *luh soh-lehy*

sunburn les coups (m. pl.) de soleil *lay kood soh-lehy*

Sunday dimanche *dee-mahnsh*

sunglasses les lunettes (f. pl.) de soleil *lay lew-neht duh soh-lehy*

suntan lotion la lotion à bronzer *lah loh-ssyohn ah brohn-zay*

supermarket le supermarché *luh sew-pehr-mahr-shay*

supper le dîner *luh dee-nay*; le souper *luh soo-pay*; **to have supper** dîner *dee-nay*; souper *soo-pay*

sure sûr(e) *sewr*

surfboard la planche de surf *lah plahnsh duh sewrf*

surgeon le chirurgien *luh sheer-ewr-zhyan*

SUV le VUS *luh vay-ew-ehss*

sweater le chandail *luh shahn-dahy*

sweet doux (douce) *doo (dooss)*

swim nager *nah-zhay*

swimming pool la piscine *lah pee-sseen*

synagogue la synagogue *lah see-nah-gohg*

synthetic synthétique *san-tay-teek*

T

table la table *lah tah-bluh*

tablecloth la nappe *lah nahp*

tablet (pill) le comprimé *luh kohn-pree-may*

taillight le feu arrière *luh fuh ah-ryehr*

tailor le tailleur *luh tah-yuhr*

take prendre *prahn-druh*

take off (clothing) ôter *oh-tay*; enlever *ahn-luh-vay*

talcum powder le talc *luh tahlk*

tampon le tampon périodique *luh tahn-pohn pay-ree-oh-deek*

tangerine la mandarine *lah mahn-dah-reen*

taste (noun) le goût *luh goo*

taste (verb) goûter *goo-tay*

taxi le taxi *luh tahk-ssee*

tea le thé *luh tay*; **iced** le thé glacé *luh tay glah-ssay*; **with lemon** au citron *oh see-trohn*; **with milk** au lait *oh leh*; **with sugar** sucré *sew-kray*

team l'équipe (f.) *lay-keep*

telephone le téléphone *luh tay-lay-fohn*; **telephone book** l'annuaire (m.) *lah-new-ehr*; **telephone call** le coup de téléphone *luh koo duh tay-lay-fohn*; **to call** donner un coup de téléphone *doh-nay uhn koo duh tay-lay-fohn*; **telephone card** la carte téléphonique *lah kahrt tay-lay-foh-neek*

television la télévision *lah tay-lay-vee-zyohn*

tell raconter *rah-kohn-tay*

temporary provisoire *proh-veez-wahr*

ten dix *deess*

tent la tente *lah tahnt*

terrific formidable *fohr-mee-dah-bluh*

terrycloth le tissu-éponge *luh tee-ssew ay-pohnzh*

thank remercier *ruh-mehr-ssyay*

thanks to grâce à *grahss ah*

thank you merci *mehr-ssee*

that ça *sah*; cela *suh-lah*

the le (m.), la (f.), les (m./f. pl.) *luh, lah, lay*

there à *lah*; **over there** là-bas *lah bah*

there is, are il y a *eel yah*; voilà *vwah-lah*

they ils (m. pl.) *eel*, elles (f. pl.) *ehl*

thief le voleur *luh voh-luhr*

thin mince *manss*

thing la chose *lah shohz*

think penser *pahn-ssay*

thirst la soif *lah swahf*; **be thirsty** avoir soif *ah-vwahr swahf*

thirteen treize *trehz*

thirty trente *trahnt*

this ceci *suh-ssee*

thousand mille *meel*

three trois *trwah*

throat la gorge *lah gohrzh*

through à travers *ah trah-vehr*

thumb le pouce *luh pooss*

Thursday jeudi *zhuh-dee*

ticket le billet *luh bee-yeh*; **child's ticket** billet au tarif enfant *bee-yeh oh tah-reef ahn-fahn*; **entrance ticket** le billet d'entrée *luh bee-yeh dahn-tray*; **student's ticket** billet au tarif étudiant *bee-yeh oh tah-reef ay-tew-dyahn*

ticket collector le contrôleur *luh kohn-troh-luhr*

ticket window le guichet *luh gee-sheh*

tie (neck) la cravate *lah krah-vaht*

time l'heure (f.) *luhr*; le temps *luh tahn*; **at what time?** À quelle heure? *ah kehl uhr*; **on time** à l'heure *ah luhr*

time (in a series) la fois *la fwah*; **one time** une fois *ewn fwah*; **two times** deux fois *duh fwah*

timetable l'horaire (m.) *loh-rehr*; l'indicateur (m.) *lan-dee-kah-tuhr*

tip (end) le bout *luh boo*

tip (gratuity) le pourboire *luh poor-bwahr*

tire (car) le pneu *luh pnuh*

tire (verb) fatiguer *fah-tee-gay*

tired fatigué(e) *fah-tee-gay*

tiring fatigant(e) *fah-tee-gahn(t)*

tissue le mouchoir en papier *luh moo-shwahr ahn pah-pyay*

title le titre *luh tee-truh*

to à *ah*

toast le pain grillé *luh pan gree-yay*

tobacco le tabac *luh tah-bah*; **tobacco shop** le bureau de tabac *luh bew-roh duh tah-bah*

today aujourd'hui *oh-zhoor-dwee*

toe l'orteil (m.) *lohr-tehy*

together ensemble *ahn-ssahn-bluh*

toilet la toilette *lah twah-leht*

tolerate supporter *sew-pohr-tay*

tomato la tomate *lah toh-maht*

tomorrow demain *duh-man*

tonsilitis l'amygdalite (f.) *lah-meeg-dah-leet*

tooth la dent *lah dahn*; **toothache** le mal de dents *luh mahl duh dahn*

toothpaste la pâte dentifrice *lah paht dahn-tee-freess*

toothpick le cure-dents *luh kewr dahn*

touch toucher *too-shay*

touch-up une retouche *ewn ruh-toosh*

tough dur *dewr*

tourist le touriste *luh too-reesst*

tourist office le syndicat d'initiative *luh san-dee-kah dee-nee-ssyah-teev*

toward vers *vehr*

towel la serviette *lah sehr-vyeht*

tower la tour *lah toor*

town hall la mairie *lah meh-ree*

track la voie *lah vwah*

traffic la circulation *lah seer-kew-lah-ssyohn*

traffic light le feu *luh fuh*

train le train *luh tran*

translate traduire *trah-dweer*

travel (verb) voyager *vwah-yah-zhay*

travel agency l'agence (f.) de voyage *lah-zhahnss duh vwah-yahzh*

traveler voyageur *vwah-yah-zhuhr*

treatment le traitement *luh treht-mahn*

tree l'arbre (m.) *lahr-bruh*

trick (verb) tromper *trohn-pay*

trip le voyage *luh vwah-yahzh*; l'excursion (f.) *lehkss-kewr-zyohn*; **business trip** le voyage d'affaires *luh vwah-yahzh dah-fehr*

trouble la difficulté *lah dee-fee-kewl-tay*

trout la truite *lah trweet*

truck le camion *luh kah-myohn*

true vrai(e) *vreh*

trunk la malle *lah mahl*; **car trunk** le coffre *luh koh-fruh*

truth la vérité *lah vay-ree-tay*

try (to) essayer (de) *eh-sseh-yay (duh)*

try (on) essayer *eh-sseh-yay*

Tuesday mardi *mahr-dee*

tuna (fish) le thon *luh tohn*

turkey la dinde *lah dand*

turn (noun) le tour *luh toor*

turn (verb) tourner *toor-nay*

twelve douze *dooz*

twenty vingt *van*

tweezers la pince à épiler *lah panss ah ay-pee-lay*

two deux *duh*

U

ugly laid(e) *leh(d)*

umbrella le parapluie *luh pah-rah-plwee*

unbearable insupportable *an-ssew-pohr-tah-bluh*

unbelievable incroyable *an-krwah-yah-bluh*

undecided indécis(e) *an-day-ssee(z)*

under sous *soo*; dessous *duh-ssoo*

undershirt le maillot de corps *luh mah-yoh duh kohr*

understand comprendre *kohn-prahn-druh*

underwear les sous-vêtements (m. pl.) *lay soo veht-mahn*

unfair injuste *an-zhewsst*

unhappy malheureux(euse) *mahl-uh-ruh(z)*

unimportant insignifiant(e) *an-ssee-nee-fee-ahn(t)*

United States les Etats-Unis *lay zay-tah zew-nee*

until jusqu'à *zhewss-kah*

up, upstairs en haut *ahn oh*

urgent urgent(e) *ewr-zhahn(t)*; **urgently** d'urgence *dewr-zhahnss*

us nous *noo*

use (verb) utiliser *ew-tee-lee-zay*; employer *ahn-plwah-yay*

use (noun) l'emploi (m.) *lahn-plwah*

used up épuisé(e) *ay-pwee-zay*

useful utile *ew-teel*

useless inutile *een-ew-teel*

V

vacation les vacances (f. pl.) *lay vah-kahnss*

valid valable *vah-lah-bluh*

value la valeur *lah vah-luhr*

varied varié(e) *vah-ree-yay*

veal le veau *luh voh*

vegetable le légume *luh lay-gewm*

velvet le velours *luh vuh-loor*

very très *treh*

vest le gilet *luh zhee-leh*

vicinity les environs (m. pl.) *lay zahn-vee-rohn*

view la vue *lah vew*

village le village *luh vee-lahzh*

vinegar le vinaigre *luh vee-neh-gruh*

vitamin la vitamine *lah vee-tah-meen*

W

waist la taille *lah tahy*

waiter le garçon *luh gahr-ssohn*

wait for attendre *ah-tahn-druh*

waiting room la salle d'attente *lah sahl dah-tahnt*

waitress la serveuse *lah sehr-vuhz*

walk (noun) la promenade *lah prohm-nahd*; **to take a walk** faire une promenade *fehr ewn prohm-nahd*

walk (verb) marcher *mahr-shay*

walker le déambulateur *luh day-ahn bew-lah-tuhr*

wall le mur *luh mewr*

wallet le portefeuille *luh pohr-tuh-fuhy*

want désirer *day-zee-ray*; vouloir *voo-lwahr*; avoir envie de *ah-vvahr ahn-vee duh*

war la guerre *lah gehr*

warm chaud *shoh*

wash laver *lah-vay*; **wash oneself** se laver *suh lah-vay*

wash and wear ne pas repasser *nuh pah ruh-pah-ssay*

washroom le lavabo *luh lah-vah-boh*

watch (noun) la montre *lah mohn-truh*

watch (verb); (look at) regarder *ruh-gahr-day*; **(supervise)** surveiller *sewr-veh-yay*

watchband un bracelet de montre *uhn brahss-leh duh mohn-truh*

watchmaker's shop l'horlogerie (f.) *lohr-lohzh-ree*

waterfall la cascade *lah kahss-kahd*

water l'eau *loh*

watermelon la pastèque *lah pahss-tehk*

waxing l'épilation (f.) *lay-pee-lah-ssyohn*

way le moyen *luh mwah-yan*; la façon *lah fah-ssohn*

weak faible *feh-bluh*

wear porter *pohr-tay*

weather le temps *luh tahn*

Wednesday mercredi *mehr-kruh-dee*

week la semaine *lah suh-mehn*

weigh peser *puh-zay*

weight le poids *luh pwah*; **weights** les haltères *lay zahl-tehr*

welcome: you're welcome de rien *duh ryan*; il n'y a pas de quoi *eel nyah pah duh kwah*

well bien *byan*

well-done (cooking) bien cuit(e) *byan kwee(t)*

west l'ouest (m.) *lwehsst*

wet mouillé(e) *moo-yay*

wet suit la combinaison (f.) de plongée *lah kohn-bee-neh-zohn duh plohn-zhay*

what que, quoi *kuh, kwah*

wheelchair le fauteuil roulant *luh foh-tuhy roo-lahn*

when quand *kahn*

where où *oo*

which quel(le) *kehl*

white blanc(he) *blahn(sh)*

who qui *kee*

whole entier(ière) *ahn-tyay (ahn-tyehr)*

why pourquoi *poor-kwah*

wife la femme *lah fahm*

willingly volontiers *voh-lohn-tyay*

win gagner *gah-nyay*

wind le vent *luh vahn*

window la fenêtre *lah fuh-neh-truh*; **ticket window** le guichet *luh gee-sheh*

window display l'étalage (m.) *lay-tah-lahzh*

windshield wipers les essuie-glaces (m.) *lay zeh-sswee glahss*

wine le vin *luh van*; **red** rouge *roozh*; **rosé** rosé *roh-zay*; **sparkling** mousseux *moo-ssuh*; **white** blanc *blahn*

wine glass le verre à vin *luh vehr ah van*

wine merchant le négociant en vins *luh nay-gohss-yahn ahn van*

wine waiter le sommelier *luh soh-muh-lyay*

winter l'hiver (m.) *lee-vehr*

wireless sans fil *sahn feel*

wish (verb) désirer *day-zee-ray*; vouloir *voo-lwahr*; avoir envie de *ah-vwahr ahn-vee duh*

wish (someone something) souhaiter *soo-eh-tay*

with avec *ah-vehk*

withdraw retirer *ruh-tee-ray*

without sans *sahn*

woman la femme *lah fahm*

wood(s) le(s) bois *luh (lay) bwah*

wool la laine *lah lehn*

word le mot *luh moh*

work (noun) le travail *luh trah-vahy*

work (verb) travailler *trah-vah-yay*; **function** fonctionner *fohnk-ssyoh-nay*; marcher *mahr-shay*

workshop l'atelier (m.) *lah-tuh-lyay*

world le monde *luh mohnd*

worn out (things) usé(e) *ew-zay*; **(people)** épuisé(e) *ay-pwee-zay*

wound (noun) la blessure *lah bleh-ssewr*

wound (verb) blesser *bleh-ssay*

wounded blessé *bleh-ssay*

wrapper l'enveloppe (f.) *lahn-vlohp*

wrap up emballer *ahn-bah-lay*; envelopper *ahn-vloh-pay*

wrist le poignet *luh pwah-nyeh*

write écrire *ay-kreer*

wrong: to be wrong avoir tort *ah-vwahr tohr*

X

X-ray la radio *lah rah-dyoh*

Y

year l'an (m.) *lahn*, l'année (f.) *lah-nay*

yellow jaune *zhohn*

yes oui *wee*

yesterday hier *yehr*

yet encore *ahn-kohr*

yield céder *say-day*

yogurt le yaourt *luh yah-oort*

you tu *tew*; vous *voo*

young jeune *zhuhn*

Z

zero zéro *zay-roh*

zipper la fermeture éclair *lah fehr-muh-tewr ay-klehr*

zone la zone *lah zohn*

zoo le zoo *luh zoh*; le jardin zoologique *luh zhahr-dan zoh-oh-loh-zheek*

FRENCH-ENGLISH DICTIONARY

A

à to, at; **à peu près** about, approximately; **prix fixe** fixed price meal; **à travers** across, through

abricot (m.) apricot

accord (m.) agreement; **d'accord** agreed, O.K.

accrocher to hang up

achat (m.) purchase

acheter to buy

addition (f.) check, restaurant bill

adresse (f.) address

aérobic (m.) aerobics

affaire (f.) matter, concern

affiche (f.) poster

agence (f.) agency, bureau; **une agence de voyage** travel agency

agent (de police) (m.) policeman

agneau (m.) lamb

aider to help

aiguille (f.) needle

ail (m.) garlic

aile (f.) fender

ailleurs elsewhere

aimer to like, love; **aimer mieux** to prefer

ajouter to add

alcool (m.) alcohol

aliments (m. pl.) food

aller to go; **aller à** to fit

allumage (m.) ignition

allumer to light

allumette (f.) match

alors then

amande (f.) almond

ambulance (f.) ambulance

amende (f.) fine, penalty

amer, amère bitter

ami(e) (m./f.) friend

amour (m.) love (noun)

ampoule (f.) bulb (electric)

amygdalite (f.) tonsilitis

an (m.) year

analyse (f.) de sang blood test

ananas (m.) pineapple

ancien(ne) former, old

anglais (m.) English

année (f.) year

anniversaire (m.) birthday

annonce (f.) advertisement

annuaire (m.) telephone book

antiseptique (m.) antiseptic

août August

appareil de photo (m.) camera

appartenir to belong

appeler to call; **s'appeler** to be called, named

appendicite (f.) appendicitis

apporter to bring

apprendre to learn

après after; **après-demain** day after tomorrow; **après-midi (m.)** afternoon

arbre (m.) tree

argent (m.) money, silver

armoire (f.) closet

arracher to pull (tooth)

arranger to adjust

arrêt (m.) a stop; **arrêt obligatoire** regular bus stop

arrêter to stop

arrière back; **en arrière** backward, behind

arrivée (f.) arrival

artichaut (m.) artichoke

artiste (m. or f.) artist

ascenseur (m.) elevator

asperge (f.) asparagus

assaisonné(e) seasoned

asseoir (s' . . .) to sit down; **asseyez-vous** sit down

assez (de) enough

assiette (f.) plate

assurance (f.) insurance

assurer (faire assurer) to insure

asthme (m.) asthma

atelier (m.) workshop, studio

attendre to wait for

attention caution

atterrir to land (plane)

atterrissage (m.) landing (plane)

attraper to catch

au to the; **au lieu de** instead of; **au milieu de** in the middle of; **au moins** at least; **au secours** help

auberge (f.) inn; **auberge de jeunesse** youth hostel

aubergine (f.) eggplant

aucun(e) any; **ne (verb) aucun(e)** not any

audiophone (m.) hearing aid

aujourd'hui today

aussi also, too

auteur (m.) author

autoroute (f.) highway

autour de around

autre other

aux to the

avant (de, que) before; **avant-hier** day before yesterday; **en avant** forward, ahead

avec with

avion (m.) airplane; **par avion** air mail, by plane

avis (m.) notice

avocat (m.), avocate (f.) lawyer

avoir to have; **avoir l'air de** to seem to; **avoir besoin de** to need; **avoir chaud** to be hot; **avoir envie de** to want to; **avoir faim** to be hungry; **avoir froid** to be cold; **avoir peur de** to be afraid of; **avoir raison** to be right; **avoir soif** to be thirsty; **avoir sommeil** to be sleepy; **avoir tort** to be wrong

B

bague (f.) ring

baguette (f.) French bread

baigner (se . . .) to bathe

bain (m.) bath

balcon (m.) balcony

ballet (m.) ballet

banane (f.) banana

banc (m.) bench

bande (f.) bandage

banlieue (f.) suburb

banque (f.) bank

barbe (f.) beard

bas (m. pl.) stockings

bas (se) low; **en bas** downstairs

base de données (f.) database

bateau (m.) boat; **bateau à voile** sailboat

bâtiment (m.) building

batterie (f.) battery (car)

beau (m.) beautiful

beaucoup (de) many, much, a lot, a great deal of

beige beige

belle (f.) beautiful

béquilles (f. pl.) crutches

berceau (m.) crib

besoin (m.) need; **avoir besoin de** to need

betterave (f.) beet

beurre (m.) butter

bibliothèque (f.) library

bien well; **bien entendu** of course

bientôt soon; **à bientôt** see you soon

bière (f.) beer

bifteck (m.) steak

bijou (m.) jewel

bijouterie (f.) jewelry shop

bijoutier (m.) jeweler

billet (m.) ticket; **billet d'entrée** admission ticket; **billet au tarif enfant** child's ticket; **billet au tarif étudiant** student's ticket

biologique organic

biscuit (m.) cookie

bistro (m.) bar, tavern, saloon

blanc(he) white

blanchissage (m.) laundering, washing

blanchisserie (f.) laundry

blessé(e) wounded

blesser to wound, hurt

blessure (f.) wound

bleu(e) blue

bleu marine navy blue

bloc (m.) writing pad

blouse (f.) chemisier

boeuf (m.) beef, ox

boire to drink

bois (m.) wood; **bois (m. pl.)** woods

boisson (f.) drink; **une boisson non-alcoolisée** soft drink

boîte (f.) box; **boîte aux lettres** mailbox; **boîte de nuit** nightclub

bol (m.) bowl

bon(ne) good

bonjour hello

bon marché cheap

bottes (f. pl.) boots

bouche (f.) mouth

boucherie (f.) butcher shop

boucle (f.) curl; **boucles d'oreille** earrings

bougie (f.) candle, spark plug

bouilli(e) boiled

boulangerie (f.) bakery

boulette (f.) meatball

bourse (f.) stock market

bout (m.) tip, point, end

bouteille (f.) bottle

boutique (f.) shop

bouton (m.) button

bracelet de montre (m.) watchband

braisé(e) braised

bras (m.) arm

brioche (f.) breakfast bun

briquet (m.) cigarette lighter

briser to break

brosse (f.) brush; **brosse à dents** toothbrush

brosser (se . . .) to brush

brouillé(e) scrambled; **les oeufs brouillés** scrambled eggs

bruit (m.) noise

brûler to burn

brûlure (f.) a burn

brun(e) brown

bureau (m.) office, desk; **bureau de change** money exchange; **bureau de location** theater box office; **bureau des objets trouvés** lost and found; **bureau de poste** post office; **bureau de renseignements** information desk; **bureau de tabac** tobacco shop

C

ça that; **ça ne fait rien** it doesn't matter

cabine téléphonique (f.) telephone booth

câbles (m. pl.) de démarrage jumper cables

cadeau (m.) gift, present

café (m.) coffee, café; **café au lait** coffee with milk; **café crème** coffee with cream; **café express** espresso; **café décaféiné** decaffeinated coffee; **café glacé** iced coffee; **café noir** black coffee

cahier (m.) notebook

caisse (f.) cash register

caissier (m.) cashier

caleçon (m.) men's shorts, undergarments

camion (m.) truck

campagne (f.) country (outside city)

canne (f.) cane

canne à pêche (f.) fishing rod

canard (m.) duck

canotage (m.) boating

caoutchouc (m.) rubber; **caoutchoucs (m. pl.)** rubbers

capot (m.) hood (car)

carburateur (m.) carburetor

carotte (f.) carrot

carré(e) square

carreaux (à carreaux) checked (material)

carrefour (m.) crossroad

carte (f.) map, card; **cartes à jouer** playing cards; **carte de crédit** credit card; **carte de débit** debit card; **carte téléphonique** telephone card; **carte postale** postcard; **carte routière** road map

cas (m.) case; **en cas d'urgence** in case of emergency

cascade (f.) waterfall

casier (m.) locker

casser to break; **casser la croûte** to get a bite to eat

cave (f.) cellar

ceci this, it

céder to yield

ceinture (f.) belt; **ceinture de sauvetage** life preserver; **ceinture de sécurité** seat belt

célibataire single (unmarried)

cendrier (m.) ashtray

cent one hundred

cerise (f.) cherry

chacun(e) each one

chaînette (f.) chain (jewelry)

chaise (f.) chair

châle (m.) shawl

chaleur (f.) heat

chambre (f.) room; **chambre à coucher** bedroom; **chambre à un lit** single room; **chambre à deux lits** double room

champignon (m.) mushroom

champ (m.) field

chance (f.) luck; **Bonne chance!** Good luck!

chandail (m.) sweater

changement (m.) change; **changement de vitesse** gearshift

changer to change

chanson (f.) song

chanter to sing

chaque each

charcuterie (f.) cold cuts, delicatessen

chasse (f.) hunting

chasseur (m.) bellboy, bellhop

chat (m.) cat

château (m.) castle

chaud hot; **avoir chaud** to be hot (person); **faire chaud** to be hot (weather)

chauffage (m.) heating

chauffer to heat

chaussettes (f. pl.) socks

chaussures (f. pl.) shoes

chemin (m.) road, way

chemin de fer (m.) railway, railroad

chemise (f.) shirt

chemisier (m.) blouse

chèque (m.) check; **toucher un chèque** to cash a check

cher, chère dear, expensive

chercher to look for

cheval (m.) (pl. chevaux) horse

cheveux (m. pl.) hair

cheville (f.) ankle

chez at the house (shop, business) of

chien (m.) dog

chirurgien (m.) surgeon

choisir to choose

chose (f.) thing

chou (m.) cabbage

choucroute (f.) sauerkraut

choux de Bruxelles (m. pl.) Brussels sprouts

ciel (m.) sky

cigare (m.) cigar

cigarette (f.) cigarette

cil (m.) eyelash

cimetière (m.) cemetery

cinéma (m.) movies

cinq five

cinquante fifty

cintre (m.) hanger

circulation (f.) traffic

cirer to shine, wax

ciseaux (m. pl.) scissors

citron (m.) lemon

citronnade (f.) lemonade

clair(e) clear, light (color)

clavier (m.) keyboard

clef (f.) key

client (m.) customer

clignotant (m.) directional signal

climatiseur (m.) air conditioner

cliquer (to) click

cloche (f.) bell

coco (m.) coconut

cocotte (en) stewed

code (m.) confidentiel PIN number

coeur (m.) heart

coffre (m.) trunk (car)

coffre-fort (m.) safe, strongbox

coiffeur (m.), coiffeuse (f.), barber, hairdresser

coin (m.) corner

col (m.) collar

colis (m.) package, parcel

collants (m. pl.) panty hose

colle (f.) glue

collier (m.) necklace

combien (de) how much, how many

combinaison (f.) slip (clothing); **combinaison de plongée** wet suit

commande (f.) order

commander to order

comme like, as

commencer to begin

comment how

commissariat (m.) police station

compagnie (f.) company

complet (m.) suit (man's)

comprendre to understand

comprimé (m.) tablet

compris(e) included

comptable (m. or f.) accountant

compter to count

concert (m.) concert; **la salle de concert** concert hall

concierge (m. or f.) house porter, caretaker, doorman

concombre (m.) cucumber

conduire to drive, take a person somewhere

confiserie (f.) confectionery store

confiture (f.) jam, marmalade

connaître to know, be acquainted

conseil (m.) advice

conseiller to advise, recommend
consigne (f.) baggage checkroom
consommation (f.) drink
contagieux(ieuse) contagious
conte (m.) short story
contenir to contain
contenu (m.) contents
contraire (m.) opposite
contre against
contrôleur (m.) ticket collector
contusion (f.) bruise
coquillage (m.) shellfish
cordonnier (m.) shoemaker
cornichon (m.) pickle
corps (m.) body
correcteur (m.) orthographique spell checker
costume (m.) suit (man's)
côte (f.) coast
côté (m.) side; **à côté de** beside, next to
côtelette (f.) cutlet, chop
coton (m.) cotton
cou (m.) neck
couche (f.) diaper
couchette (f.) berth
coude (m.) elbow
coudre to sew
couleur (f.) color
coup de téléphone (m.) phone call
coupe de cheveux (f.) haircut
coupe de glace (f.) sundae
couper to cut
cour (f.) courtyard
courir to run
courrier (m.) mail
courroie (f.) de ventilateur fan belt
cours du change (m.) exchange rate
court(e) short
couteau (m.) knife
coûter to cost

coûteux(euse) costly
couvert (m.) cover charge; place setting
couverture (f.) blanket
couvrir to cover
crabe (m.) crab
crampe (f.) cramp
cravate (f.) tie
crayon (m.) pencil
crème (f.) cream; **la crème anglaise** custard; **la crème fouettée** whipped cream
crêpe (f.) thin French pancake
crevette (f.) shrimp
cric (m.) jack (auto)
croire to believe
croisement (m.) intersection
croissant (m.) crescent-shaped breakfast pastry
croûte (f.) crust; **casser la croûte** to get a bite to eat
cru(e) raw, uncooked
cruche (f.) pitcher
cuiller (f.) spoon; **cuiller à soupe** tablespoon; **cuiller à café** teaspoon
cuillerée (f.) spoonful; **cuillerée à soupe** tablespoonful; **cuillerée à café** teaspoonful
cuir (m.) leather
cuisine (f.) cooking, kitchen
cuisinier (m.) the cook
cuisse (f.) thigh; **les cuisses de grenouille** frog's legs
cuit(e) cooked
cure-dent (m.) toothpick
curseur (m.) cursor
cybercafé (m.) Internet café

D

d'abord at first
d'accord agreed, O.K.
daim (m.) suede
dangereux(-euse) dangerous
dans in

danse (f.) the dance
danser to dance
date (f.) date
datte (f.) date (fruit)
de of; **de bonne heure** early
déambulateur (m.) walker
débarquement (m.) landing (boat)
débarquer to land (boat)
décharger (to) download
décider to decide
déclarer to declare
déçu(e) disappointed
dedans inside
défendre to forbid; **défense de cracher** no spitting; **défense d'entrer** no entry; **défense de fumer** no smoking
défendu(e) forbidden
dehors outside
déjà already
déjeuner (m.) lunch
déjeuner to eat lunch
demain tomorrow
demander to ask (for)
démarrer to boot
démarreur (m.) starter
demeurer to live, reside
demi(e) half
démodé(e) old-fashioned
dent (f.) tooth; **mal (m.) de dent** toothache
dentelle (f.) lace
dentiste (m. or f.) dentist
déodorant (m.) deodorant
dépêcher (se . . .) to hurry up; **dépêchez-vous** hurry up
dépenser to spend money
déranger to bother
dernier(ière) last
derrière behind
des some
descendre to go down, get off
désirer to desire, wish, want
désolé(e) sorry; **être désolé(e)** to be sorry

dessous under, beneath
dessus over, above
deux two
devant in front of
devenir to become
devoir to owe, have to, ought to
dictionnaire (m.) dictionary; **dictionnaire de poche** pocket dictionary
Dieu God
différent(e) different
difficile difficult
dimanche Sunday
diminuer to diminish
dinde (f.) turkey
dîner (m.) dinner
dîner to dine
dire to say
discothèque (f.) discotheque
dispute (f.) dispute, argument
dix ten
dix-huit eighteen
dix-neuf nineteen
dix-sept seventeen
docteur (m.) doctor
doigt (m.) finger
donner to give
dormir to sleep
dos (m.) back
douane (f.) customs
douanier (m.) customs official
doucement softly
douche (f.) shower
douleur (f.) pain
doux, douce sweet, mild, soft
douzaine (f.) dozen
douze twelve
droit (m.) right; **à droite** to the right
du some
dur hard, tough
durer to last

E

eau (f.) water; **eau courante** running water; **eau chaude**

hot water; **eau froide** cold
water; **eau glacée** ice water;
eau minérale mineral water
eau dentifrice (f.) mouthwash
échanger to exchange
échantillon (m.) sample
échappement (m.) exhaust
écharpe (f.) scarf
école (f.) school
écouter to listen to
écran (m.) screen
écrire to write
égarer (s' . . .) to lose one's
way, to get lost
église (f.) church
élargir enlarge
elle she
elles they
e-mail (m.) e-mail
emballer to wrap up
embrasser to kiss
emploi (m.) employ, use
employer to use
emporter to carry, take away
emprunter to borrow
en in; **en arrière** behind; **en
avant** ahead; **en bas**
downstairs; **en ce moment**
right now; **en face de**
opposite, facing; **en retard**
late; **en voiture** all aboard
encaisser to cash
enceinte pregnant
encore yet, still; **encore une
fois** again
endosser to endorse
endroit (m.) place
enfant (m. or f.) child
engrenage (m.) gears
ennuyer to annoy, bother
enregistrer to check bags
enseigne (f.) sign
ensemble together
entendre to hear
entier (entière) entire, whole
entre between

entrée (f.) entrance
entrer to enter
enveloppe (f.) envelope,
wrapper, cover
envelopper to wrap up
environ about
environs (m. pl.) vicinity
envoyer to send
épaule (f.) shoulder
épeler to spell
épicerie (f.) grocery store
épicé spicy
épilation (f.) waxing
épinards (m. pl.) spinach
épingle (f.) pin
époux (épouse) spouse
épuisé(e) exhausted, used up
équipe (f.) team
équitation (f.) horseback
riding
escalier (m.) stairs
escargot (m.) snail
espace (f.) space
espérer to hope
escale (f.) stopover
essayer (de) to try (to)
essence (f.) gas; **le réservoir
à essence** gas tank
essuie-glaces (m. pl.)
windshield wipers
est (m.) east
estomac (m.) stomach
et and
étage (m.) story, floor
étalage (m.) window display
état (m.) state
Etats-Unis (m. pl.) United
States
été (m.) summer
étiquette (f.) label
étranger(ère) foreign; **à
l'étranger** abroad
être to be; **être d'accord** to
agree; **être de retour** to be
back
éviter to avoid
excellent(e) excellent

excursion (f.) excursion, trip
exemple (m.) example; **par exemple** for example
express (m.) express

F

facile easy
façon (f.) way, style, fashion
facteur (m.) mailman
facture (f.) bill, invoice
faible weak
faim (f.) hunger; **avoir faim** to be hungry
faire to make, do; **faire beau** to be beautiful weather; **faire chaud** to be hot weather; **faire des achats** to go shopping; **faire des emplettes** to go shopping; **faire du soleil** to be sunny; **faire du vent** to be windy; **faire froid** to be cold weather; **faire la connaissance de** to make the acquaintance of; **faire la correspondance** to change trains or planes; **faire la queue** to form a line; **faire une promenade** to take a walk; **faire venir** to send for
fait(e) à la main handmade
famille (f.) family
farci(e) stuffed
fard (m.) à paupières eye shadow
fatigant(e) tiring
fatigué(e) tired
fatiguer to tire
faubourg (m.) suburb
faut: il faut it is necessary
faute (f.) mistake, error
fauteuil (m.) roulant wheelchair
faux, fausse false
félicitations (f. pl.) congratulations

femme (f.) woman, wife; **femme de chambre** chambermaid
fenêtre (f.) window
fer (m.) iron
ferme (f.) farm
fermer to close
fermeture éclair (f.) zipper
fête (f.) festival, feast, holiday
feu (m.) fire, traffic light; **feu arrière** taillight
feuille (f.) sheet, leaf
feutre (m.) felt
février February
fiche (f.) form
fichier (m.) file
fièvre (f.) fever
figue (f.) fig
figure (f.) face
fil (m.) wire; **sans fil** wireless
fille (f.) girl, daughter
film (m.) film
fils (m.) son
fin (f.) end
finir to finish, end
flan (m.) custard
flanelle (f.) flannel
fleur (f.) flower
fleuriste (m.) florist
fleuve (m.) river
foie (m.) liver
foire (f.) fair, market
fois (f.) time in a series; **une fois** one time, once; **deux fois** two times, twice
foncé(e) dark (color)
fonctionner to function, work
fontaine (f.) fountain
forêt (f.) forest
formidable terrific
formule (f.) form
fort(e) strong

four (m.) oven; **four à micro-ondes** microwave oven

fourchette (f.) fork

frais, fraîche fresh

frais (m. pl.) expense, charge, cost

fraise (f.) strawberry

framboise (f.) raspberry

français (m.) French

frappé (m.) milk shake

frapper to knock, hit, strike

freins (m. pl.) brakes

frère (m.) brother

frit(e) fried

froid (m.) cold; **avoir froid** to be cold (person); **faire froid** to be cold (weather)

fromage (m.) cheese

front (m.) forehead

frontière (f.) border

fruit (m.) fruit

fruits de mer (m. pl.) seafood

fumer to smoke

fumeur (m.) smoker

G

gabardine (f.) gabardine

gagner to earn, win

gant (m.) glove

garçon (m.) boy

garder to keep

gare (f.) station

garer to park a car

gare routière (f.) bus station

gâteau (m.) cake

gauche left; **à gauche** to the left

gencives (f. pl.) gums

gendarme (m.) policeman

gêner to bother, annoy

genou (m.) knee

genouillères (f. pl.) kneepads

gens (m. or f. pl.) people

gérant (m.) manager

gibier (m.) game (meat)

gigot (m.) leg of mutton

gilet (m.) vest

glace (f.) ice, ice cream

glacé(e) iced

glaçon (m.) ice cube

gomme (f.) eraser

gorge (f.) throat; **avoir mal à la gorge** to have a sore throat

goût (m.) taste

goûter to taste

goyave (f.) guava

grâce à thanks to

grafique (f.) graphics

grand(e) big

gratiné(e) browned

gratte-ciel (m.) skyscraper

gratuit(e) (adj.) free

gratuitement (adv.) free of charge

grave grave, serious

grillé(e) grilled, broiled

grippe (f.) the flu

gris(e) gray

gros(se) fat

guerre (f.) war

guichet (m.) ticket window; banking window

guichet (m.) **automatique** ATM

guide (m.) guide; **guide touristique** guidebook

gymnase (m.) gym

H

habiller (s'. . .) to dress oneself

habiter to live in

habits (m. pl.) clothes

haltères (m. pl.) weights

hamburger (m.) hamburger

hanche (f.) hip

handicapé(e) handicapped

hareng (m.) herring; **hareng fumé** smoked herring

haricot (m.) bean
haricots verts (m. pl.) string beans
haut(e) high
hauteur (f.) height, elevation
haut-parleur (m.) loudspeaker
herbe (f.) grass
heure (f.) hour; **à l'heure** on time; **de bonne heure** early
heureux(euse) happy
hier yesterday
histoire (f.) story
hiver (m.) winter
hockey (m.) hockey
homard (m.) lobster
homme (m.) man
homme (femme) d'affaires businessperson
hôpital (m.) hospital
horaire (m.) schedule, timetable
horloge (f.) clock
horlogerie (f.) watchmaker's shop
hôte (m.) host
hôtel (m.) hotel
hôtesse (f.) hostess
huile (f.) oil; **l'huile d'olive** olive oil
huit eight
huître (f.) oyster

incapable incapable
incendie (m.) fire
incroyable unbelievable
indécis(e) undecided
infection (f.) infection
informaticien(ne) computer scientist
informatique (f.) computer science
informatiser to computerize
infirmière (f.) nurse
infroissable permanent press
injuste unfair
insignifiant(e) unimportant
insomnie (f.) insomnia
insuffisant(e) insufficient
insupportable unbearable
intelligent(e) intelligent
interdire to prohibit, forbid
interdit(e) prohibited, forbidden
intéressant(e) interesting
interprète (m. or f.) interpreter
interpréter to interpret
inutile useless
inviter to invite
invraisemblable improbable, unlikely
itineraire (m.) itinerary, route
ivre drunk

I

ici here
il he
île (f.) island
ils they
il y a there is, are; **il y a + time** ago
immédiatement immediately
imperméable (m.) raincoat
important(e) important
impossible impossible
imprécis(e) indefinite
imprimante (f.) printer; **laser** laser; **jet d'encre** ink jet

J

jamais never; **ne . . . jamais** never
jambe (f.) leg
jambon (m.) ham
janvier January
jardin (m.) garden
jarre (f.) jar
jaune yellow
je I
jean denim
jetable disposable
jeu (m.) game
jeudi Thursday

jeune young
jogging (m.) jogging suit
joli(e) pretty
joue (f.) cheek
jouer to play; **jouer à** to play a game, sport; **jouer de** to play a musical instrument
jour (m.) day
journal (m.) newspaper
juge (m.) judge
juger to judge
juillet July
juin June
jupe (f.) skirt
jupon (m.) slip
jus (m.) juice
jusqu'à until

K

ketchup (m.) ketchup
kiosque (m.) stand; **le kiosque à journaux** newsstand
klaxon (m.) horn

L

là there; **là-bas** over there
lac (m.) lake
lacet (m.) lace (shoe)
laid(e) ugly
laine (f.) wool
laisser to let, leave behind
lait (m.) milk
laitue (f.) lettuce
lampe (f.) lamp; **la lampe de poche** flashlight
langue (f.) language, tongue
lapin (m.) rabbit
laque (f.) hairspray
lard (m.) bacon
lavabo (m.) washroom
laver to wash; **se laver** to wash oneself
laverie automatique (f.) launderette

leger(ère) light (weight)
légume (m.) vegetable
lent(e) slow
lentement slowly
lettre (f.) letter
lever: se lever to get up
lèvre (f.) lip; **rouge à lèvres (m.)** lipstick
librairie (f.) bookstore
libre free
ligne (f.) line
limette (f.) lime
lin (m.) linen (material)
lire to read
liste (f.) list
lit (m.) bed
livre (m.) book
livre (f.) pound (weight)
livrer to deliver
loger to stay at
logiciel (m.) software
logis (m.) lodging
loin far; **loin de** far from
long(ue) long
lotion (f.) lotion; **la lotion à bronzer** suntan lotion
lourd(e) heavy; **il fait lourd** it's hot and humid
louer to rent, hire
loyer (m.) the rent
lumière (f.) light
lundi Monday
lunettes (f. pl.) eyeglasses; **les lunettes de soleil** sunglasses
luxe (m.) luxury
luxueux(euse) luxurious
lycée (m.) high school

M

macédoine de fruits (f.) fruit salad
mâchoire (f.) jaw
madame Mrs.
mademoiselle Miss

magasin (m.) store; **de chaussures** shoe store; **un grand magasin** department store; **de jouets** toy store; **de photographie** camera store; **de souvenirs** gift shop; **de spiritueux** liquor store; **de vêtements** clothing store; **magasin multimédia** multimedia store

magazine (m.) magazine

mai May

maillot (m.) de bain bathing suit; **de corps** undershirt

main (f.) hand

maintenant now

mairie (f.) town hall

mais but

maïs (m.) corn

maison (f.) house; **à la maison** at home

mal (m.) ache; **mal de dents** toothache; **mal d'estomac** stomachache; **mal de gorge** sore throat; **mal de tête** headache

malade sick

maladie (f.) sickness, illness

malentendu (m.) misunderstanding

malgré in spite of

malheureux(euse) unhappy

malle (f.) trunk; **malle arrière** auto trunk

manche (f.) sleeve

mandarine (f.) tangerine

manette (f.) de jeux joystick

manger to eat

mangue (f.) mango

manque (m.) lack

manquer to lack, miss

manteau (m.) overcoat

marchand (m.) merchant

marchandise (f.) merchandise

marché (m.) market

marcher to walk

mardi Tuesday

margarine (f.) margarine

mari (m.) husband

marque (f.) brand (of product)

marron brown

marron (m.) chestnut

mars March

matin (m.) morning

mauvais(e) bad

mauve purple

mayonnaise (m.) mayonnaise

mécanicien (m.) mechanic

médecin (m.) doctor

médicament (m.) medicine

meilleur(e) better (adj.)

melon (m.) melon

même same; **le/la même** the same

mémoire (f.) memory

menton (m.) chin

mer (f.) sea; **au bord de la mer** at the seashore

merci thank you

mercredi Wednesday

mère (f.) mother

mériter to deserve

merveilleux(euse) marvelous

mesure (f.) measurement

mesurer to measure

métro (m.) subway

mettre to put, put on

meublé(e) furnished

midi noon

mieux better (adv.)

milieu (m.) middle; **au milieu de** in the middle of

mille thousand

million (m.) million; **un million de + noun** a million

mince thin

minuit midnight

minute (f.) minute

miroir (m.) mirror

mode (f.) style; **à la mode** stylish, in style

modem (m.) modem

modifier to modify, change

moins less

mois (m.) month

moitié (f.) half

monde (m.) world; **tout le monde** everybody

moniteur (m.) monitor

monnaie (f.) coin money, change

monsieur (m.) mister, Mr., sir

montagne (f.) mountain

montant (m.) sum total

monter to go up

montre (f.) watch

montrer to show

morceau (m.) piece

mosquée (f.) mosque

mot (m.) word

moteur (m.) motor

moteur (m.) de recherche search engine

mouchoir (m.) handkerchief; **le mouchoir en papier** tissue

mouillé(e) wet

moule (f.) mussel

mousseline de soie (f.) chiffon

moutarde (f.) mustard

moyen (m.) way

mur (m.) wall

musculation (f.) bodybuilding

musée (m.) museum

musique (f.) music

N

nager to swim

nappe (f.) tablecloth

nationalité (f.) nationality

nausée (f.) nausea

ne; ne . . . aucun(e) not . . . any; **ne . . . jamais** never; **ne . . . pas** not; **ne . . . plus** no longer, not . . . anymore; **ne . . . que** only; **ne . . . rien** nothing

nécessaire necessary

neige (f.) snow

neiger to snow

nettoyer to clean

nettoyer à sec to dry-clean

neuf nine

nez (m.) nose

noir(e) black

noix (f.) walnut

nom (m.) name; **nom de famille** family name; **prénom (m.)** first name; **surnom (m.)** last name, nickname

nombre (m.) number (quantity)

non no

non-fumeurs non-smoking

nord (m.) north

note (f.) bill (hotel)

nourriture (f.) food

nous us

nouveau (m.) new

nouveauté (f.) novelty

nouvelle (f.) new

nuit (f.) night

numéro (m.) number; **le numéro de téléphone** telephone number

nylon (m.) nylon

O

observer to observe

obtenir to obtain

occasion (f.) opportunity, bargain; **marchandise d'occasion (f.)** secondhand (used) goods

occupé(e) busy

océan (m.) ocean

oeil (m.) eye; **(pl.) les yeux** eyes

oeuf (m.) egg; **au plat** fried; **brouillé** scrambled; **dur** hard-boiled; **frit** fried; **mollet** medium-boiled;

à la coque soft-boiled; **poché** poached; **poêlé** sunny-side up
offrir to offer
oie (f.) goose
oignon (m.) onion
olive (f.) olive; **l'huile (f.) d'olive** olive oil
ombre (f.) shade (tree)
omelette (f.) omelet; **l'omelette norvégienne** baked Alaska
ongle (m.) nail (finger); **la lime à ongle** nail file
onze eleven
opéra (m.) opera, opera hall
opticien (m.) optician
or (m.) gold; **en or** of gold
orage (m.) storm
orange (f.) orange
orangeade (f.) orangeade
orchestre (m.) orchestra
ordinateur (m.) computer
ordinateur (m.) portable laptop computer
ordonnance (f.) prescription
oreille (f.) ear; **boucle (f.) d'oreille** earring
oreiller (m.) pillow
orteil (m.) toe
os (m.) bone
ôter to take off, remove
ou or
où where
ouate (f.) absorbent cotton
oublier to forget
ouest (m.) west
oui yes
outre-mer overseas
ouvert(e) open (adj.)
ouvrir to open

P

paille (f.) straw (material)
pain (m.) bread; **baguette (f.)** French bread; **pain**

blanc white bread; **pain bis** pumpernickel; **pain de froment** whole wheat; **pain grillé** toast; **pain de seigle** rye bread; **petit pain** roll
paire (f.) pair
palais (m.) palace
palourde (f.) clam
pamplemousse (m.) grapefruit
panier (m.) basket
panne (f.) breakdown, mishap; **en panne** broken down
pantalon (m.) pants
pantoufle (f.) slipper
papier (m.) paper; **papier à lettres** note paper; **papier d'emballage** wrapping paper; **papier hygiénique** toilet paper
paquet (m.) package
par by; per; **par avion** air mail, by plane; **par exemple** for example; **par ici** this way; **par jour** per day
parapluie (m.) umbrella
parc (m.) park
parce que because
pardessus (m.) overcoat
pardon excuse me
pardonner to excuse
pare-choc (m.) bumper
parfait(e) perfect
parfum (m.) perfume, flavor
parler to speak
parmi among
partager to share
partenaire (m. or f.) partner, significant other
parterre (m.) mezzanine
partie (f.) part
partir to leave
partout everywhere
pastèque (f.) watermelon
pâte (f.) paste; **la pâte dentifrice** toothpaste

patin (m.) à glace ice-skating; **patin à roulettes** roller skating

pâtisserie (f.) pastry, pastry shop

patron (m.) boss

pauvre poor

payer to pay

pays (m.) country (nation)

paysage (m.) countryside

peau (f.) skin

pêche (f.) peach; fishing; **la pêche sous-marine** deep-sea fishing

pêcher to fish

peigne (m.) comb

pellicule (f.) roll of film

pendant during

pendule (f.) clock

penser to think

pension (f.) boardinghouse

perdre to lose

père (m.) father

permanent(e) permanent

permettre to permit; **permis** permitted

permis (m.) permit; **permis de conduire** driver's license

personne (f.) person

persuader to persuade

perte (f.) loss

peser to weigh

petit(e) small

petit déjeuner (m.) breakfast

peu (adv.) little, not much

peuple (m.) people (nation)

peur (f.) fear; **avoir peur de** to be afraid of

peut-être maybe, perhaps

phare (m.) headlight

pharmacie (f.) pharmacy

photo (f.) photograph

photocopie (f.) photocopy

photographier to photograph

phrase (f.) sentence

pièce (f.) room, play

pied (m.) foot; **à pied** on foot

pierre (f.) stone

piéton (m.) pedestrian

pile (f.) battery (watch)

pilule (f.) pill

pince (f.) à épiler tweezers

pipe (f.) pipe

piscine (f.) swimming pool

piste (f.) runway; **piste de ski** ski slope

place (f.) square (public); seat in conveyance

plafond (m.) ceiling

plage (f.) beach

plainte (f.) complaint

plaire (à) to please

plaisanterie (f.) joke

plaisir (m.) pleasure

plan (m.) plan; **plan de ville** street map of city; **plan à vue d'oiseau** bird's-eye view of the city

planche de surf (f.) surfboard; **planche (f.) à roulettes** skateboard

plancher (m.) floor

plat (m.) dish of food

plat(e) flat

pleurer to cry

plongeon (m.) diving

pluie (f.) rain

plume (f.) pen

plusieurs several

plutôt rather

pneu (m.) tire; **pneu crevé** flat tire

poche (f.) pocket; **livre de poche** paperback

poids (m.) weight

poignet (m.) wrist

poire (f.) pear

pois (m.) pea; **pois chiches (m. pl.)** chick-peas; **à pois** polka-dotted

poisson (m.) fish

poitrine (f.) chest

poivre (m.) pepper

pomme (f.) apple
pomme de terre (f.) potato
pompe (f.) à essence fuel pump
pont (m.) bridge
porc (m.) pork
portable (m.) cell phone
portatif(ive) portable
porte (f.) door
porte-bonheur (m.) charm
portefeuille (m.) wallet
porte-monnaie (m.) purse
porter to carry, wear
porteur (m.) porter
posséder to possess, own
poste (f.) post office; **poste aérienne** air mail
poste (m.) station; **poste d'essence** gas station
potable drinkable; **eau potable** drinking water
potage (m.) soup
poterie (f.) pottery
pouce (m.) thumb
poulet (m.) chicken
poumon (m.) lung
pour for, in order to
pourboire (m.) tip (gratuity)
pourquoi why
pousser to push
pouvoir to be able to, can
préférer to prefer
premier(ière) first; **premier secours (m.)** first aid
prendre to take
prénom (m.) first name
préparer to prepare
présenter to present, introduce
préservatif (m.) condom
presque almost
pressé(e) hurried, rushed
presse-papiers (m.) clipboard
prêt(e) ready
prêter to lend
printemps (m.) spring

prise de courant (f.) socket
privé(e) private
prix (m.) price, prize
prochain(e) next
proche near, neighboring
profession (f.) profession
promenade (f.) walk; **faire une promenade** to take a walk
promesse (f.) promise
promettre to promise
prononcer to pronounce
propre clean
propriétaire (m. or f.) owner
propriété (f.) property
protéger to protect
protester to protest
provisoire temporary
provisoirement temporarily
prudence (f.) carefulness
prune (f.) plum
pruneau (m.) prune
public(ique) public
purée (en) mashed
pyjama (m.) pajamas

Q

quai (m.) platform
qualité (f.) quality
quand when
quantité (f.) quantity
quarante forty
quart (m.) quarter
quartier (m.) district
quatorze fourteen
quatre four
quatre-vingt-dix ninety
quatre-vingts eighty
que that
que? what?
quel(le) which
quelque chose something
quelquefois sometimes
quelque part somewhere
quelques some
quelqu'un someone

question (f.) question
queue (f.) line (of people); tail; **faire la queue** to form a line
qui who
quincaillerie (f.) hardware store
quinze fifteen
quitter + place *or* **person** to leave
quoi what
quotidien(ne) daily

R

rabais (m.) reduction
raconter to tell
radio (f.) radio, X-ray
radis (m.) radish
rafraîchissements (m. pl.) refreshments
ragoût (m.) stew
raifort (m.) horseradish
raisin (m.) grape; **raisin sec** raisin
raison (f.) reason; **avoir raison** to be right
raisonnable reasonable
rang (m.) row
rapide fast
rapidement quickly
rappeler: se rappeler to remember
rare rare
raser: se raser to shave oneself
rasoir (m.) razor; **le rasoir électrique** electric razor
rayon (m.) shelf; department (of a store)
rayure (f.) stripe; **à rayures** striped
récemment recently
recevoir to receive
réclame (f.) advertisement
recommander to recommend
récompense (f.) reward

récompenser to reward
reçu (m.) receipt
récupérer to recuperate
réduction (f.) discount
refuser to refuse
regarder to look at
règle (f.) rule, ruler
régler to settle, adjust, regulate
regretter to regret, be sorry
regulier(ière) regular
regulièrement regularly
relier to connect
remarquer to notice
rembourser to reimburse, refund
remède (m.) remedy
remercier to thank
remettre to put back; **se remettre** to recover (health)
remplacer to replace
remplir to fill (out)
rencontrer to meet
rendez-vous (m.) meeting
rendre to return, give back
renseignement (m.) a piece of information; **les renseignements** information
renvoyer to send back
réparer to repair
repas (m.) meal
repasser to iron; **ne pas repasser** wash and wear
répéter to repeat
répondeur (m.) automatique answering machine
répondre to answer
réponse (f.) the answer
repos (m.) rest, relaxation
reposer: se reposer to rest
représentation (f.) performance
requin (m.) shark
réseau (m.) network
réservation (f.) reservation

réserver to reserve
résoudre to resolve
responsable responsible
ressembler à to resemble,
  look like
restaurant (m.) restaurant
rester to stay, remain
résultat (m.) result
retard (m.) delay; **en retard**
  late
retenir to retain
retirer to withdraw
retouche (f.) touch-up
retourner to return, go back
retraite (en) retired
retrouver to retrieve
réveil (m.) alarm clock
réveiller: se réveiller to
  wake up
revenir to come back, return
rez-de-chaussée (m.) ground
  floor
rhume (m.) cold; **rhume des
  foins** hay fever
rien nothing; **ne . . . rien**
  nothing; **de rien** you're
  welcome
rire to laugh
rive (f.) bank, shore
rivière (f.) river, stream
riz (m.) rice
robe (f.) dress; **robe de
  chambre** bathrobe; **robe
  de soir** evening gown
robinet (m.) faucet
robot (m.) ménager food
  processor
roman (m.) novel
rond(e) round
rose pink, rose
rôti(e) roasted
rouge red
route (f.) route, road
rue (f.) street
ruelle (f.) lane, alley

S

sable (m.) sand
sac (m.) bag, pocketbook
saignant(e) rare (food)
saison (f.) season
salade (f.) salad
sale dirty
salé(e) salted; salty
salle (f.) room; **salle à manger**
  dining room; **salle d'attente**
  waiting room; **salle de bains**
  bathroom; **salle de concert**
  concert hall; **salle de repos**
  recovery room
salon (m.) de beauté beauty
  salon
saluer to greet
samedi Saturday
sandales (f. pl.) sandals
sang (m.) blood
sans without
santé (f.) health
sardine (f.) sardine
satin (m.) satin
satisfait(e) satisfied
saucisse (f.) sausage
saumon (m.) salmon
savoir to know (facts)
savon (m.) soap
scanneur (m.) scanner
scaphandre (m.) diving suit
sec, sèche dry
sèche-cheveux (m.) hair dryer
sécher to dry
secours (m.) help; **au secours!**
  help!
secrétaire (m. or f.) secretary
sécurité (f.) security; **la
  ceinture de sécurité** seat
  belt
seize sixteen
séjour (m.) stay, sojourn
sel (m.) salt
selon according to
semaine (f.) week

sembler to seem

sentier (m.) path

sentir: se sentir to feel

sept seven

sérieux(ieuse) serious

serrure (f.) lock

serveuse (f.) waitress

service (m.) service

serviette (f.) towel, napkin, briefcase; **serviette hygiénique** sanitary napkin

servir to serve

seul(e) alone, only (adj.)

seulement (adv.) only

shampooing (m.) shampoo

si if; yes (to a negative question)

siège (m.) seat

signer to sign

signification (f.) meaning

signifier to mean

s'il vous plaît please

six six

ski (m.) ski; **les skis nautiques** water skis

slip (m.) panties

soda (m.) soda

soeur (f.) sister

soie (f.) silk

soif (f.) thirst; **avoir soif** to be thirsty

soin (m.) care; **avec soin** carefully

soir (m.) evening

soixante sixty

soixante-dix seventy

soldes (m. pl.) sales, bargains

sole (f.) sole, flounder

soleil (m.) sun; **il fait du soleil** it is sunny; **les coups (m. pl.) de soleil** sunburn

sommeil (m.) sleep, sleepiness; **avoir sommeil** to be sleepy

sommelier (m.) wine waiter

somnifère (m.) sleeping pill

sonner to ring

sorbet (m.) sherbert

sortie (f.) exit

sortir to leave

souhaiter to wish (someone something)

soûl(e) drunk

soulier (m.) shoe

souper (m.) supper

souper to have supper

souris (f.) mouse

sous under

sous-titre (m.) subtitle

sous-vêtement (m.) undergarment; **les sous-vêtements (m. pl.)** underwear

soutien-gorge (m.) bra

souvent often

spectacle (m.) show

stade (m.) stadium

station-service (f.) service station; gas station

stylo à bille (m.) ball-point pen

succursale (f.) branch of a bank, etc.

sucre (m.) sugar

sucre artifiel (m.) artifical sweetener

sud (m.) south

suivant(e) following, next

suivre to follow

supermarché (m.) supermarket

supporter to tolerate

sur on

sûr(e) sure

surnom (m.) last name, nickname

surtout especially

surveiller to watch, supervise

survêt (m.) jogging suit

synagogue (f.) synagogue

syndicat (m.) d'initiative tourist office

synthétique synthetic, polyester

système (m.) de navigation GPS GPS

T

tabac (m.) tobacco
table (f.) table
tableau (m.) picture, painting
tache (f.) stain
taille (f.) size, figure (body), waist
taille-crayon (m.) pencil sharpener
tailleur (m.) tailor, woman's suit
talc (m.) talcum powder
talon (m.) heel (of foot)
tampon (m.) **périodique** tampon
tapis (m.) rug
tard late
tarif (m.) rate
tartan (m.) plaid
tarte (f.) pie
tasse (f.) cup
taxi (m.) taxi
teinturerie (f.) dry cleaner's
téléphone (m.) telephone
téléphoner to call on the phone
téléphoniste (f.) operator
téléski (m.) ski lift
télévision (f.) television
tempête (f.) storm
temple (m.) church (Protestant)
temps (m.) weather, time; **de temps en temps** from time to time
tenir to hold
tente (f.) tent
terminer to finish
terrain (m.) ground; **terrain de camping** camping grounds; **terrain de golf** golf course; **terrain de sport** playing field

terre (f.) land, earth; **par terre** on the ground
tête (f.) head
thé (m.) tea; **au citron** with lemon; **au lait** with milk; **glacé** iced; **sucré** with sugar
thon (m.) tuna (fish)
timbre (m.) stamp
tire-bouchon (m.) corkscrew
tirer to pull
tissu (m.) material
tissu-éponge (m.) terry cloth
titre (m.) title
toit (m.) roof
tomate (f.) tomato
tomber to fall; **tomber malade** to become ill
tort: avoir tort to be wrong
tôt early
touche (f.) key (computer)
toucher to touch; **toucher un chèque** to cash a check
toujours always
tour (f.) tower
tour (m.) trip, turn
touriste (m. or f.) tourist
tourner to turn
tout (m. s.); **tous** (m. pl.); **toute** (f. s.); **toutes** (f. pl.) all, every; **tous les jours** every day; **tout le monde** everybody; **tout le temps** all the time
tousser to cough
toux (f.) the cough; **la pastille contre la toux** cough drop; **le sirop contre la toux** cough syrup
traceur à paupieres eyeliner
traduire to translate
train (m.) train; **être en train de** to be in the act of
traitement (m.) treatment
trajet (m.) distance, journey, trip
tranche (f.) slice

travail (m.) work
travailler to work
travers: à travers across, through
traverser to cross, go across
treize thirteen
trente thirty
très very; **très bien** very well
triste sad
trois three
tromper to deceive, trick; **se tromper** to be mistaken, make a mistake
trop (de) too much, many (of)
trottoir (m.) sidewalk
trou (m.) hole
trouver to find
truite (f.) trout
tu you

U

un (m.) a, an, one
une (f.) a, an, one
uni(e) solid (color)
unique only
unité centrale (f.) CPU
urgent(e) urgent; **cas urgent** (m.) emergency; **d'urgence** urgently
usage (m.) custom, practice
usagé(e) secondhand
usé(e) worn out, threadbare, hackneyed
usine (f.) factory
utile useful
utiliser to use

V

vacances (f. pl.) vacation
valable valid
valeur (f.) value
valise (f.) suitcase
vapeur (à la) steamed
varié(e) varied
veau (m.) veal

velours (m.) velvet; **velours côtelé** corduroy
vendeur(euse) salesman, saleswoman
vendre to sell
vendredi Friday
venir to come; **venir de** to come from; **faire venir** to send for
vent (m.) wind; **il fait du vent** it is windy
vente (f.) sale; **en vente** for sale
ventilateur (m.) fan, blower
verglas (m.) ice, frost
vérifier to check
vérité (f.) truth
verre (m.) glass; **le verre à vin** wineglass; **le verre de contact** contact lens
vers towards
vert(e) green
vestiaire (m.) coat checkroom
veston (m.) jacket
vêtements (m. pl.) clothing
viande (f.) meat
vide empty
vie (f.) life
vieille (f.) old
vieux (m.) old
village (m.) village
ville (f.) city
vin (m.) wine; **vin blanc** white wine; **vin mousseux** sparkling wine; **vin rosé** rosé wine; **vin rouge** red wine; **le négociant en vins** wine merchant
vinaigre (m.) vinegar
vingt twenty
violet(-ette) purple
virage (m.) turn, bend, corner
visage (m.) face
vitamine (f.) vitamin
vite quickly
vitesse (f.) speed; **vitesse maximum** speed limit

vitrine (f.) shop window
vivre to live
voici here is, are
voie (f.) route, path, track
voilà there is, are
voir to see
voisin(e) neighbor
voiture (f.) car
vol (m.) flight
volant (m.) steering wheel
voler to fly, steal
voleur (m.) thief, robber
volontiers gladly, with
    pleasure, willingly
vouloir to wish, want; **vouloir
    dire** to mean, signify
vous you
voyage (m.) trip; **voyage
    d'affaires** business trip
voyager to travel
voyageur (m.) traveler
vrai(e) true

vraiment really
vue (f.) view
VUS (m.) SUV

W

wagon (m.) railroad car
wagon-restaurant (m.)
    dining car
W.C. toilet

Y

y there
yaourt (m.) yogurt
yeux (m. pl.) eyes

Z

zéro zero
zone (f.) zone
zoo (m.) zoo

INDEX